INTERNATIONAL CRIMINAL LAW

INTERNATIONAL AND COMPARATIVE CRIMINAL JUSTICE

Series Editors:

Mark Findlay, *Institute of Criminology, University of Sydney, Australia*
Ralph Henham, *Nottingham Law School, Nottingham Trent University, UK*

This series explores the new and rapidly developing field of international and comparative criminal justice and engages with its most important emerging themes and debates. It focuses on three interrelated aspects of scholarship which go to the root of understanding the nature and significance of international criminal justice in the broader context of globalization and global governance. These include: the theoretical and methodological problems posed by the development of international and comparative criminal justice; comparative contextual analysis; the reciprocal relationship between comparative and international criminal justice and contributions which endeavor to build understandings of global justice on foundations of comparative contextual analysis.

Other titles in the series:

The Dual State
Edited by Eric Wilson
ISBN 978 1 4094 31077

Policing in Hong Kong
Kam C. Wong
ISBN 978 1 4094 1060 7

Criminal Law Reform and Transitional Justice
Human Rights Perspectives for Sudan
Edited by Lutz Oette
ISBN 978 1 4094 3100 8

Codification, Macaulay and the Indian Penal Code
The Legacies and Modern Challenges of Criminal Law Reform
Edited by Wing-Cheong Chan, Barry Wright and Stanley Yeo
ISBN 978 1 4094 2442 0

Exploring the Boundaries of International Criminal Justice
Edited by Ralph Henham and Mark Findlay
ISBN 978 0 7546 4979 3

International Criminal Law
Using or Abusing Legality?

EDWIN BIKUNDO
Griffith University, Australia

Routledge
Taylor & Francis Group
LONDON AND NEW YORK

First published 2014 by Ashgate Publishing

2 Park Square, Milton Park, Abingdon, Oxon OX14 4RN
711 Third Avenue, New York, NY 10017, USA

Routledge is an imprint of the Taylor & Francis Group, an informa business

First issued in paperback 2016

British Library Cataloguing in Publication Data
A catalogue record for this book is available from the British Library

The Library of Congress has cataloged the printed edition as follows:
Bikundo, Edwin, author.
International criminal law : using or abusing legality? / by Edwin Bikundo.
pages cm. -- (International and comparative criminal justice)
Based on the author's thesis (doctoral--University of Sydney, 2010).
Includes bibliographical references and index.
ISBN 978-1-4094-3867-0 (hardback)
1. International criminal law. I. Title.
KZ7000.B55 2013
345--dc23

2013031080

ISBN 978-1-4094-3867-0 (hbk)
ISBN 978-1-138-24693-5 (pbk)

To Janice and Hector.

Thank you

Contents

Table of Cases *ix*
Table of Legal Instruments *xiii*
Preface *xv*

1 The Responsibility to Protect Civilians from Political Violence: Locating Necessity between the Rule and its Exception 1

2 International Criminal Law: From *Hostis* to *Hostia Humani Generis* 15

3 Between Necessity and Contingency: Representing Legality as a Faustian Pact 33

4 Global Law: From Force and Law to Aggression and Legality 47

5 The Deficiencies of Law before Overwhelming Violence 69

6 A Possible Methodology of Judicial Discourse in Marshalling, Interpreting, and Construing Aggression Clauses 89

7 Exclusion and Inclusion: From Biopolitics to Biolegality 113

8 Abuse of Legality: The Illegal Use of the Legal 131

9 Reframing Criminal Aggression from Outside to Inside Law 147

10 Legality and Resolving Ambiguity 159

References *167*
Index *191*

Table of Cases

A v Secretary of State for the Home Department, 8 December 2005, [2005] UKHL 71, [2005] 3WLR 1249, [2006] 1 All ER 575, [2006] HRLR 6, para 9

Akdivar v Turkey Application Eur. Ct.H.R No: 21893/93 Judgment of 1 April 1998

Atlee v Laird 339 F. Supp. 689 (E. D. Pa. 1972)

Barton v The Queen (1980) 147 CLR 57

Bowman v Secular Society Ltd. [1917] AC, 406

C.R v C.R, 22 November 1995, Case 48/1994/495/577

Clyne v NSW Bar Association (1960) 104 CLR 186

Connelly v DPP [1964] A. C. 1254

Democratic Republic of the Congo v Belgium – Case Concerning the Arrest Warrant of 11 April 2000 – Judgment – General List No. 121 [2002] ICJ 1 (14 February 2002) Majority Judgment

Democratic Republic of the Congo v Uganda – Case Concerning Armed Activities On The Territory of the Congo – General List No. 116 [2005] (19 December 2005)

Dole Chadee et al. v Trinidad and Tobago of 29 July 1998 CCPR-14-1/CCPR-OP-3

DPP v Humphrys [1977] A.C. 1

Engel and Others v the Netherlands (1976) Series A no. 22

Ex P Badhan [1991] 2 QB 78

Ex P Dean [1993] QB 769

Ex P Schmidt Div. Ct. Roch L J & Sedley J 26 November 1993

Ex Parte Brookes (1984) 80 C. Appeal R. 164

Ex parte Quirin 317 U.S. 1 (1942) 1

Frisbie v Collins 342 U.S. 519 (1952)

Greece v the United Kingdom decision of 2 June 1956, 7

Green v U.S. 184 (1957)

Hamdan v Rumsfeld, Secretary of Defense, et al. Certiorari to the United States Court of Appeals for The District of Columbia Circuit No. 05–184. Argued 28 March 2006 and decided 29 June 2006

Holtzman v Richardson 484 F. 2d. 1307 (2d. Cir. 1973)

Hui Chi-Ming v R [1992] 1 AC 34, 57

International Military Tribunal (IMT) Judgment, 30 September 1946 in 22 Trial of German Major War Criminals: Proceedings of the International Military Tribunal Sitting at Nuremburg 411, 444(1950) Opinion and Judgment, International Military Tribunal at Nuremberg (1 October 1946), reprinted in

Jordan J Paust et al., *International Criminal Law: Cases and Materials* (1998) 900, 904

International Military Tribunal at Nuremburg. HMSO Cmd 6964 (1946) 13, reprinted in (1947) 41 *American Journal of International Law* 186

Ireland v United Kingdom Judgment of 18 January 1978, Eur. Ct. H.R,. Series A, no. 25

Jago v District Court (NSW) (1989) 168 CLR 23

Jean-Bosco Barayagwiza v The Prosecutor Appeals Chamber Case no. ICTR-97-19-I l decision of 3 November 1999 before: Judge Gabrielle Kirk McDonald (P), Mohamed Shahabuddeen, Lal Chand Vohrah, Wang Tieya, Rafael Nieto-Navia JJA (Barayagwiza I for convenience)

Judgment of German Major War Criminals. Proceedings of the IMT, Nuremberg, Official Documents vol. I. (1947) 223

Ker v Illinois, 199 U.S. 436 (1886)

Keyowski v R. (1988) 62 CR (3d) 349, 550 per Wilson J

Lakhdar Boumediene et al., Petitioners v George W. Bush, President of the United States et al. Supreme Court of the United States, unreported No. 06–1195. Decided 12 June 2008

Lawless v Ireland Eur. Ct. H.R Judgment of 1 July 1961, Series A, no. 3

Libyan Arab Jamahirya v UK (Lockerbie case) [1992] ICJ Rep 3

Loizidou v Turkey Application No. 15318/89 judgment of 23 March 1995

Luftig v McNamara 252 F. Supp. 819 (D.D.C. 1966)

Mabo and Others v The State of Queensland (No. 2) (1992) 175 CLR 1

Madzimbamuto v Lardner-Burke [1969] AC 645 (PC)) per Lord Reid at 723–4

Marbury v Madison, 1 Cranch 137, 177 (1803)

Maxwell v The Queen (1996) 184 CLR 501

Mellifont v AG (1991) 173 CLR 289

Metropolitan Bank v Pooley (1885) 10 App. Cases 210 per Lord Blackburn, 220–21

Military and Paramilitary Activities in and against Nicaragua (Nicaragua v the United States of America), Decision on Jurisdiction and Admissibility (1984) ICJ REP. 392, 27June 1986

Military and Paramilitary Activities in and against Nicaragua (Nicaragua v the United States of America), Decision on the Merits (1986) 14 ICJ, 62*Mills v Cooper* (1967) 2 ALLER 100

Mitchell & Ors v DPP & Ano. CLR (1987) 127. Per Haynes P. at 129

Moevao v Dept of Labour [1980] I NZLR 464

Municipality of Mombasa v Nyali Limited [1963] E.A. 371

Murphy v Ramsey, 114 U.S. 15, 44 (1885)

North Sea Continental Shelf [1969] ICJ Rep paras 73–7

Ol Ole Njogo and Others v The Attorney General Civil Case No. 91 of 1912 (E.A.P. 1914), 5 E.A.L.R. 70

Proprietary Articles Trade Assoc. & Others v Att-Gen of Canada & others [1931] AC 310 per Lord Atkin

Prosecutor v Akayesu Case No. ICTR-96–4-A (Appeals Chamber), 1 June 2001. Decision of 2 September 1998

Prosecutor v Brima, Kamara and Kanu, Written Reasons for the Trial Chamber's Oral Decision on the Defence Motion on Abuse of Process due to infringement of Principles of Nullum Crimen Sine Lege and Non-Retroactivity as to Several Counts, SCSL-04-16-PT 31 March 2004

Prosecutor v Deronjic, Miroslav ICTY Case Number: IT-02-61-S, 30 March 2004 Sentencing Judgment

Prosecutor v Dragan Nikolic Decision on Defence Motion Challenging the Exercise of Jurisdiction by the Tribunal Case No. IT-94-2-PT

Prosecutor v Drazen Erdemovic, Majority Opinion and Separate and Dissenting Opinion of Judge Cassese, ICTY Appeals Chamber Judgment of 7 October 1997

Prosecutor v Dusko Tadić a/k/a 'Dule'. Case No. IT-94-1 (Appeals Chamber) Unanimous Decision of 2 October 1995, 'On The Defence Motion For Interlocutory Appeal On Jurisdiction' 2 October 1995

Prosecutor v Jean-Bosco Barayagwiza Appeals Chamber Case no. ICTR-97-19-I Decision on Prosecutor's Request for Review or Reconsideration dated 31 March 2000 before: Navanethem Pillay (P), Asoka de Zoysa Gunawardana, Erik Møse JJ. (Barayagwiza II)

Prosecutor v Slobodan Milošević Richard May (P), Patrick Robinson, Mohamed Fassi Fihri JJ. Decision on Preliminary Motions dated 8 November 2001 ICTY Case No IT-02-54

Prosecutor v Thomas Lubanga Dyilo Case No. ICC- 01/04-01/06 Decision on the consequences of non-disclosure of exculpatory materials covered by Article 54(3)(e) agreements and the application to stay the prosecution of the accused, together with certain other issues raised at the Status Conference on 10 June 2008. Before: Adrian Fulford (P), Elizabeth Odio Benito, René Blattmann JJ, dated 13 June 2008

Prosecutor v Thomas Lubanga Dyilo Case No. ICC- 01/04-01/06 Judgment on the appeal of the Prosecutor against the decision of Trial Chamber I entitled 'Decision on the release of Thomas Lubanga Dyilo' The Appeals Chamber, Sang-Hyun Song (P), Philippe Kirsch, Georghios M Pikis, Erkki Kourula, Daniel David Ntanda Nsereko JJ, dated 21 October 2008

Questions of Interpretation and Application of the 1971 Montreal Convention arising from the Aerial Incident at Lockerbie (*Libyan Arab Jamahiriya v United Kingdom*), Provisional Measures Order of 14 April 1992

R (on the application of Al-Jedda) (FC) (Appellant) v Secretary of State for Defence (Respondent) [2007] UKHL The UK House of Lords

R v Conway (1989) 1 SCR 1659

R v Conway [1989] 70 CR (3d)

R v Forbes ex p. Bevan (1972) 127 CLR 1

R v Jones and others [2006] UKHL 16

Radhabinod Pal, *Dissentient Judgment of Justice Pal: International Military Tribunal for the Far East* (1953)

Randu Nzai Ruwa & 2 Others v Internal Security Minister & Another [2012] eKLR

R. v Horseferry Road Magistrates' Court, Ex parte Bennett [1994] 1 A.C. 42

R. v Horseferry Road Magistrate's Court, ex p Bennett (No3) [1995] 1 Cr App R 147, 149

R. v Dedan Kimathi S/o Wachiuri [1956] eKLR*Republic of Fiji v Prasad* (Unreported, Court of Appeal of Fiji, 1 March 2001, Civil Appeal No. ABU0078/2000S)

Ridgeway v The Queen (1994–1995) 185 CLR 19

S.S. Lotus (France v Turkey) (1927), Permanent Court of International Justice Publications, Series A, No. 9, at 18 (Sept. 7)

Southeast Mortg. Co. v Sinclair, 632 So. 2d 677(1994)

The State v Dosso [1958] 2 PSCR 180

The Legality of the Threat or Use of Nuclear Weapons, International Court of Justice (Advisory Opinion of 8 July 1996) General List no. 95

The Prosecutor v Jean-Paul Akayesu Case No. ICTR-96-4-T Decision of 2 September 1998 at para 521

The Prosecutor v Siméon Nchamihigo Case No. ICTR-2001-63-DP before Navanethem Pillay J. Decision of 8 May 2002 On the Defence Motion Seeking Release of yhe Accused Person and/or Any Other Remedy on the Basis of Abuse of Process by the Prosecutor

The Prosecutor v Théoneste Bagosora, Gratien Kabiligi, Aloys Ntabakuze and Anatole Nsengiyumva Case No. ICTR-98-41-T ICTR Judgment and Sentence of 18 December 2008

Uganda v Commissioner of Prisons, Ex parte Matovu [1966] EA 514

United States of America v Alstötter et al. (The Nuremberg Trials: 'The Justice Case') 3 T.W.C. 1 (1948), 6 L.R.T.W.C. 1 (1948), 14 Ann. Dig. 278 (1948) <http://www.law.umkc.edu/faculty/projects/ftrials/nuremberg/Alstoetter.htm#War%20Crimes%20and%20Crimes%20Against> at 6 August 2009

United States v Alvarez-Machain, 504 U.S. 655 (1992)

United States v Araki, Dissenting Opinion of Justice Pal, in 105 The Tokyo Major War Crimes Trial 36-7 (R. John Pritchard, ed.) (1998) at 37

US v Marion 404 US 307, 324 (1971) 61

USA v Von Leeb et al. (The German High Command Trial) Case No. 72 United States Military Tribunal, Nuremberg (1948) Law-Reports of Trials of War Criminals, The United Nations War Crimes Commission, Volume XII, London, HMSO, 1949

Velvel v Johnson 287 F. Supp. 846 (D. Kan. 1968)

Walton v Gardiner (1993) 117 CLR 378

Williams v Spautz (1991–1992) 171 CLR 509

Table of Legal Instruments

1215 Magna Carta 25 Edw. I, c. 29 (1297) (1215)

1814 United States Constitution

1899 *Hague Convention For the Pacific Settlement of International Disputes (Hague I)* (29 July 1899)

1907 *Hague Convention on the Opening of Hostilities* (Hague III); 18 October 1907

1907 *Pacific Settlement of International Disputes (Hague I)*; 18 October 1907

1919 *The Covenant of the League of Nations*

1928 'Kellogg–Briand Pact; 1928' *United States Statutes at Large*, vol. 46, part 2, 2343 Articles 1–3

1945 London Agreement of 8 August 1945 with the Charter Annexed, subsequent trials on Control Council Law No. 10, Punishment of Persons Guilty of War Crimes, Crimes Against Peace and Against Humanity, 20 December 1945, 3 Official Gazette Control Council for Germany 50–55 (1946)

1945 *Agreement for the Prosecution and Punishment of the Major War Criminals of the European Axis, and the Charter of the International Military Tribunal*, London, 8 August 1945

1945 *Charter of the United Nations*

1946 *The Charter of the International Tribunal for the Far East*

1946 *Affirmation of the Principles of International Law recognised by the Charter of the Nuremberg Tribunal*, Resolution 95 (I) of the United Nations General Assembly, 11 December 1946

1970 *Resolution on Principles of International Law concerning Friendly Relations and Co-operation among States in accordance with the Charter of the United Nations,* UNGA Resolution 2625 (XXV) (24October 1970)

1974 *Definition of Aggression,* United Nations General Assembly Resolution 3314 (XXIX) of 14 December 1974

1976 *International Covenant on Civil and Political Rights*, 999 U.N.T.S. 171, entered into force 23 March 1976, Article 9 (1)

1978 *Declaration on the Preparation of Societies for Life in Peace,* UNGA/ Res/33/73 (15 December 1978)

1981 *African [Banjul] Charter on Human and Peoples' Rights*, adopted 27 June 1981, OAU Doc. CAB/LEG/67/3 rev. 5, 21 I.L.M. 58 (1982), 1520 UNTS 217, entered into force 21 October 1986

1982 *Canadian Charter of Rights and Freedoms*, Part I of the Constitution Act, 1982 assented to 29 March 1982

1984 *Declaration of the Right of Peoples to Peace,* UNGA Res 39/11 (12 November 1984)

1993 United Nations Security Council Resolution 827(1993) with the Statute of the International Criminal Tribunal for the Former Yugoslavia Annexed

1994 *Statute of the International Criminal Tribunal for Rwanda*, annexed to *Resolution 955*, SC Res 955, UN SCOR, 49th sess, 3453rd mtg, UN Doc S/RES/955 (1994)

1995 *International Criminal Tribunal for Rwanda, Rules of Procedure and Evidence* Adopted on 29 June 1995 pursuant to Article 14 of the *Statute of the International Criminal Tribunal for Rwanda*, annexed to *Resolution 955*, SC Res 955, UN SCOR, 49th sess, 3453rd mtg, UN Doc S/RES/955 (1994).

1998 *Rome Statute of the International Criminal Court*, opened for signature 17 July 1998, 2187 UNTS 3, art 83(2) (entered into force 1 July 2002).

2002 Agreement between the United Nations and the Government of Sierra Leone on the Establishment of the Special Court for Sierra Leone, signed on 16 January 2002, Statute of the Special Court Annexed

Preface

Law and violence have a deeply ambiguous relationship to each other. The law is supposedly the antithesis of violence and yet the law is at the same time the legitimation and institutionalization of some forms of violence. This collection of essays weaves disparate threads together organized around the core argument that criminalizing violence involves imposing a monopoly on the legitimate use of force. This inquiry seeks to construct and unpack a legal argument for a legal answer to a legal problem: namely, whether (and if so how) the law itself provides an answer to the question of whether law is a suitable medium or not to resolve the related issues of the prevention of violence, the illegal use of force and the criminality of aggression in international law. It looks at the law on the use *for* force (in saving and protecting life) rather than the use *of* force (in inflicting death, destruction and injury). The stakes raised in this inquiry reveal the law as a line that separates, as well as invests with meaning, the boundary dividing life and death. These lines of inquiry therefore have implications in both law and jurisprudence generally.

The inquiry was prompted by a certain discrepancy (or development) in legal opinion regarding legally regulating violence that has arisen in the past 60 years or so. Justice Robert Jackson, speaking for the United States of America at the end of the first Nuremberg Trial in 1945, punctuates this period at one end. He said it was illegal and criminal for any 'nation to redress grievances or seek expansion by resort to aggressive war'. At the other end of the period is Mr Bill Richardson, again speaking for the United States, at the United Nations Conference on the establishment of the International Criminal Court in 1998. He said that acts not clearly criminalized under international law should be excluded from the definition of aggression and that it was therefore premature to attempt to define aggression in terms of individual criminal responsibility.

This project takes its cue from the arguments, exemplified by Bill Richardson's statement, against legally defining the crime of aggression. These arguments by default (either designed or accidental) favour instead political action such as in the United Nations Security Council against the International Criminal Court in framing matters of aggression and the use of force. The focus on the United States is in recognition of both its indispensable role and pivotal influence in developing international criminal law and its preponderant military force. This correlation of law-making power with preponderant force is no coincidence at all.

Although an adequate definition of aggression is itself not the core problem, issues resulting from the history of defining aggression arise once the chequered evolution of attempts at codification is examined. The focus is therefore on the conceptual definability of a crime of aggression, which is a legal-theoretical matter, and not on the actual process of providing a definition, which is a matter decided by the political process that achieved the necessary consensus. It is therefore not so much an issue of the lack of law in defining aggression in international criminal law as it is one of assembling adequate political consensus to craft an objective legal standard sufficiently oblivious of military might.

The inquiry here tests whether the power to inflict death and injury is outside or inside the law. This project questions whether using the law to address political violence would legally entail an abuse of legality or not. Abuse of legality means capturing legal rules, principles and processes in ways that undermine the rule of law and human rights, but doing this in the name of upholding the rule of law or protecting human rights. This takeover or mimicry of law makes it difficult to discern between what is good faith application of legal principle and what is a travesty of it.

My intuition is that even in the absence of specific laws governing an ambiguous state of facts, there is always legality as an approach to unstructured situations. This legality (as a way of doing things) exists side-by-side with, and even without, specific laws. Laws are evidence of legality and not the other way round. Legality in that way justifies acts even in the absence of clearly enabling structures. Given this, the task I set out to do is to trace a line dividing politics and law that assigns the characterization of aggression to legality. The argument therefore contends that there is an emerging but contested global monopoly on the legitimate use of force. This monopoly is oriented towards future human security and global stability that are necessarily predicated upon legality as a stabilizer of future expectations.

In other words, when confronted with the threat or use of violence, the questions posed are recast to whether there is a distinction between just and unjust force and violence, who decides this, how, and with reference to what. Couched like this, the questions are more amenable to processing within the legal system from legislation to adjudication and enforcement, rather than by brute force, which would be the default mode of dispute resolution in the absence of peaceful dispute settlement. Most importantly, and this is the crux of the matter, even though brute force is brought to bear, this will in itself not change the law but only breach it.

Further, where it is claimed that such use of force in fact has changed the law, this violence is not just *contrary* to law but also *against* the law. That is, it is simultaneously a crime of aggression and an abuse of the legal process and undermines global order. This is violence against the notion of law itself, not only against its provisions but against the very order of normality that makes the law intelligible. This is demonstrably on the wrong side of the line separating self-defence from taking the law into one's own hands. Actors that claim the justification of law deserve, as it were, 'their day in court' to prove or have their claims disproven in an appropriate manner and forum.

Consequently, the argument is that law is the appropriate medium within which to discuss regulating violence in a globalized society. The thesis pursued is that 'peace', normatively speaking, does not require the absence of coercion but merely presupposes a monopoly on the legitimate use of force. This legitimacy should be considered as a matter of and for pre-existing standards of greater or lesser detail (that is, legality). To orient the debate, this relates to considerations associated with consolidating the international community as a multifaceted pluralistic society. These considerations increasingly indicate legality as the means to approach the use of force from the local to the global level as it affects individuals, communities, States and humanity alike.

Further, using legality would substitute the terrorist/freedom fighter paradox for a general objective legal standard instead of singular subjective self-interested stances. Therefore, in place of mutually exclusive self-justified violence by States, an all-inclusive framework of rules and exceptions would generally apply in discerning competing claims. In criminal law terms, possible exceptions, justifications, excuses or defences may include self-defence, humanitarian intervention, the responsibility to protect, measures undertaken to combat terrorism and the like.

To summarize, the project is organized by arguing against the objections opposing further legalization of the use of force and consequently proposing rendering inapplicable the relevant customary international law. These revolve around the propositions that law is either unable or unsuitable to resolving the role of force in international relations and that this is best left to the political sphere (effectively therefore in the realm of combat with no normative distinction between sides). However, implicit in the argument is that the usefulness or inability of the law is for the law to decide, not a literal trial by battle. This is because the legal system is itself best placed to judge on its own misuse or any abuse of legal process, which would essentially involve taking life (and liberty or property, which relate to quality of life) without due process of law; in other words, *violently*, which is precisely what is at stake.

The method used here analyses of the observation and description of the legal/illegal distinction when applied to force, violence or aggression. This distinction is drawn through an exclusion and inclusion mechanism that alternately protects life from and exposes it to force/violence. This process is underwritten by a functional, but not essential, distinction between force (which is sanctioned by law) and violence (which is outside or contrary to law according to law).

Specific to this process is criminalizing violence and institutionalizing force by withholding legitimacy from the latter and granting it to the former through a claimed monopoly on a legitimacy that is politically contestable but beyond legal reproach. The work addresses this process by highlighting the dialectic of inclusive exclusion and exclusive inclusion through the deconstructive parsing and examination of the language contained in critical phrases and terms that were arrived at, or departed from, through the political process.

I employ a critical theoretical methodology to interrogate the relationship between law and violence in the context of communal order and disorder. Critical theory makes it possible to analyse international society as a whole in terms of place and time but also values interdisciplinary perspectives to supplement the law, including politics and not ignoring economics. This is to make the implicit deep structural debate explicit and, incidentally but more importantly, bring to light a method for discerning between competing teleological claims that pit law against politics and vice versa in defining violence and aggression.

In bringing to light this method for discerning between legal and political claims, I need an analytical and descriptive theory that purportedly considers different social perspectives simultaneously yet separately, while leaving each supreme in its domain. That is, what is required is a meta-narrative or paradigm that provides some measure of objectivity without solely relying on legal arguments to promote exclusively legal solutions for a social problem. For this purpose, sociological systems theory saves the argument from lifting itself up by its own bootstraps because it assigns certain characteristics to social systems, which are reducible in inner logic to binary coding both in political communication (friend/enemy) and legal communication (lawful/unlawful); all of which much simplifies the task of classification.

I contribute a prescriptive and normative perspective on the back of this descriptive systems theory. This is accomplished through utilizing the descriptiveness in assigning a truth/untruth value to competing teleological arguments. These arguments dispute between what is and what is not customary international law, in terms of what use the law is in the context of violence.

The methodology brings together (in an overall framework of a shared relation to 'life') Niklas Luhmann's description of humans as divided into mind and body (or in his terms, 'psychic' and 'organic systems'), as well as Michel Foucault's 'biopolitics' and Giorgio Agamben's conjunction of *Zoë* or 'bare life' and *Bios* or 'social life' in the human, as all describing an identical phenomenon. This phenomenon is the contemporary centrality of 'life and death' in social control as means and end, tool and material. This phenomenon may be named 'biolegality', meaning law oriented to life as its referent and justification and therefore legitimacy. Elements of Niklas Luhmann's sociological systems theory inform the research paradigm within which I work. It focuses on communication and assigns humans a decentred role as part of society's environment, comprising of the mind and body as separate systems unified in the human. Further, because Niklas Luhmann regarded the law as society's immune system, he explicitly inflected it within a biological register. The layered method chosen reflects that the social debate sought to be untangled and unpacked is convoluted with political arguments dressed up as legal ones and with legal arguments disparaged as political ones.

Consequently, critical theory is the genre within which I write, with a systems theoretical sensibility. Luhmann, Foucault and Agamben provide for both theoretical conceptualization and empirical practice in their identification of social processes linked to or mimicking life processes, thereby demonstrating that life is itself conceptually both the subject and object manipulated in the process. I scrutinize not the human actors as such but their communicative acts. Communication and language are the core concerns and the specific subject and focus of my work.

This study distinguishes force from violence by initially uniting them in the value-neutral concept of coercion. It subsequently distinguishes them as force being coercion used for social ends (for example, law enforcement or self-defence), while violence is coercion for anti-social ends (here the crime of aggression is portrayed as threatening collective security and peaceful change). With reference to human society writ large, social/anti-social is congruent with friend/enemy in the political sphere and lawful/unlawful in the legal system. The resolution therefore to the current debate is more legalization that deeper embeds the use of force in society for social ends and either blackens or whitens the current grey areas that are still rhetorically insisted upon as a matter for politics. This is especially relevant in highly politicized contexts, such as war or revolution and the transition through to peace and justice.

The project therefore observes the manipulation, apportionment and direction of life and death processes in society by tracing an overarching but contingent trajectory of an expanding and consolidating line that draws and dissolves boundaries within it. This is theory building that looks upon law and violence as a self-referential bundling in which the terms opposed only make sensible meaning in relation to each other. At its simplest, law is not violent and violence is not lawful. This thesis will propose some amelioration in the actual application of law through debating its effects on individuals and communities.

Chapter 1 inquires into the responsibility to protect civilians from political violence. The chapter inquires into the expansion of the rule of law in international law as it relates to the use of force. The consequential but regrettable necessity of a forcible response to real or threatened mass atrocities underscores this fundamental undesirability of violence versus its inevitability. The compromise reached is that force, although inevitable, should only be used sparingly. Chapter 2 is a theoretical and empirical investigation into whatever causal link there may be between international criminal trials and preventing political violence through exemplary prosecutions. Specifically how do representative trials of persons accused of having the greatest responsibility for the most serious crimes of concern to the international community as a whole, supposedly bind recurrent violence? The argument pursued is that by using an accused as an example, a court engages in an indirect and uncertain substitution of personal rights for social harmony and order. Chapter 3 argues that in international law the Hobbesian social contract intended to prevent violence works in exactly the same way as a Faustian pact. That is to say, even when it is effective whatever it achieves could still have been realized without it. But once utilized there is no objective proof of its contingency likewise just as before it is resorted to there is no proof of its necessity. Essentially it creates its own reality poised as it is between necessity and contingency.

Chapter 4 expounds on the linkages between the crime of aggression and the abuse of legal process. It explores how the doctrine of the abuse of legality relates to aggression from local to global contexts. This chapter argues that society politicises violence when it is indistinguishable from force by dividing it into a binary pairing of social/anti-social. Society permits, if not encourages, the former (as law enforcement) and abhors the latter (as law-transgressing violence). This is how force is developed conceptually through legal tools by being accorded social recognition. What is therefore value-neutral in a mythical state of nature becomes decried in society (partially) and exalted (partially), dependent on whether society characterizes it as social or anti-social. Chapter 5 describes a legal methodology for determining matters of aggression. It argues that society overall has separated law from politics by imposing rules on utilizing force, thereby separating power from authority: that is, mere ability from legitimacy. Therefore, in pondering the applicability of legality (the effect of rules) versus the inapplicability of legality (the freeing up from rules), judges look to the society's general will as constructed via the prism of legal text.

Chapter 6 discusses aggression in the context of international criminal justice as opposed to other possible alternatives. The argument pursued is that, viewed through the prism of law, the debate on prosecuting criminal aggression at the International Criminal Court, while explicitly referring to criminality, implicitly refers to an international legal order. This order promotes obeying the force of law rather than the law of force. Chapter 7 examines biolegality or the 'law of life itself'. This chapter argues that the law not only regulates both the states of life and death but also defines the boundary between them. The law does this by assigning rights and duties between the living to create different forms of and entitlements to life. This 'vital' process of the law profoundly influences social relations and can be abused with deadly consequences. Chapter 7 discusses the deficiencies of law when facing overwhelming violence. The chapter explains that extreme violence shows up certain inadequacies in law that go beyond mere systemic lack (of law and order resources) to conceptual befuddlement (given a monopoly on violence, when is might not right?). Nevertheless, the argument is that there is a meaningful and consequential distinction between a *monopoly* on the legitimate use of force and a *legitimate* monopoly on the use of force.

Chapter 8 addresses the illegal use of the legal system. The argument is that globally, society functions optimally when social systems, such as the legal system, have overall control of their processes, especially in terms of being independent of unmediated political intervention. With law specifically in mind, the chapter reconstructs the notion of abuse of legality as expressing the teleology of law according to the law and therefore as the principal juridical weapon against political machination in discerning between law creating and law destroying violence.

Chapter 9 examines the law on aggression up to immediately after the Second World War and as reflected by debate around the setting up of the International Criminal Court. The argument is that, in discussing the legality or illegality of the use of force in its normative manifestation, there is a universal yet inarticulate major premise posited, which at its simplest says 'there is a right to peace'. This right to peace and concomitant duty to keep the peace inheres in the nation state but also, as the chapter argues, in individuals through the operation of international human rights instruments and customary international law. Peace at its most basic is the absence of violent struggle. Armed conflict is the resort to force by State or non-state actors, which may be legal or illegal.

Finally, Chapter 10 brings the disparate threads together and consolidates the thesis. This chapter re-addresses the basic research question posed in the opening hypothetical case study: *Must a judicial entity decline to entertain a prosecution for criminal aggression as* ipso facto*, an abuse, or misuse of legal procedure?* Previous chapters have traced the genealogy of aggression through its criminalization to its relationship to law and deriving meaning, as well as illustrated how it applies in actuality. Based on that preliminary effort, this chapter argues that suspending the law leads to irresolvable ambiguities between those entitled to life and those deserving of death. Such ambiguities arise between war and peace, norms and exceptions, law and fact, sanctioned and unsanctioned and so forth. The chapter addresses these ambiguities by recommending that politicians leave the law to its devices, free of direct everyday political interference, to delineate progressively the expanding boundaries of its application to life. In this instance, the solution is specifically to provide an acceptable legal definition of aggression for the purposes of the Rome Statute. This would frame the debate as law distinct from politics and move away from the political decision-making procedure such as say that of the United Nations Security Council, to an adjudicatory forum as exemplified by the International Criminal Court.

A court, as a judicial proceeding with the potential to be or not to be, would then have the necessary independence and impartiality to decline to exercise jurisdiction in order to protect the integrity of its proceedings, and therefore of the legal system as such, by preferring not to proceed with politically motivated prosecutions. That is, if we in the final analysis understand legality and violence as a mutually exclusive but nevertheless entwined dyad, then our approach to aggression as either a non-justiciable act of state violence or as a justiciable legal fact constitutes a normative choice (that is in turn socially constituted). However, the only legally defensible position is that the use of force is a justiciable legal fact.

Chapter 1

The Responsibility to Protect Civilians from Political Violence: Locating Necessity between the Rule and its Exception

The promise of international law to promote and protect human welfare is limited by the means at the disposal of the international community where, normatively speaking, peace is the rule and armed conflict the exception. The consequential but regrettable necessity of a forcible response to real or threatened mass atrocities underscores this fundamental undesirability of violence versus its inevitability. The compromise forged is that force, although inevitable, should be used sparingly and only where necessary: specifically in emergencies and especially to protect civilians from mass atrocities. There are two, on the face of it contradictory, approaches clear in the debate on the role of force or violence in international law. The first relates to the fundamental undesirability of violence generally. The second relates to the inevitability of violence and consequential regrettable *necessity* of a forcible response in defence. The role of law in this debate is to navigate between these two coasts of undesirability and inevitability on the ship of necessity. This meandering approach is crystallized in the rules relating to the use of force, which try to restrict force only to extreme circumstances. The compromise reached is that force, although inevitable, should only be used sparingly.

Managing the Necessity to Use Force

The principled management of necessity therefore increasingly governs how the responsibility to protect civilians is achieved in international affairs. The responsibility to protect (R2P) is not of itself a legal concept. It is better viewed as a meta-legal concept from which a number of legal rules and principles can be derived. These include the rules and principles regarding the protection of civilians (POC). Force is made available to protect human life and violence is outlawed precisely because it is targeted against human life. In order to counter illegal violence, R2P may be viewed as reconciling the undesirability of violence to the inevitability of lawful force. Force is in this way legitimated as a means by which the ends of POC are to be achieved.

Linking force and the sanctity of human life through a means–ends relationship, where force is the means by which the sanctity of human life is protected, reconciles otherwise intractable contradictions. This approach can be seen in the UN Charter's preamble when reciting the background to the United Nations, its aims and the means to achieve those aims. The foundational principles of the United Nations are to save humanity from war, reaffirm human rights, establish the conditions for achieving justice and the international rule of law and to promote social progress and better living standards in enlarging freedom. These principles of course are accompanied with the sovereign equality of states, the self-determination of peoples and non-intervention in essentially domestic issues. The ends of the United Nations are to be achieved by practising tolerance and peaceful coexistence and uniting in strength to maintain international peace and security. Most crucially for this discussion, armed force shall not be used except in the common interest, and the international machinery shall be employed for the promotion of the economic and social advancement of all peoples. As a rule the use of force is generally prohibited. The traditionally accepted exceptions to this rule are legitimate self-defence and action taken under the UN Charter for the restoration and maintenance of international peace and security. Peace is the rule and war (armed conflict) the exception. In fact, armed force is only justifiable for facilitating the return to peace. This is why it is notable, for example, that even United Nations Security Council (UNSC) resolutions authorizing the use of force do not do so explicitly but instead use wording referring to *all necessary* means or measures to achieve their object. Such wording is deemed sufficient to permit the use of force without specifically recommending it (Freudenschuß 1994: 492, Baker and DeFrank 1995: 304–305). That in principle is what the member states of the United Nations have signed up to, to pool their collective capacities for the maintenance of peace and security within a legal framework. This legalization of the legitimate use of force by progressively outlawing political violence is supposed to promote and provide the rule of law in international affairs. This rule of law discourages war/armed conflict and instead promotes peace principally through differentiating of the legal regimes that are applicable during war and peace. Consequently this chapter's thesis is that a rule and exception scheme where peace is the norm and violence the exception generates an outlawing and criminalization of political violence.

The recent return to UNSC resolutions to authorize the use of force under Chapter VII of the UN Charter in the Libyan Arab Jamahiriya and Côte d'Ivoire appear to continue the long-term trend towards bringing violence within the ambit of legality. This relationship brought about between law and violence has at least two facets. The first involves criminalizing political violence. The second increasingly invokes legality to justify or excuse the use of force against political violence. The occurrences of political violence in Libya and Côte d'Ivoire that are now under consideration by the International Criminal Court (ICC) can be used as examples of political violence, not of criminal aggression. The broad question of the illegal use of violence brings together international humanitarian law/the law of armed conflict, public international law and both international and domestic criminal law. The legitimacy and legality of the use of force has two senses: not only a negative prohibition on deliberately targeting civilians but a positive obligation that any use of armed force is to protect civilians. Or at the very least that civilians must not be deliberately targeted (even when states use force to ensure self-determination or to protect against secession or insurgencies). As is to be demonstrated below, the responsibility to protect (R2P) can be conceived of as a subset of the POC.

Reconciling Sovereignty and Intervention

In conceptualizing R2P the International Commission on Intervention and State Sovereignty (ICISS) managed to reconcile the ostensibly incompatible principles of sovereignty and humanitarian intervention (Knight 2011: 34). Indeed one contributing factor animating the ICISS was to avoid any terminology that espoused military force as either the primary or the sole way to respond to actual or impending mass atrocities (ICISS 2001: 40). Apart from the use of force as a last resort other criteria for using force during R2P intervention are: the right authority, a just cause, the right intentions, a proportionate response and a reasonable likelihood of success (ICISS 2001: 47). These are substantially a reiteration of *jus ad bellum* principles enjoying a long pedigree (Aquinas 1981, Augustine 2003, Walzer 1977).

R2P principles hold that each state has the responsibility to protect its populations from genocide, war crimes, ethnic cleansing and crimes against humanity (UNGA 2005, paras 138 and 139). The international community should encourage and help states to exercise this responsibility. There is a view that the United Nations through then Secretary-General Kofi Annan's reform agenda established the responsibility to protect as a new norm legalizing humanitarian intervention (Stedman 2007: 938). The Security Council likewise has a responsibility to protect populations by using appropriate collective action via diplomatic, humanitarian and other peaceful means under Chapters VI and VIII of the UN Charter. Should peaceful means be inadequate and national authorities fail to protect their populations as required, then resort may be had to Chapter VII of the UN Charter, which authorizes the use of necessary measures including armed force. UN Secretary-General Ban Ki-moon (UNSG 2009) refers to these as three equal and mutually reinforcing pillars. A contrary take on this is that the 2005 World Summit agreement and the affirmation of this agreement in Security Council and the General Assembly resolutions in themselves did not constitute new legal norms about the responsibilities of the international community to protect populations from genocide, ethnic cleansing, war crimes and crimes against humanity. They merely contributed to interpret and clarify existing international legal responsibilities in customary international law (Rosenberg 2009: 445–6).

The Obama administration's National Security Strategy appears to reaffirm America's commitment to pursue its interests through an international system in which all nations have both rights and responsibilities. These include preventing genocide and mass atrocities under the UN auspices via R2P (US National Security Strategy 2010: 48). This recognizes that, although the primary responsibility for preventing genocide and mass atrocity rests with sovereign governments, this responsibility passes on to the broader international community either when it is sovereign governments themselves who commit genocide or mass atrocities, or when they prove unable or unwilling to take necessary action to prevent or respond to such crimes inside their borders (US National Security Strategy 2010: 48). This is a departure by Obama in relation to R2P from the Bush era doctrine of pre-emptive and if necessary unilateral use of force (Reinold 2011). R2P, including its potential for collective action, is increasingly supported by globally shared understandings (Brunnée and Toope 2010: 211). It is, however, considered a threat to national sovereignty (Eckhard 2011: 90); moreover, there is a predominant view that it is yet to become a binding norm of international law (Matthews 2008, Stahn 2007: 102).

Concepts of Sovereignty

The European Treaty of Westphalia in 1648 marked the first phase in the development of modern notions of sovereignty, which established a system of modern nation states in which the sovereign reigned supreme domestically as well as in the state's international relations (Deng 2010: 356). As early as 1651 Thomas Hobbes wrote that the end for which sovereigns were entrusted with authority was the protection of the safety of the people (Hobbes 1996: 222). Even in international law 'the raison d'être of the State is the protection of its citizens' (Brownlie 1963: 289). R2P has conceptualized sovereignty as responsibility rather than only authority (Thakur 2006: 255). This means that current understandings hold that the international community is obligated by humanitarian and human rights norms to protect populations from mass deprivation and death, all of which make humanitarian intervention imperative (Deng 2010: 354).

The second phase in conceptualizing sovereignty is traceable to the end of the Second World War in 1945 in which sovereign power was challenged by the domestic development of democratic values and institutions and by accountability to an international community that sought adherence to human rights and humanitarian standards (Deng 2010: 356). The third phase was brought about during the 1990s through the end of the Cold War, which rendered state sovereignty vulnerable to international scrutiny (Deng 2010: 356). The fourth phase of this phenomenon is the contemporary pragmatic attempt to reconcile state sovereignty over domestic affairs with responsibility for the welfare of its citizens (Deng 2010: 356). To sum up, the current normative status of sovereignty is derived from humanity, as the legal principle that human rights, interests, needs and security must be respected and promoted, and this is also the *telos* or final purpose of the international legal system (Peters 2009: 514).

The Law on the Use of Force

Ramesh Thakur (2010: 10) recently observed that 'repeated US assaults on UN-centred law governing the international use of force have undermined the norm of a world of laws, international law's efficacy and the UN's legitimacy as the authoritative validator of international behaviour'. According to Thakur, because international law is intended to align political power to legal justice, when the powerful subvert the law to make it serve their agenda for keeping others in line, many will resist such perversion of justice (2010: 24). Taking a cue from Thakur's admonition regarding aligning political power to legal justice, this chapter argues that civilians are increasingly protected by both the regimes of law relating to the law on the use of force, *jus ad bellum*, and the law relating to the resort to force, *jus in bello*. The chapter does this principally by examining recent UNSC practice evidencing the coordination and convergence of the Protection of Civilians, the Responsibility to Protect and referrals to the ICC for political violence. In the light of recent practice an argument can be made that the international community bears a moral, legal and political responsibility to protect (Glanville 2010).

POC, moreover, seems to be emerging as more than mere political rhetoric and more of a *jus cogens* norm in the following ways. First it is impermissible for states themselves to use violence against their own citizens in a way that would cause atrocity crimes to happen (Stahn 2007). Second and following on from the first, it is at the very least permissible for the international community to intervene under the Third Pillar of R2P to protect civilians from political violence leading to atrocity crimes. In other words, high-level and sustained armed force may not be used deliberately contrary to the welfare of civilians and, if it is nevertheless consciously used against them to the level of committing mass atrocities contrary to this stipulation, then that would be criminal under international law *and* a justification for armed force against the responsible government.

In public international law, the central provision relevant to R2P and now POC is the United Nations Charter's Article 39:

> The Security Council shall determine the existence of any threat to the peace, breach of the peace, or act of aggression and shall make recommendations, or decide what measures shall be taken in accordance with Articles 41 and 42, to maintain or restore international peace and security.

Historically, the origin of the Article as reflected in the framer's intent was to give as unrestricted a hand as possible to the UNSC for freedom of action (Frowein and Krisch 2002: 718–19). With reference to international criminal law, it and related articles were expansively construed in the Tadić case discussed below (*Prosecutor v Tadić* 1995). More recently, it was considered by the ICC state parties to be closely related to the ICC Statute's (Rome Statute) Article 15 (UN Diplomatic Conference 1998), which was drafted in contemplation of the UN Charter. Prior to the state parties agreeing to a definition, the connection between the identical word 'aggression' in public international law and international criminal law was by no means co-extensive. The same word in the same language and discipline could nevertheless have different semantic effect, let alone tenor and import; for instance, aggression under the UN Charter and aggression in the Nuremberg Charter, Judgment and Principles. The former relates to law on the use of force by states under public international law, and the latter to individual criminal responsibility under international criminal law by natural persons. Now the Rome Statute has blurred the boundary between the two meanings to a certain extent. Additionally R2P is specifically tied to four core international crimes: genocide, war crimes, ethnic cleansing and crimes against humanity (Orford 2009: 1006). R2P was therefore boosted by the establishment of the ICC (Sarkin 2010). Even the International Court of Justice (ICJ) has ruled that states are obliged to take all reasonable measures within existing international law to prevent genocide and punish the perpetrators (*Bosnia v Serbia* [2007]: para. 425). R2P's First Pillar is therefore a *jus cogens* or peremptory norm of customary international law, imposing on states the legal responsibility to protect their populations from genocide, war crimes, ethnic cleansing and crimes against humanity (Bellamy and Reike 2010: 285–6). Côte d'Ivoire and Libya before the UNSC serve as locations where R2P, POC and international criminal responsibility are utilized in tandem to address international peace and security challenges.

Côte d'Ivoire

Following disputed presidential elections and civil armed conflict in Côte d'Ivoire, the UNSC authorized the UN Operation in Côte d'Ivoire (UNOCI) to use 'all necessary means' under Chapter VII of the UN Charter to carry out its mandate of protecting civilians under threat of imminent physical violence (UNSC 2004: para. 8, UNSC 2007: para. 5). The UNSC also authorized French forces stationed in Côte d'Ivoire to use 'all necessary means' in order to help protect civilians (UNSC 2004: para. 16, UNSC 2010: para. 17). Furthermore, the UNSC urged Laurent Gbagbo, the previous incumbent president, to hand over power to Alessane Ouattara, the internationally recognized winner of the elections, in accordance with the voting result. The ICC Prosecutor on his part stated that widespread or systematic killings in Côte d'Ivoire might trigger an investigation (ICC 2011). Alessane Ouattara, the incoming president, promised legal action against Laurent Gbagbo for atrocities committed during the post-election violence (Kaka 2011).

Libya

Regarding Libya, on 26 February 2011 the UNSC unanimously adopted Resolution 1970 under Chapter VII, Article 41 (measures not involving the use of armed force) of the UN Charter (UNSC 2011a). This was in consideration of 'widespread and systematic attacks' taking place in Libya against the civilian population, possibly amounting to crimes against humanity. Invoking the Libyan authorities' responsibility to protect its population, the UNSC decided to refer that situation dating from 15 February 2011 to the ICC Prosecutor. Speaking in favour of the resolution, Nigeria's representative was convinced not only would it address the ongoing violence, but it would also provide for the protection of civilians as well as enhance respect for international humanitarian and human rights law. The Brazilian representative agreed that the measures adopted were meant to halt the violence, ensure the protection of civilians and promote respect for international law (except for the exemption from jurisdiction of nationals of those countries not parties to the Rome Statute). In fact the Prosecutor was reported as being confident of charges ultimately being brought against Muammar Gaddafi, the now deceased Libyan leader (Richey 2011). On 17 March 2011 the UNSC adopted Resolution 1973 (UNSC 2011b) by a vote of 10 in favour to none against (Brazil, China, Germany, India and the Russian Federation all abstained). In it, while reiterating the primary responsibility of the Libyan authorities to protect the Libyan population, the Council authorized member states, acting nationally or through regional organizations or arrangements, to take *all necessary measures* to protect civilians under threat of attack in the country, outside deploying ground troops (UNSC 2011b).

The representatives of the United Kingdom, Lebanon and Colombia stated that the Libyan authorities had lost all their legitimacy and therefore the UNSC resolution was aimed at protecting Libyan civilians. Lebanon's representative hoped that the resolution would have a deterrent role and end the Libyan authorities' use of force against its civilians. Germany's representative, for their part, said the UNSC's intention was to stop the violence in Libya. The United States agreed, saying the Council had responded to the Libyan people's cry for help and the purpose was to protect Libyan civilians. Bosnia and Herzegovina's representative was of the view that the Libyan people desperately needed humanitarian assistance, and the unimpeded access of that relief was an absolute *necessity*. He therefore called on the Libyan authorities to end their violence against the Libyan people and believed that the resolution was an answer to their legitimate call.

Colombia's representative said his delegation was convinced that the purpose of the new resolution was essentially humanitarian and was conducive to bringing about conditions that would lead to the protection of civilians. In their view the Council had acted because the Libyan government, through its actions, had shown that it was not up to protecting and promoting the rights of its people. The Russian Federation abstained, while making clear their opposition to violence against civilians. Portugal's representative said his country had voted in favour of the text because the attacks against civilians had continued after the passage of the last Council resolution, and affirmed that today's resolution addressed his country's priorities, including protecting civilians and the facilitation of unimpeded humanitarian aid.

Nigeria's representative said the resolution had been *necessitated* by the persistently grave and dire situation in Libya. This created the need to ensure the protection of civilians and the delivery of humanitarian assistance to those most in need, adding that when the fate of innocent civilians was in question, the international community must be ready to respond. The League of Arab States and the African Union had spoken with one voice in condemnation of the situation in Libya. South Africa agreed the Council had acted responsibly to answer the call of Libyan people. It would also speed humanitarian assistance to those that needed it most. China said that the continuing deterioration of the situation in Libya was of great concern. However, the UN Charter must be respected and the crisis ended through peaceful means, not the use of force, until peaceful means were exhausted. It did not, however, veto the resolution because it attached great importance to the requests of the Arab League and the African Union. Brazil, on their part, were not convinced that the use of force as provided for in the resolution would lead to the realization of the immediate end to violence and the protection of civilians. These, according to the Brazilian representative, demanded a political process.

There was therefore a broad consensus discernible that the Libyan government had used force on its citizens contrary to human rights and R2P norms which led to the regime losing its legitimacy in the eyes of the international community that necessitated both the referral to the ICC and the taking of all necessary means or measures including the use of armed force to protect Libyan citizens. According to Alex Bellamy (2011: 263) the adoption of Resolution 1973 ‘reflected a change in the Security Council's attitude toward the use of force for human protection purposes’. In spite of identifying this means–ends relationship where force is used to protect human beings, Bellamy (2011: 265–6) considers R2P in relation to Libya as being more the exception than the rule. He identifies three factors that lead to this conclusion. First was the clear threat of mass atrocity, second was an extremely short time frame for an appropriate response, and third was the support of regional organizations, especially the Arab League. According to Simon Chesterman (2011: 280–81) the intervention in Libya, while interesting, was not exactly ground-breaking. But, as he points out, there was no need to employ phraseology referencing ‘unique’ and/or ‘exceptional’ circumstances that were used earlier in order to avoid vetoes by some Security Council Permanent Members. This can be viewed as the real difference offered by Resolution 1973: it referred to no unique or exceptional circumstances but only ‘necessity’ because it was a *normative* development. It was normative in the sense that it relied on necessity as the justification for the use of force while not relying on unique or exceptional circumstances to justify the use of force. This was the distinction between the Libyan intervention and all previous interventions.

Yugoslavia

The clear capacity of the UNSC's power to generate law and indeed even create judicial institutions was affirmed by the jurisprudence of the International Criminal Tribunal for the former Yugoslavia (ICTY). That court's decision also had a clear influence on the drafting of the Rome Statute for the ICC. Article 13 of the Rome Statute provides the trigger mechanism for the ICC's jurisdiction. The article codifies three separate modes for exercising jurisdiction. The first is the traditional basis of the consent of states. The second (already used in the case of Libya) is through a referral of the UNSC by a resolution under Chapter VII of the UN Charter. The third provides for the independent prosecutorial power to refer a case. The first and the third are directly derived from state consent and also flow from specific articles of the Rome Statute, namely Articles 14 and 15, respectively. The second, however, is conceptually a very different proposition in that the power therein flows from UNSC action. This UNSC power received judicial affirmation in the Tadić case (*Prosecutor v Tadić* 1995: paras 26–8). According to Jose E. Alvarez (1996: 245) the Tadić decision was foundational because among others things it indirectly reinvigorated the rule of law. It was also political, given that its intention was to help restore peace. Alvarez (1996: 263) argues that the appellate judges in that case turned to 'necessity' as the ultimate justification to dismiss Tadić's arguments. That court said, with reference to UNSC Resolution 808 setting up the tribunal, that 'neither the text nor the spirit of the [United Nations] Charter conceives of the UNSC as *legibus solutus* (unbound by law)'. Mia Swart (2011: 986) on her part is of the view that, whether or not the ICTY initially had a defect in its legitimacy, this could subsequently be remedied by its moral power and the fairness of its proceedings. Yet, the court essentially recognized a power of UNSC that did not proceed from anything more than the acts of the UNSC itself. However, as the court pointed out, because that power was not limitless or subject to no review, the power had to comply with the conditions of its exercise, which in this case were the restoration and maintenance of international peace and security. The inherent jurisdiction of the Court to decide was described as inversely proportional to the textual discretion of the UNSC to act. In other words, the UNSC could act to give jurisdiction to the ICTY only insofar as doing so was consistent with the Council's mandate. Further, the court clarified that the Charter conceived of the Council as having specific powers (not absolute fiat), which could not exceed those of the United Nations itself: it was instead limited by the jurisdiction of and the internal division of power within the United Nations. The power of the UNSC to invoke Chapter VII powers to initiate or indeed stop an investigation by the ICC in Article 15 of the Rome Statute historically originated from UNSC Resolution 808 of 1993 as affirmed by the ICTY. The essential connectedness between the UNSC's power to regulate international violence and the ability to set up criminal tribunals was first confirmed in the Tadić case explicating *legibus solutus* and only then did it subsequently found its way to Article 13 of the Rome Statute.

The United Nations Security Council as Bound by Law

What can a concept drawn from twelfth- and thirteenth-century canon and civil law teach us about the contemporary regulation of violence in international law? Well, a lot more than would be considered obvious, if the recent developments in the application of R2P and POC are anything to go by. It is mildly interesting that when the ICTY needed to explain and justify the then novel idea that the UNSC could create an international tribunal, it reached for a rather arcane expression in order to state what the Security Council *is*, that is, a creature of law in comparison to what it is *not*, that is, a lawless entity. Thanos Zartaloudis (2010: 102) painstakingly traces how the Latin maxim was transferred from the Roman Empire to medieval ecclesiastical authorities and onward to the notion of 'the people' as a politically legitimizing entity. Kenneth Pennington (1993: 90–91) in turn provides four different but related meanings for *legibus solutus*.

1. The prince's authority to change, derogate, or dispense from positive law (shared with all governmental legislative bodies);
2. The prince's immunity from prosecution;
3. The prince's authority to transgress or dispense from the normal rules governing the legal system;
4. The prince's power to transgress the rights of the subject.

Pennington's classification above seems to indicate that the ICTY in Tadić only applied the third meaning encompassing the authority to transgress or dispense from the normal rules governing the legal system. So the ICTY were saying the UNSC was not *legibus solutus* in the sense that it did not have the authority to transgress the system's normal legal rules. According to Christian Tomuschat (2006: 830) the Nuremberg trials following the Second World War (coupled with the UN Charter) brought forth the international community as a legal concept that placed the leaders of all human communities under the rule of international law. Therefore, a state (actually a government) should never be above the law. The principle elevating the king above the law, *rex legibus solutus*, and its equivalent raising the republic above the law, *res publica legibus solute*, were resoundingly rejected.

In a recent case, the British House of Lords found a clash between the power and duty to detain exercisable on the express authority of the UNSC and fundamental human rights (*R v Secretary of State for Defence* 2007). It held, however, that the United Kingdom could lawfully, where *necessary* for imperative security reasons, exercise this power to intern so as to minimize human rights infringements. The reason for holding the proscription on internment to be qualified or displaced was that Article 25 of the UN Charter requires member states to accept and carry out UNSC decisions, while Article 103 provides that, in the event of a conflict between that obligation and the member state's obligations under any other international agreement, the Charter prevails. This would mean that the UNSC is *legibus solutus* in Pennington's third sense.

The point is that this does not mean that the UNSC is absolved of legal obligations (*Prosecutor v Tadić* 1995: para. 35, Gill 1995: 48). This is the only legally defensible position because a legal system is the weaving of legal rules to legally regulated institutions, leaving no power in the state or in society that is *de legibus solutus* (O'Donnell 2001). That is, all powers are subject to the legal authority of other powers and nobody is supposed to be above or beyond the rules. However, given the centrality of necessity to our inquiry what about the well-known maxim that 'necessity knows no law'? The ICJ (which was evenly split with seven votes to seven, only resolved by the presiding judge's casting vote) had this to say on the legality of the threat or use of nuclear weapons in the Legality of the Threat or Use of Nuclear Weapons case (ICJ 1996: para. 105):

> It follows from the above-mentioned requirements that the threat or use of nuclear weapons would generally be contrary to the rules of international law applicable in armed conflict, and in particular the principles and rules of humanitarian law.
>
> However, in view of the current state of international law, and of the elements of fact at its disposal, the Court cannot conclude definitively whether the threat or use of nuclear weapons would be lawful or unlawful in an extreme circumstance of self-defence, in which the very survival of a State would be at stake.

This case is extraordinary in that the ICJ essentially ruled that it was unable to answer a question before it: it was unable to distinguish between the lawful and the unlawful even after accepting jurisdiction. It was clearly a reaffirmation of the principle 'necessity knows no law', which renders definition and decision impossible in that indistinct boundary between law and politics. This *non-liquet* or identification of a gap in the law that the law cannot answer illustrates a 'state of exception' contemplated by the law (Agamben 2005). Actions taken by the Security Council in addressing aggression and breaches of the peace are paradoxically unbound by law but sanctioned by the law (Noll 2008: 578–9). Indeed, the UNSC's Chapter VII powers, especially as read with Article 25 (which binds all members to UNSC decisions) and Article 103 raise obligations to the Charter above all other legal obligations (*Libyan Arab Jamahiriya v United Kingdom* (Lockerbie case) [1992] paras. 39–46). In my view, this in principle shows the rejection of incorporating violence into law by law. This rejection of violence (and assimilation of force) by law means that the law is permanently at work defining and limiting the exception and in that way, *manages* it as a matter of necessity. To sum up: the UNSC is not *legibus solutus* because its legally mandated ends bind it – and the protection of civilians is coming to assume a central place in those ends, by force if necessary.

State Use of Force

The legal formulation by *all necessary* means or measures is a familiar one in the law on the use of force. However, linking it explicitly to POC and to R2P of both the nation state and the international community, coupled with a referral to the ICC, annexes the regulation of violence to a means–ends economy. Economy, in this instance, is an assembly of means and methods for the ad hoc realization of abstract principles (justice or the welfare of humanity) linking contingent means (including armed force) for realizing permanent humanitarian ends. In *Politics as a Vocation*, Max Weber (2004: 77–8) set out to sociologically define a 'state'. According to him, the state could not be defined in terms of its *ends*, because there was scarcely any task that the state has not taken in hand, and there was no task that one could say has always been exclusive and peculiar to it. Ultimately, the modern state can only be defined sociologically in terms of the specific *means* peculiar to it (including presumably, the international community), that is, the use of physical force. Intriguingly enough, Weber linked this force to violence without specifying their difference (if any) and indeed further links this to the law itself, arguing that anarchy follows lack of violence. He was of the view that every state was founded on force and that if no social institutions existed which knew the use of violence, then the concept of 'state' would be eliminated, and anarchy, in its specific sense would emerge.

Weber concedes that force is neither normal nor the exclusive means open to the state. He nevertheless holds that the relationship is an intimate one because it is the means specific to the state. However, Weber distinguishes the use of force as normal before the modern state and then goes on to give his famous and influential definition of the state as 'a human community that (successfully) claims the monopoly of the legitimate use of physical force within a given territory'. Weber noted that the right to use physical force is ascribed to other institutions or to individuals only to the extent to which a state permitted it. This was because the state is considered the sole source of the 'right' to use violence. Weber here appears to refer to a normative rule-generative *claim* as opposed to descriptive fact-based assertion.

Whatever else that may be said about this definition, its sole referent is a state in control of territory. This in itself tends to sound a bit dated to current readers. With globalization, the state is increasingly marginalized and the monopoly on the use *of* force is becoming a monopoly on the use *for* force. That is, humanitarian and security concerns increasingly underpin resort to force. Claims to sovereignty in justifying resorts to force are no longer legitimate as such. Weber's approach is strikingly similar to Walter Benjamin's (1986: 277) own take. Benjamin sets out his own purpose as explicating the relationships between violence, law and justice. He said that 'it is clear that the most elementary relationship within any legal system is that of ends to means, and, further, that violence can first be sought only in the realm of means, not of ends'. This teleological approach taken to violence meant that his criterion for judgement was the intention of the violence. Therefore, violence without any intention other than to be violent did not fall under his critique. However, from the legal perspective a crime is either an unlawful act or a lawful act done by unlawful means. Therefore legitimate self-defence is excluded from the prohibition of the use of force, just as is the action of the UNSC under Chapter VII of the UN Charter. Weber, therefore, is now superseded. Were he alive to see contemporary developments he would be compelled to revise his definition of the state and its supposed monopoly on the legitimate use of force. Nowadays the state is defined in terms both of its end of civilian welfare and protection, which are the only justification for its means, and its means, which *ultimately include* the use of force. In sum, we are entering a situation in law where the state can no longer be defined in terms of its (Weberian) monopoly on forceful means, but rather must be defined in terms of the ends that it pursues without excluding the use of force.

Conclusion

What therefore legitimates and legalizes the international community's use of force in R2P contexts is precisely because it is used to protect civilians despite their own state having the primary responsibility to protect them. This is why POC is at the centre of both legality and legitimacy in both international and domestic law and practice. This means that both means and ends are liable to criminalization. In terms of means and ends, POC is covered under both legal regimes of resort to force and the use of force. This is despite there being no defence of humanitarian intervention being made explicitly available for criminal aggression as defined under the Rome Statute. Does this mean that the time-honoured public international law distinction between the law of war and the law of peace has now been replaced by an emerging normative monopoly on the legitimate use of force? If such a monopoly has arisen it can only be a normative claim as opposed to a descriptive statement of the status quo. POC nevertheless now governs both how and why force is used globally and, as such, protection of human life is now elevated to front and centre in the legal regime. This legal regime is such that force is not the sole or even the primary means for the protection of civilians but is nevertheless the ultimate means of protection. In other words, the relationship between the responsibility to protect and the protection of civilians is one of means and ends. The use of armed force is the means by which civilians are protected and civilian protection is the end of any legitimate use of force.

Chapter 2
International Criminal Law: From *Hostis* to *Hostia Humani Generis*

As a term, 'Crimes against Humanity' is on the face of it eternally open to signifying too much. Even when championing the ethical treatment of animals for instance nobody deploys terms such as crimes against the bovine for cows, or the canine for dogs, or the equine for horses or the feline for cats, etc., but instead universally call for their 'humane' treatment. This is because all crimes are in the literal sense against humanity (just as all lawyers are in the same sense human rights lawyers despite appeals to the divine and other abstractions). It takes human beings to legislate the law, breach it, try and then punish the perpetrators even when the offence has an animal subject. This is why to call for the humane treatment of humans is the highest point of self-reflexivity making crimes against humanity the most self-reflexive criminal category where we reflect on the human *qua* human.

Larry May's conception of crimes against humanity is probably the most well known. It describes protective and security principles as underlying the international jurisdiction over the crimes. May's approach, however, does not really take into account the normative and descriptive elements of the law where 'humanity' has both qualitative and quantitative elements. Christopher Macleod (2010) for one identifies a certain ambiguity of the term 'humanity' which can refer either to a species or the quality of being humane, that is, humaneness (Macleod: 283). Macleod helpfully reviews eight different conceptions of crimes against humanity in the relevant literature. In the end he favours a definition where 'an action is a crime against humanity if and only if it is a crime that damages humankind' (Macleod: 287), very literally, an offence committed against humanity as such (Macleod: 287). This comes at some cost though because the author readily admits to making humanity a metaphysical object (Macleod: 295). How it makes the transition from the metaphysical to the physical is the subject of this chapter. The chapter examines the divergence and convergence of the theory and practice of international criminal justice in order to provide a factual, textual and legal background that sketches out its redemptive sacrificial economy. Synthesizing some common themes encountered in the subject area (including global politics, exemplary trials, community-formation via exclusion and inclusion, secular and religious mystification, symbolism and perpetual promise), this chapter's thesis is that international criminal law processes embody the international community through iconic presentation. The phrase *hostis humani generis* or enemy of all mankind has been identified as being at the very beginning of international criminal law. It was used to establish jurisdiction especially over but not necessarily limited to pirates. A counterpart phrase *hostia humani generis* or sacrifice for all mankind would have explanatory value indicating as it does that those accused of crimes against humanity are also tried for and on behalf of redeeming all of humanity.

International criminal justice is here portrayed as a political apparatus for generating humanity. International criminal law's contribution to this anthropological machine is the constant generation of social scapegoats through a sacrificial economy. The chapter stages an engagement between international criminal law and an innovative theoretical framework, essentially sketching out an iconography of the criminal trial as being dependent upon a sacrificial economy.

Individual Criminal Responsibility for Mass Political Violence

There is always it seems something new from Africa in the International Criminal Court's (ICC) case docket. As of this writing, that Court has five situations and cases from Uganda, Sudan, the Democratic Republic of Congo, the Central African Republic, Kenya, Libya and Côte d'Ivoire (ICC 2011c). All these in a court that was set up, it is said, to punish those most responsible for 'the most serious crimes of concern to the international community as a whole' that 'deeply shock the conscience of humanity' (Rome Statute of the International Criminal Court 1998: Preamble and Article 1 afterwards the Rome Statute). Faced with this rhetorical claim, surely the proper scholarly attitude then can only be an inquisitively open-minded scepticism towards Africans having a near monopoly of these crimes and prescribing select criminal trials as being the panacea. This chapter casts a critical eye at two apparently unrelated fields of inquiry, both addressing an ethical gap between the theory and the practice of international criminal justice. The first regards a certain ethical ambivalence about whether a criminal trial relying on individual criminal responsibility can prevent the recurrence of mass violence. The second highlights the ethical ambiguity of how a universal court, designed and intended to prosecute those most responsible for the worst crimes known to humanity, only has cases from a single continent whether by coincidence or not. The problematic link between those otherwise unrelated questions in the context of international criminal justice is the continent and peoples of Africa. In theory, at least as per the rhetoric of the then UN Secretary-General Kofi Annan, the establishment of the ICC in 1998 was a historical moment gifting hope to future generations, and a great step towards universalizing human rights and the rule of law (ICC 1998). Annan, quoting Marcus Tullius Cicero's declaration that 'in the midst of arms, law stands mute': *inter armes silent leges* said that there was now real hope that Cicero's cynicism would be less justifiable in the future than it had been in the past (ICC 1998). According to Annan, until the moment establishing the ICC when powerful men committed crimes against humanity, they had known 'that as long as they remained powerful no earthly court could judge them'. Indeed even when they were judged here on earth (as happened in 1945) they could protest that it was merely a form of vengeance: 'victors' justice'. Consequently the accused could explain their guilt away by claiming their prosecution was really a persecution only occasioned by others who proved more powerful than they and those more powerful were in that way able to sit in judgement. At the same momentous occasion Philippe Kirsch, the chairman of the diplomatic conference setting up the Court and later a president of the ICC, concurred that setting up the Court had established solid foundations of an institution, which would have a major impact for future generations. According to Kirsch, the international community had acted to show that it would not stand silently by as genocide was committed. The adoption of the Statute furthermore was 'really the future of humanity in many ways' (ICC 1998).

The central question structuring this piece is how do representative trials of persons accused of having the greatest responsibility for the most serious crimes of concern to the international community as a whole supposedly bind recurrent violence?

The Universality and Promise of International Criminal Justice

Arguably, universal justice has tensions within and between justice and universality. The opposition within justice regards simultaneously addressing individual criminal responsibility and mass violence that implicates a substantial segment of a population. The contradiction within universality is how a court set up by the international community with the potential to cover all states, whether members of the Rome Statute or not, only has African cases even after utilizing all the various means by which it may be seized of jurisdiction. This is in the context of it only being able to act where the state that would otherwise do so is either unable or unwilling to perform its prosecutorial duty (Rome Statute 1998: Article 17).

Community-Formation and Secular Mystification

Sarah Nouwen and Wouter Werner have argued and demonstrated empirically that international criminal trials are an irreducibly political process (Nouwen and Werner 2010). Marti Koskenniemi says that the symbolism of the international criminal trial enables the formation of a moral community (Koskenniemi 2002). Koskenniemi also says that international law, although secular, has a horizon of transcendence couched in messianic language, whose present imperfections only set off its yet-to-be fulfilled promises the brighter (Koskenniemi 2004b: 507). Immi Tallgren points out that international criminal justice, following the rhetoric of domestic criminal justice, sees all criminals (whether robbers or genocidaires) as having a single disease whose cure is deterrent punishment (Tallgren 2002). Given such rhetoric, the logic of both domestic and international criminal justice is that achieving general prevention requires 'exemplary decisions' (Tallgren 2002: 576). This rhetoric and consequent logic are, however, inadequate to serve fully its expressive purpose, which is the prevention of criminality (Tallgren 2002: 571–2). International criminal justice in this way attracts attention to itself and therefore away from what it is intended to address. International criminal law is consequently a 'kind of religious service of hope that is stronger than the desire to face everyday life' that enables the avoidance of the *why* question in international criminal law (Tallgren 2002: 593). To put it baldly, international criminal law enables global governance by simultaneously rationalizing and mystifying political control (Tallgren 2002: 594–5).

Taking a cue from Koskenniemi, Nouwen, Werner, Simpson and one of their common interlocutors, Carl Schmitt, who stated that all 'significant concepts of the modern theory of the state' are secularized theological concepts because of their 'historical development' and 'systematic structure' (Schmitt 2005: 36), I argue that the iconographic symbolism of a few representative trials in The Hague, an iconic city ('the legal capital of the world'), to prevent mass organized political violence, may be both irreducibly political and irreducibly theological. This argument demonstrates that unpacking the iconography of international criminal justice reveals that iconic trials in an iconic city by an iconic prosecutor have their own rhetoric, logic and aesthetic. The rhetoric is organized around achieving universal justice on behalf of the international community/humanity through singular trials of particular individuals. The logic follows an exchange of responsibilities between individuals and their communities via an uncertain and indirect substitution of personal rights for social harmony and order. The aesthetic presents and represents the ICC prosecutor as an image and icon of the international community's justice.

The logic, rhetoric and aesthetic all combine to provide an assemblage of means and methods for the ad hoc realization of abstract principles, that is, an economy. This is specifically a sacrificial economy linking contingent means for realizing permanent ends. All that is in order to visualize the invisible, and hear the inaudible international community through its icons as embodied representations of something that has its own existence, yet which is only visible and audible through those icons (Mondzain 2005: 86). The icon sets up a relation between the visible and invisible without any respect for realism or neglect for the material (Mondzain 2005: 85). The question therefore is not whether the icon is by nature or by definition true or false, or even good or bad, because its truth is derived not from itself but from its founding cause (Mondzain 2005: 82). The essence of the *iconic* image is not its visibility (which belongs to imagery and not to iconicity); 'it is its economy, and that alone, that is visible in its iconicity' (Mondzain 2005: 82). To belabour the point, the rhetorical, logical and aesthetical substitution of a flesh and blood prosecutor for the immaterial international community is precisely what visualizes and renders audible that international community for the purposes of international criminal justice. The ethical position of this, however, falls short of that to which it aspires.

The occurrence of post-electoral violence in Kenya is a case study referred back to repeatedly in this chapter to illustrate different facets of the main argument as they develop. Although it is an example drawn from an African case before the

ICC it has general insights to contribute that are generally applicable to evaluating other courts and tribunals both historical and contemporary. According to the then ICC prosecutor Luis Moreno-Ocampo, the leadership of Kofi Annan was essential for his office (ICC 2009e). A practical illustration of the working of the Court pursuant to the theory of universal justice was when Annan, in his capacity as chair of the African Union Panel of Eminent African Personalities, submitted to the ICC prosecutor a sealed envelope containing a list of persons allegedly implicated in post-electoral violence occurring in Kenya (ICC 2009e). Annan explained that in Kenya there was no opposition between a truth commission and justice and suggested a three-pronged approach with the ICC prosecuting those most responsible, national accountability proceedings for other perpetrators, as well as reforms and mechanisms such as the Truth, Justice and Reconciliation Commission (ICC 2009e).

Pursuant to this prompting from Annan, the ICC prosecutor subsequently said more than once that Kenya would be an example to the world/international community on managing and preventing recurrent political violence (ICC 2009c, ICC 2009d):

> The Prosecutor emphasized that Kenya would prove an example of how to work together with the international community and the Court to end impunity and prevent future crimes. 'Kenya will show how to manage past violence and how to create a peaceful process for the upcoming elections in 2012. Kenya will be an example to the world.' … 'We all agree that impunity is not an option,' he stressed, 'and that to prevent new violence in 2012 it is necessary to prosecute those responsible for the crimes committed during the post election violence.' (ICC 2009c)

To be fair, it was the Kenyan government itself that originated the idea in the first place of using international criminal prosecutions to prevent the recurrence of political violence:

> Regarding Kenya, I met on 3 July with a Government delegation from Kenya, led by Justice Minister Kilonzo. They informed me that, in order to prevent a recurrence of violence during the next election cycle, those most responsible for the previous post-election violence must be held accountable. They are committed to ending impunity, and committed themselves to refer the situation to the Court if efforts to conduct national proceedings fail. (ICC 2009e).

For one thing, preventative exemplification to prevent mass violence is problematic because the law only provides the Court with jurisdiction over natural persons who are to be individually responsible and liable for punishment without allowing corporate or group liability (Rome Statute 1998, Article 25). The selection of accused, however, does seem to be with a view to how they exemplify acts committed *en masse* and in concert. Indeed the then prosecutor has assured that, the 'persons bearing the greatest responsibility for the most serious crimes are being brought to justice' (ICC 2010b). What therefore does the ICC prosecutor *mean* when he constantly repeats the refrain that the Kenya situation would be an *example* supposedly to *prevent* recurring violence. Did the then prosecutor speak *literally* or *literarily*? Is peace a cause or an effect of justice? A literal analysis of the trial process would only reveal an individual in jeopardy of his or her own life, liberty or property. This, bar a mysterious link, does not directly translate to communal peace. How does one prosecute their way to peace? Perhaps there is some indirect analogical relation amenable to elucidation.

A literary or figurative analysis by contrast to a literal one could link individual trials to communal peace, precisely through analogy by making an example of the accused to other potential accused. The point is that there is neither empirical proof nor factual analysis relied on or referred to linking peace and criminal trial, only hopes, promises, suppositions, assumptions and, central to this chapter, ritualized conduct. Indeed interlocutors such as the then prosecutor are not concerned with the actual reality of their intended results but only with their meaning in terms of iconicity to the various constituencies of international criminal justice. The then prosecutor and the Kenyans therefore speak of more than merely law and, to understand those statements better, we need to rely on more than a purely legal analysis of the pacifying preventative exemplar being brought to bear.

The example as a category is used for reasoning analogically by comparing a particular case to a particular case as opposed to either deduction (comparing from the universal to the particular) or induction (comparing from the particular to the universal) (Agamben 2009: 19). The example is a curious case because, while at the same time it belongs to and defines a category, it does so simultaneously as part of and yet outside the same category it defines and to which it belongs (Agamben 1998: 22 and Agamben 2009: 24). Because there is no such thing as absolute guilt, insofar as an accused is made an example of by being tried and punished for the *future* possible actions of *others* he or she cannot help but be innocent. Yet at the same time he or she is guilty for his or her own past conduct making him or her simultaneously belong and not belong wholly to both the categories of innocence and guilt. That innocence, although perhaps miniscule in the scheme of things, is nevertheless critical. According to René Girard, innocence is esssential in creating a social scapegoat in order to prevent recurrent violence because it renders the sacrificial ritual different from vengeance and, in that way, arrests any spiral into endless mutually destructive violence through, for instance, vendettas without end (Girard 1977: 14 and 22–6).

Selective Universality

The rhetoric is therefore that humanity sits in judgement over inhumanity. Given the geographic selectivity of the cases though, it would rather more accurately be put as one segment of humanity sits in judgement over another. One cannot help but detect a note of amphiboly here where Africans are *exclusively* responsible for *all* of humanity's very *worst* problems. Such indiscriminating use of universal sets in international criminal law, not just humanity but closely related terms – the international community and mankind – is under critiqued within the discipline. That lack of sufficient critique is probably because those sets are precisely what make the field itself intelligible and one cannot very well question them and remain comfortably meaningful within the field. These sets, moreover, are crucial and deployed at strategic moments in discourse.

They are crucial in providing a basis for both galvanizing action and paralysing dissent and they are strategic in how they artfully structure the field into insiders and outsiders, while at the same time claiming to act on behalf of both. Moreover, this acting on the behalf of both involves self-selected active insiders acting against more or less passively acquiescent outsiders. The outsider, in terms of humanity, nonetheless remains human and part of humanity. This stands to reason because non-humans could never be guilty of inhumanity. These sets of sets therefore paradoxically include and exclude at the same time insiders and outsiders. The insiders are included as actors but excluded as the acted upon, while the outsiders are excluded as actors but included as the acted upon. Humanity therefore is the set of sets that simultaneously includes and excludes itself. That exclusive-inclusion and inclusive-exclusion dynamic is what makes the international system actually work in the first place and, without it, the system is again unintelligible and paralysed. Universality is arguably at present a useful legal fiction that on occasion cloaks injustice. Suppose, for a moment, we entertain the somewhat unusual thought (elaborated below) that a secular sacrificial economy lies at the root of international criminal justice, what would it mean if, as according to Edward Carr, this ethical system were built on the sacrifice of the weaker brother? (Carr and Cox 2001: 49, Koskenniemi 2005: 499).

Africa is the example *par excellence* of the outside and Africans are the perennial outsiders. However, following from the argument outlined above, Africa and Africans constitute the international community's boundary as such via international criminal justice. In an empirical sense, Africans are the only ones currently under active investigation and trial at the ICC. This is not because of any deliberate intention of a prosecutor or any vast racial plot but follows through from the structure of a faith-based and piety-dependent criminal justice system where judges are not judged and trials are not tried. The reason why Africa is and shall remain the focus of international criminal law is that the boundary of the set of sets that is and contains humanity is under-developed and, in the interim, requires to be conjured up through configuring beings that are simultaneously outside and inside by insiders that are at the same time inside and outside. The beings tried are broadly familiar as sacrificial scapegoats while those doing the trying are familiar as sovereigns. A very specific form of scapegoating is done in international criminal law. The accused are supposed to bear the highest responsibility for the worst crimes known to humanity. The selection of Africans exclusively for this dubious honour, while not random, is definitely arbitrary. It is not random because there are real prima facie grounds indicating that persons from the region selected are responsible in some way for the commission of absolutely heinous acts. It is arbitrary, however, because out of a total human population in the billions the few Africans selected neither have the monopoly on international criminality (not even in Africa) nor can they be singled out solely as the very worst offenders.

A completely reasonable counter-argument, however, could be made that African states and African people are the most supportive group of the ICC. What is more, the African continent not only has the worst crimes but, most significantly, also has the least infrastructure to deal with these crimes. So is Africa and are Africans the sole focus of international criminal law because of their high enthusiasm for international criminal justice, culpability for international crimes or structural and political weaknesses or some admixture of all three? Article 13 of the Rome Statute provides the trigger mechanism for the ICC's jurisdiction. This Article codifies three separate modes for exercising jurisdiction. The first is the traditional basis of the consent of states. The second is through a referral of the United Nations Security Council by a resolution (UN Charter 1945, Chapter VII). The third provides for an independent prosecutorial power to refer a case. The first and the third are directly derived from state consent and also flow from specific articles of the Rome Statute, 14 and 15 respectively. Plainly because *all* the modes of triggering jurisdiction have been exhausted exclusively in relation to Africa, it is both culpability and weakness. That is precisely why the selection, while arbitrary, is not random. The inability to prosecute implies weakness but being unwilling to do so constitutes culpability. It would appear then that the pious hope by which punishment will surely follow crime is not perfectly congruent with this reality. Why is it that Africans appear to have the monopoly on the worst crimes that humanity has to offer along with the weakest infrastructure to deal with them? Coincidence? Or is this structural weakness precisely why Africa is targeted and not any others.

Another objection raised could be that the case often celebrated as heralding the birth or beginning of international criminal law (that of Peter von Hagenbach) is, after all, neither from Africa nor of an African (Schabas 2007: 1). Likewise, the trials after the Second World War of the Nazis, the Imperial Japanese and their Axis partners, were also nothing to do with Africa. Even more so Italy, which could have provided some accused criminals for their wartime actions in Ethiopia, was not part of these post-war trial processes (Pankhurst 1999). However, precisely those exceptional and therefore oft-cited cases make the point that now international criminal justice has been normalized by setting up a permanent court, the usual suspects are exclusively African and as yet not even exceptionally non-African. However, given the glacially developing trend whereby the exception gradually becomes the rule (Benjamin 1996: 392), Africans are only the vanguard for a globalizing international criminal justice. Indeed Giorgio Agamben finds it unsurprising 'that there is a predilection to resort to exemplary punishment in a state of exception' (Agamben 1998: 23). The then prosecutor himself said that the 'court is really helping to establish a new idea in the world with state parties and non-state parties. It will take time. In 30 years, all the world will be a member of the court but in the meantime we are progressing' (Menya and Reuters 2009). The Court thus starts with Africans in order to cut its teeth before promising to sink its talons on bigger prey.

This is the point made again and again that a court that is yet to gain credibility and respect begins with going after the weakest and not necessarily the most criminal. Therefore it targets Africans not because they are the worst but because they are the weakest. This is supposed to somehow redeem the whole of humanity, thus making Africa the perpetually scapegoated *pharmakos* that is given up and giving itself up to sacrifice in order to embody the international community through criminal justice. This is neither the time nor the space within which a comprehensive and satisfactory explanation of such a complex and long-standing social phenomenon as the scapegoat mechanism can be elucidated. However, various writers from both inside and outside the traditional international criminal law canon may enrich the discussion and shed some light on the particular concerns raised.

The characterization 'universal justice' has the international community performing a seemingly external sacrifice (because the accused is taken out of the normal communal relations as a rogue, terrorist, pirate, outlaw, etc.) (Simpson 2004: xi). On the other hand, the accused's community, which is also the 'accused community', provides an internal scapegoat to redeem itself. Socially unsanctioned violence violates that most sacred value (sanctity of human life), which requires a sacrifice (trial and sentencing of criminals) that produces a scapegoat (Noll 2008: 563; Girard 1986) through the punishment of individuals as responsible for *future* collective breaches of the peace by *others*. Such ambivalent figures are conceptually similar to persons declared anathema (Gignac 1907, Hubert and Mauss 1964, Agamben 1998, Simpson 2004: 325). The sacrificial economy particularly clarifies inclusion and exclusion mechanisms in the construction and reconstruction of the relationship between the particular (a specific set of facts) and the universal (the general system of law) (Fox 2007: 563).

Substitutive Logic

The logic underpinning the rhetoric of universal justice through individual criminal responsibility is one where the responsibilities of the whole are substituted for those of a part. To refer once more to the Kenyan case in the then prosecutor's words: the 'whole international community is with the Kenyans, all Kenyans must come together and use the law and justice as a basis for their common future. The common goal is to ensure there is no repeat of violence in the 2012 elections' (ICC 2010e). This is intended to 'end impunity to prevent future crimes' (Menya and Reuters 2009). The then prosecutor said that 'Kenya will provide a historic example on how one country chose to address and prevent massive crimes'; furthermore, 'Kenyans, including women, youth, tribal groups, judicial, political, and religious leaders have a role. This is their court' (Mwanzia 2011). As per the then prosecutor's rhetoric, the international community is the community of communities in that it contains all Kenyan communities and individuals.

The then prosecutor's own original contribution to the Kenyan situation was to add exemplification as the means by which to achieve such a preventative approach to violence. He then proceeded to extend its effective reach from Kenya and Kenyans to the wider international community by saying: 'Kenya could be an example of how to manage this type of conflict because Kenya had a problem but Kenya stopped the crimes in two months. Now they have to do more to prevent repetition and ensure the next election is an example' (Thomasson 2011). This preventative exemplification to ward off violence thus became a running theme covering not just a specific election in time and space (Kenya in 2012) but also 15 other elections elsewhere and at different times; moreover, all of them in the future:

> The best example is Kenya. Justice for the post-electoral violence in Kenya will ensure a peaceful election in 2012. Additionally, it will send a clear message for the 15 elections to come in the region: violence during electoral times cannot be a tool to retain or to gain power; but it is a sure avenue towards a one-way ticket for prison in The Hague. That is the message we need to send in Kampala. (ICC 2010d)

Thus futurity is linked to collective liability to scapegoat the accused by apportioning responsibility for what has not yet occurred and is by no means certain to occur apparently on ultimate behalf of all of humanity. It was as though this is a liturgical exercise that has the then prosecutor effectively intoning: 'here judged today is the individual responsible for the communal violence you have suffered (and perpetrated) whom is now punished. Peace be with you for now and ever more'. The recipients of this message of the trial as a spectacle shall, it is hoped, respond affirmatively: 'there, but for toeing the peaceful line, go I'. And if violence were to be no more, peace would surely follow. Once again: '[t]he results of our investigations in the Kenya situation will be presented to the Judges in December. We are preparing two cases against six individuals. These cases could have a critical role to play in preventing violence in the next election in Kenya and in another fifteen countries of the region' (ICC 2010g).

This exemplary preventative approach is to be achieved by only trying those accused with the greatest responsibility for the worst crimes (ICC 2009):

> The investigation will focus on those most responsible for the most serious incidents. We will try to conduct an expeditious investigation, aiming to present a sample representative of the crimes committed. We envision at least two cases against one to three persons in each case. We will focus on those who, according to the evidence that will be collected in the course of our independent investigation, are most responsible. (ICC 2010c)

When examining relevant national proceedings of potential cases prosecutorial policy seems to follow the same line of holding a few individuals responsible for the mass by focusing on those who appear to bear the greatest responsibility for the most serious crimes (ICC 2010f). This approach is applied in enabling the selection of cases based on 'persons most responsible' or 'those bearing the greatest responsibility' but not making those standards legal preconditions for admissibility, which would be a hindrance to the then prosecutor (ICC 2011a). The Assembly of State Parties to the ICC appears to endorse the view that the ICC has had to take a policy decision to focus prosecutions on 'those bearing the greatest responsibility for the most serious crimes' even though it is not prescribed in the Statute (ICC 2006). However, among professional criminologists there seems to be a broad consensus that the efficacy of punishment in acting as a general deterrent is not the most important factor in lowering crime rates (Bernard et al. 2010: 20–24). Moreover, international criminal trials do little to deter violence or promote reconciliation (Snyder and Vinjamuri 2003–2004, Shaw, Waldorf, and Hazan 2010: 31–2, Justice Report 2011).

Images and Icons of the International Community

Tallgren proposes that perhaps the purpose of international criminal law is less the prevention or suppression of criminality than the establishment of symbols, which enable belief in a legitimate international community that can be governed analogously to the nation state (Tallgren 2002: 594–5). Tallgren suggests one way to focus differently on international criminal justice is as a continuous remembrance service, akin to divine religious services, which meaningfully targets the questions of life and death, good and evil, as well as the promises of justice, peace and love (Tallgren 2002: 593). Girard and Agamben have outlined the sacrificial and juridical logics inherent in such an exercise (Jenkins 2004). Lior Barshack, for one, conceives of the court as a social mechanism providing the centre of contemporary civil religion (Barshack 2000). Both Girard and Gregor Noll have noted before the proximities of sacrifice to violence and of the trial to the sacrifice (Girard 1977, Noll 2008). Secularization is inadequate as a remedy because it is the shifting (rather than abolition) of concepts from one sphere (religion) to another (for example, politics or law), consistently with their erstwhile function (Agamben 2009: 77). Secularization can therefore mean the obscured continuation of practices of religious origin, more or less unrecognized or unacknowledged (Löwith 1949, Kantorowicz 1997, Schmitt 2005, Schmitt 2008, Gillespie 2008). Presently, therefore, sacrifice as a social function has shifted register in moving into law through politics from theology.

Aesthetics is central to law generally but international law in particular because such central features structuring it, for example, the aforementioned humanity but also sovereignty, the rule of law, human rights, etc., can only be interacted with indirectly in terms of their positive (actual performance) or negative (perceived lack) manifestation. This means that all of its main principles and concepts are always *presented* but never present in the real sense. That is to say they are not to be found as themselves within the material physical realm open to the senses except in and by representation. This is because – it is believed – they are to be found either above or perhaps below but in any event beyond the directly perceptible. Yet they remain in some normative sense the 'truth' behind the representative 'façade'. This briefly passes for the aesthetics of law. The argument indicates that any efforts directed towards interacting with these necessarily transcendent concepts could only be grounded in a secular sacrificial economy (Goodrich 1990: 59, Zartaloudis 2010: 16). That is to say, if trial works by displacing social and individual perceptions of guilt onto the accused (who is selected for his or her sins but not only for his or her sins is he or she punished but also those of others), then it displays an irrepressible sacrificial economy.

What is a Sacrifice? Core and Collateral Effects and Affects

What would happen if a would-be sacrificial victim were given a voice? There are three examples of human sacrifice documented in the Christian Bible. To start with probably the least known, that of Jephthah of his daughter (we are not even told her name): she was sacrificed in exchange for victory in war over the Ammonites by her father. Apparently, although unhappy, she accepted her fate quietly and was duly sacrificed (Carroll and Prickett 2008: 310–12). The case of Abraham and his first-born son Isaac is probably more familiar than the first. Abraham was instructed to sacrifice Isaac to prove his piety towards God. While on the way to the altar when the unsuspecting son innocently inquired as to the whereabouts of the sacrificial lamb, he received the response that God would provide. Indeed God did, but only after Abraham was about to slit his own son's throat as an offering (Carroll and Prickett 2008: 23–4). We therefore are not told what view Isaac would have had of the proceedings had he been fully appraised of them beforehand. The last example is probably the most well known and influential where Jesus Christ, simultaneously both God and man, was given over in sacrifice by God his Father to humanity in order to redeem that humanity (Carroll and Prickett 2008: 39). Jesus, while fully aware of and initially willing to go along with the sacrificial elements of his death, nevertheless expressed some reluctance that was subsequently overcome to accept it (Carroll and Prickett 2008: 41). More to the point, the last is a profoundly influential sacrifice because its daily ritual re-enactment and reaffirmation does not require an actual death but only simulates the original foundational sacrifice of Christ's crucifixion. One does not have to be a Christian believer to appreciate the value of a simulated death underpinning such a nevertheless efficacious sacrifice.

A sacrifice is therefore not a simple word at all. It requires at a bare minimum three elements: the person, animal or object offered up for sacrifice itself; the individual or community making the sacrifice; and the immaterial but representable idea, being or deity to whom the sacrifice is being made (Hubert and Mauss 1964). The relationship between these various elements is an additional layer of complexity. The sacrifice and the person making the sacrifice must be somehow connected without necessarily being identical. The relationship between the person making the sacrifice and the entity to which the sacrifice is addressed can only be representative. That is, both indirect and uncertain. This interaction is therefore not one of direct exchange or a trading of favours, as it were, but more one of supplication, which if performed in the ritually correct manner promises to bring about the desired response.

Sacrifice is a transcendental concept, which as such is a necessary condition of possibility for the international criminal justice system. As seen above, the phenomenon of redemptive sacrifice is not new or even new in its theological aspects to international law (Beard 2003, 2006, Grbich 2006, Orford 2006b). The elements of sacrifice most relevant to international criminal justice are redemption, atonement, expiation and purification. Redemption connotes deliverance from sin and damnation, including by atonement or expiation. Expiation is a means by which redress (for a crime or offence) is made by an accused through, for instance, punishment. Atonement connotes restoration or reconciliation of friendly relations by reparation of wrong or injury through making amends or providing satisfaction and, in that way, purifies society of the pollution of the harm done.

By empathizing with sacrificial victims it is imperative to note that a sacrifice, by its very nature, is just a performative exercise that it is never literally *true* but only either efficaciously or inefficaciously performed. There can never be any *real* sacrifices because it is all about figuratively indirect and therefore necessarily uncertain substitutions. They are all simulations, ritualized exercises to bind society through compelling spectacle. As a virtual activity, therefore, they do not need the collateral real and repetitive spilling of blood, as it were, to impress their core moral or political lessons upon pious or impious onlookers. The affective states that trials are intended to produce on the audience are not directly linked to their punitive effects on the accused.

Social Catharsis

Richard Dawkins's notion of memetic transmission encapsulates nicely the cultural shifting of the trial-as-sacrifice by explaining how the descent (if not the origin) of law and the legal system from the sacred could occur (Dawkins 2006: 192). The trial can be seen in the form of a morality tale rippling across space and time through a series of memes; peace is good and beneficial while war is bad and attended with prohibitive cost. The trial is subsequently installed as an archive and repository of communal values. By linking prosecution of the accused to achieving peace, the court makes the virtual sacrifice paradigmatic of the international criminal trial. The trial-as-sacrifice through the scapegoated *pharmakos* provides both social bonding and the binding of violence. This is how international criminal trials build the international community up through instrumentalizing empathy or identifying the self with the other in the dock, which enables formation of society via outlawry, etc., where the excluded provides the boundary for inclusion (Simpson 2004: xi).

To summarize the line of argument pursued to this point, the two limbs of the central ethical problem identified – the ambivalence of justice (by making an example of one from the past to others in the future) and ambiguity of universality (exclusive focus on Africa) – are linked by the *pharmakos* mechanism (explained below) through preventative approaches to legal justice. In the Kenyan case study chosen both the Kenyans and the then prosecutor share a common faith in the value of this preventatively sacrificial economy in hopefully eradicating violence. If the Kenyans initiated the process, then the ICC prosecutor continued and extended it. Even so, as we shall see below, defence counsel note it with alarm and, likewise, the then prosecutor actually charges some accused with practising it themselves. Therefore, in international criminal justice as social catharsis, the international community is making the sacrifice, Africans (who both belong to and are excluded from the international community) are the sacrifice, and the entity they are sacrificed to is a 'justice' that is never present but is only ever presented.

The paradox of individual criminal responsibility for mass communal violence has led defence counsel to go on record with misgivings about this approach on the basis that it is liable to generate scapegoats:

> When it comes to crimes in Ituri, those who are the most powerful are spared. Thomas Lubanga is charged in place of those who should have been prosecuted, and so the accused is placed in an unacceptable situation. The International Criminal Court is put before an immense danger, a fearsome danger, because the International Criminal Court cannot prosecute all of the suspects. And because it can never prosecute all of the suspects, international criminal justice must necessarily face the temptation to convict by proxy those who are absent. The danger is tremendous, because beyond the prosecution of an individual, an attempt is made to prosecute a criminal phenomenon which is far greater than him. The accused then becomes or risks becoming a scapegoat. (ICC 2009b: 31)

The defence counsel further expanded upon the idea portraying the accused as a scapegoat:

> As regards scapegoats, we must ensure that the concept of individual criminal responsibility is applied. Only this vigilance on the principles and on the evidence can enable the International Criminal Court to meet the challenges of justice, the human and symbolic challenges inherent in any trial before it; and that double vigilance is all the more important, your Honours, in that in bringing before you to be judged Thomas Lubanga, and bringing before you Thomas Lubanga to be judged in the place of those who bear the greatest responsibility for the crimes

> committed in Ituri, one is seeking to have you play a role which is not yours, one which cannot be yours, one which must not be yours. (ICC 2009b: 33)

The spectre of the scapegoat also crops up in yet another case on this occasion, introduced by the prosecution this time, explicitly linked to the notion of sacrifice and as evidence to prove knowledge of serious crimes against a civilian population by the accused:

> Witness 45 provides further details in regard to the trials. He states that none of the soldiers served a full prison sentence. The witness further states that Jean-Pierre Bemba reassured the ones tried that, and I quote: 'It was done for outside people, and after that they would be released.' …
>
> Approximately one month following their convictions, Jean-Pierre Bemba granted them amnesty and they were reintegrated into the MLC force. In referring to the case of Commander Ngalimo, who was the MLC commander, your Honours, in the Mambasa sector, the witness states that he was found guilty for the murders – for murders and pillaging and sentenced to five years' imprisonment. And he further states that when Ngalimo complained of having been sacrificed and being used as a scapegoat, Jean-Pierre Bemba sent someone to reassure and promise him that he would be released soon thereafter. Only one month later, Ngalimo was granted *amnesty and received a promotion to the rank of a colonel*. (ICC 2009a: 106)

In keeping with the perception of a redemptive sacrificial economy a former Kenyan Member of Parliament, Ms Jayne Kihara, of whom it is alleged that she financed and bought machetes for gangs involved in attacks, chimed into the debate and referred to herself as a 'sacrificial lamb' (Gekara 2009). Sacrifice therefore meaningfully links even primarily oral and primarily literary communities. The example, which appears in such different guises as precedent, or case study, even acts as a morality tale linking literal and figurative statements. It is therefore clear that potential accused, the then prosecutor and defence counsel, are all alive to the idea and dangers of using legal processes to generate scapegoats in a sacrificial context. To summarize the workings of the iconography envisaged, politically motivated violence in Kenya, although unique, once dealt with serves as an exemplary case to influence in future the international community generally and at least 15 other African countries in particular. This renders any convicted individuals responsible not only for their own past actions, but also for the potential actions of others in the future. On the face of it, this is a departure from the norm, because past rules guiding present actions provide the usual basis for the criminal law in which each person is individually responsible for wrongs already committed by them and not for the wrongs of others that are yet to be committed and indeed may never be committed.

The afflicted (and afflicting) communities are a singled out part of the international community and therefore the scapegoat is simultaneously from both local and global communities; this is why the useful paradox of sacrality/*homo sacer*/scapegoat is relevant to explain how a being can be inside and outside at the same time. According to Jacques Derrida, the scapegoat or *pharmakos* is a being that simultaneously belongs and does not belong to society (Derrida 1981: 130–34). This coincidence between outsider and insider makes the scapegoat more easily amenable to sacrifice for communal atonement or expiation. They belong to the community enough to be associated with it but are just vulnerable enough within it to be picked on as the victims of sacrifice. The *pharmakos* therefore exemplifies a vehicle through which a social body figuratively expels evil, harm or wrongdoing from itself as a purificatory process. The scapegoat is paradoxical because it is the border between inside and outside, making it both and neither. In this way society consitutes and reconstitutes both its make up and its moral values.

Frazer, in his magisterial ethnographic study of the scapegoat, meticulously documents examples from all over the world, demonstrating the theory and practice behind how to ritually transfer the guilt of a whole people onto an individual human, animal or object (Frazer and Fraser 2009: 557). If we think of the human as a hyphen that connects god to animal, the dividing line between the two necessarily passes through the human that is a sort of divine animal (Derrida and Bennington 2009: 13, Agamben 2004: 37). According to Frazer 'when a nation becomes civilized, if it does not drop human sacrifices altogether, it at least selects as victims only such wretches as would be put to death at any rate. Thus the killing of a god may be confounded with the execution of a criminal' (Frazer and Fraser 2009: 588–9). Further:

> a common and successful device is to consummate the sacrifice on the person of a malefactor, whose death at the altar or elsewhere is little likely to excite pity or indignation, since it partakes of the character of a punishment, and people recognize that if the miscreant had not been dealt with by the priest, it would have been needful in the public interest to hand him over to the executioner. (Frazer and Fraser 2009: 660)

The ambivalence and ambiguity outlined make it possible to draw both distinctions (within universality and humanity) and comparisons (between separate cases both actual and potential) where there otherwise were none. Describing the exemplification process is therefore a foray into representations in the realm of law, that is, legal aestheticization (Simons 2008: 227). In being a cautionary example to others, the accused is a peace sacrifice in a literary, or figurative, or iconographic sense. This 'sacrifice for peace' element gives the entire international criminal trial a decidedly quasi-religious aspect with the trial standing in as a secular sacrifice that casts the accused as a social scapegoat for the preservation of peace. There are at least two challenges of representation here. One might be how to ground the real and immediate jurisdiction of the court over perpetually potential cases. The other is attendant upon portraying Africa as a terrain of, and Africans as, a cipher for *all* the worst of humanity's ills. The mysterious link between the two is the scapegoat/*pharmakos* mechanism already encountered in several instances above.

Although sacrifice links simultaneously both violence and trial in international criminal justice, nothing has as yet been written on it as being explanatory of Africa's peculiar position within it. This chapter noted the sacrificial economy of law not merely to note or even applaud its potentials and redemptive capacity, but it is also a directed critique suggesting that international criminal justice is all and only about affects and icons; that such a sacrificial economy of law could potentially be organized without any actual victims. One possible way towards this is to shift emphasis from law enforcement, aimed at redressing breaches once they occur, to law fulfilment, addressed at achieving the promise of the law before it is breached (Agamben 1991, 2011). All we should unflinchingly acknowledge is the anarchic core of international justice where violence is both benediction and malediction simultaneously. Consequently short-term interventionist and, in the end, ineffectual responses to political violence should be abandoned. The study began by attempting a partial demystification of basic concepts in the panoply of international criminal justice, not in order to advocate abolishing or abandoning them immediately, but to suggest finally positive ethical transformations in their use in order to align those practices more closely to the aims of apportioning responsibility equitably, promoting reconciliation in affected communities, and encouraging remorse in convicted offenders in order to prevent the recurrence of political violence. This would hopefully bind the sacrificial logic, rhetoric and aesthetic of international criminal justice to an ethic of empathy that strives to be truly universal and truly just.

Chapter 3
Between Necessity and Contingency: Representing Legality as a Faustian Pact

> The conquest of the earth, which mostly means the taking it away from those who have a different complexion or slightly flatter noses than ourselves, is not a pretty thing when you look into it too much. What redeems it is the idea only. An idea at the back of it; not a sentimental pretence but an idea; and an unselfish belief in the idea something you can set up, and bow down before, and offer a sacrifice to … . (Conrad, Matin and Stade 2003: 50)

The Faustian Pact as a Legal Exemplar

This chapter argues that the use of legality to prevent violence is akin to a Faustian pact. The evidence examined ranges from the literary to the legal and theoretical. The minorities in question are the indigenous Australians and the coastal inhabitants of Kenya, both of whom pose broadly similar but contextually different challenges to state territoriality. These challenges to sovereignty reveal the sacrificial economy grounding the relationship between legal force and lawless violence. In the end the problematic triumph of law reveals the paradigm of legality as a Faustian pact. Which is to say that before the Faustian pact is resorted to, there is no conclusive proof of its necessity. Whenever it appears effective whatever it achieves could potentially have been realized without it. Once utilized, however, there is no objective proof of its contingency. It is in this way profoundly ambivalent.

The conclusion reached is that it is impossible to demonstrate empirically either the necessity or superfluity of legality in preventing violence. This ambiguity is why precisely it is so useful in wielding power. It simply enables the glorification of that power giving it a legitimation beyond mere violence. This study aims to draw the veil from some of that mystification in relation to the glorified formations of political communities in the space between international and domestic law – a space occupied by individuals of varying personal status. The specific query is how do sacrificial themes function and enable social relations through the expedient form of an inclusivity that necessarily accompanies exclusivity.

As good a place to start as any is engaging with Giorgio Agamben whose work meditates upon similar themes. Agamben, however, is often criticized for sloppiness with his sources most especially Foucault and classical authors (Lemke 2011: 53ff.). Further, his thought is accused of neither explaining nor providing political programmes (Bailey 2009: 113–32), and his paradigmatic method itself sacrifices history with its ahistorical use of exemplars like the Roman Law's *homo sacer*, or 'sacred man' who-may-be-killed-but-not-sacrificed, 'the camp', etc. (Gratton 2011: 599–613). Finally, Agamben is charged too with making hyperbolic claims derived from minimal evidence or relying on particularly exceptional circumstances to explain an entire epoch of Western political history (Gratton 2011: 599–613). In spite of all these misgivings his work admittedly provides unique insights into the contemporary global political situation, nevertheless (Ross 2012: 421–34).

Mitchell Dean argues against a formalistic approach to studying power. Instead using Agamben's work among others he opts for the substantive use of paradigmatic cases, analogies and exemplars (Dean 2012: 101–17). Agamben defines a paradigm as having the following features (Agamben 2009: 31). A paradigm is analogical. It moves from singularity to singularity being as it is neither deductive (from universal to particular) nor inductive (from particular to universal. A paradigm neutralizes the general/particular dichotomous logic with a bipolar analogical model containing fields of tension approximating a magnetic field. A paradigmatic case as such suspends even as it exposes its belonging to its group. An example (insofar as it is as an example) gestures towards a group that it is a part and representative of at the same time. It mimics the single sided Möbius strip in forming a definitional boundary that simultaneously contains and excludes the group it belongs to. Therefore it is never possible to separate its exemplarity from its singularity. It follows that the paradigmatic group is itself immanent in each particular instance of the paradigm but at the same time it is neither presupposed nor derived from them. Each exemplar singly can stand in for the group's membership. It other words in the paradigm there is no origin or *archē* because each occurrence of the phenomenon is originary or archaic. This locates the paradigm's site in history on a crossing between occurrence at the same instant and occurrence over time. This chapter takes a similar approach methodologically by looking for 'signatures' in Agamben's sense of the term as an indicator in a latter-day concept that refers back to the concept's origins in a separate sphere of thought (Agamben 2009). Therefore in the various exemplars of the Faustian pact each instance while unique has general lessons as member of a group, which can be drawn from regarding each member of them as a paradigm for each other.

Being and Essence in Australia

The *Mabo* case is most noteworthy for overturning the international legal doctrine of Australia having been *terra nullius* (land with no owner) and in that way establishing the existence and persistence of native title claims to land in Australia. The following discussion, however, will focus on examining the introduction of new legal orders, the effect of these upon property rights specifically relating to land and therefore in effect the construction of identity, order and hierarchy in society.

According to the High Court of Australia, the notion that under Australian common law the sovereign acquired absolute beneficial ownership of all land was wrong.[1] That disavowed proposition had had four bases, one negative and three positive (*Mabo* [No 2]: para. 31). The negative basis was simply that the Crown was absolute owner for the reason that there was no other (or no other recognizable) proprietor. The three positive bases were first, that when English law was brought to Australia, the common law to be applied included the feudal doctrine of tenure. This meant that just as the Crown acquired or was deemed to have acquired universal ownership of all land in England, likewise the Crown became the owner of all land in the Australian colonies. The second positive ground for absolute beneficial ownership of the sovereign was that all land in any colony was 'the patrimony of the nation' and, upon that basis, the Crown acquired ownership of this patrimony on behalf of the nation. The third and final positive basis for the absolute beneficial ownership of all land was simply through the sovereign exercising his or her own prerogative to this effect.

A closer look at these bases, all of which were examined and rejected by the High Court, reveals a peculiar ontology of the negative in that the first so-called negative basis underpins the three apparently positive bases. That is to say only by the lack of any other sovereign could feudal law be imported, and land can be deemed the patrimony of any nation, and a sovereign be able to exercise their prerogative. In fact, the three positive bases are not legally examinable as such because they are in their very nature non-justiciable. The court can only examine their effects and not their legitimacy.[2] This is simply because the Crown's acquisition of sovereignty over the territory of Australia cannot be challenged in an Australian court (*Mabo* [No 2]: para. 83).

The High Court instead decided that acquisition of sovereignty confers a radical title to the land.[3] Although native title to land survived the Crown's acquisition of both sovereignty to the territory and accompanying radical title to the land, crucially, native title rights (but not them exclusively) were exposed to extinguishment by any valid exercise of sovereign power (*Mabo* [No 2]: para. 83), which was inconsistent with the continued right to enjoy native title.[4] In other

1 Native title survives the Crown's acquisition of sovereignty. The common law of Australia rejects the notion that, when the Crown acquired sovereignty over Australia it thereby acquired the absolute beneficial ownership of the land therein. The court accepted that the antecedent rights and interests in land possessed by the indigenous inhabitants of the territory survived the change in sovereignty and thus constituted a burden on the radical title of the Crown. *Mabo* [No 2] at 62.

2 The Court held that although the question of acquisition of sovereignty was a non-justiciable question in a municipal court, the effect of such acquisition of sovereignty upon native title was nevertheless a justiciable question. *Mabo* [No 2] at 31–2, 81–2 and 129–30.

3 Sovereign power enabled the Crown to extinguish native title; however, any instrument purporting to exercise that power was to be construed rigorously. Such legislative or executive instrument would have to reveal a clear and plain intention to do so. *Mabo* [No 2] at 64, 110–11 and 195–6.

4 The court rejected the notion of 'terra nullius' and held that native title survived the acquisition of sovereignty. *Mabo* [No 2] at 57–8, 109, 180, 182, 192 and 216.

words the legitimacy of the sovereign, supreme and undivided, and their power and authority were never legally in question. Indeed they could never be in question without irresolvable self-contradiction. Only the legality of acts purportedly done under the sovereign's name were and not the legitimacy or even the justness of those acts. Having said that, if more than one possible reading were possible legal doctrine would require that the court select the more just or legitimate choice over any others.

It is clear that *Mabo* [No 2] is legal authority for the proposition that the sovereign's mere existence and the actual exercise of that sovereignty are separate and distinct.[5] Sovereignty's existence (being a non-legal question; one that the court must assume in order to be and remain a court) cannot be questioned in a court of law but its exercise can be examined legally for both its propriety and its effects. This is deeply intriguing because it is arguably the pivot upon which the entire case turned. To start with, the decision rests on a fundamental paradox being that the only direct experience we can have of sovereignty is when it is exercised and yet sovereignty is only exercised because it already exists. Existence and exercise are inseparable and co-dependent. Each presupposes the other. To develop this further, the existence/exercise distinction neatly maps onto that mainstay of democratic monarchies, the separation of reign from governance, which conceptually separates power from its legitimation. It does this by introducing an internal division within power – which is to say – that of the existence of a power that is distinguishable from its exercise. This acquisition/consequences of acquisition or existence/exercise distinction neatly folds onto potentiality/actuality, glory/power, etc. where one of the pair is transcendent while the other is immanent. The transcendent moreover mysteriously legitimizes the immanent, which is after all the whole point of the distinction.

Real sovereignty then seems to subsume within itself both actualized and potential sovereignty. The actualized sovereignty is immanent and thus able to be questioned in the here and now but the potential sovereignty is transcendent and cannot be questioned in a court without the foundational system that makes law intelligible collapsing. Moreover, if we focus for a moment on the question of a sovereignty that exists without being exercised, a sovereignty that is never present directly but must always be *re*presented in *all* its manifestations, then we enter the realm of pure potentiality. This sovereignty exists merely as the potential to be exercised or not exercised and not otherwise.

How would a sovereignty that is not exercised look like? Would it have concrete effects? It would seem that in *Mabo* [No 2] the non-exercise of sovereignty was made the basis for the continued existence of native title. Interestingly enough the court did this while overruling *terra nullius*, which in turn had been based on a cascading series of negative ontologies or lacks as shown above. Most important was that of the indigenous Australians not having any (or perhaps more accurately

5 There was no necessary link between acquiring sovereign power and acquiring beneficial ownership of land. *Mabo* [No 2] at 57, 80–81 and 180.

any recognized) system of law and thus not having any legal title and thereby rendering the territory open for settlement. Indeed to accentuate on the negativity-as-grounding theme, native title is extinguished if the particular clan or group ceases to acknowledge traditional laws and fails to observe its customs (*Mabo* [No 2]: para. 83).

This negative ontology is the productivity of the void, the amazing fecundity of nothing that opens the way for active intervention in creating legal orders 'out of nothing', literally *ex nihilo* in Christian theological terms (as opposed to the Ancient Greek idea of creating order out of chaos) (Close 2009: 8). The court therefore consciously or unconsciously utilized a structural grammar and semantic form of reasoning that was irreducibly if not obviously theological. In this way it was possible to disavow any responsibility for any prior, current and future dispossession while deriving the benefit of that dispossession and by this move cementing the possessory legitimacy upon surer foundations. The reason for the somewhat muted shift into a theological register is, in my view because of the complex relationship and interplay between force or violence, law and religion, theology and philosophy, et cetera.

Take *terra nullius*, which was the fountain and origin as it were of the dispute. It is itself traceable back to fourteenth-century papal bulls to Roman Catholic sovereigns giving carte blanche over non-Christian's lives and over their lands. Protestant sovereigns likewise issued charters of similar import and effect even as they repudiated the pope's authority to make similar claims. Again, this was a dispute about the exercise and not the existence of the power necessary. The power to go forth and occupy land bears that originally religious signature.

The principle difference between *Mabo* [No 2] and the cases it overruled was the status of the doctrine of *terra nullius* as having been shifted to be a contestable question of fact away from being a matter of binding law. A principal previous judgment examined and overruled by the High Court was *Milirrpum v Nabalco Pty Ltd. (Gove Land Rights Case)* (1971) 17 FLR 141 (hereafter *Milirrpum*). In that case Blackburn J found that Australia was not *terra nullius* as a matter of fact at all but was only *terra nullius* as a matter of settled law, which law he as a judge bound by precedent could not disturb being as he was too low down in the judicial hierarchy. However, the High Court did not labour under his particular disability. It was open to it to reconsider this question as the highest court in the land and therefore one not subject to a superior binding authority. This judicial intervention was richly generative of legal consequences. The difficulty, however, is to discern as to whether the fact that the issues selected and rejected for judgment were based on anything other than legally sanctioned violence – whether actual or potential – backing up the enforcement of the decision, from historical times to the present.

According to Blackburn J the principles that relate to the acquisition of colonial territory were not simply of law but also included Christian ideas. These ideas posited that the whole earth and its resources were open to the industry and enterprise of the human race as a duty and a right. Not the entire human race of course but only the more 'advanced' peoples within it who were justified in dispossessing, of necessity, the less advanced. This religious notion was supported not just by the Bible, but also by that celebrated jurist-theologian Emmerich de Vattel and indeed was the basis upon which the Puritans of Massachusetts acquired territory in America. Related to this was the doctrine that discovery was at the root of title in international law. This meant that any sovereign whose subjects discovered new territory acquired the title to that territory by the fact of such discovery. Therefore only that sovereign and not the sovereign's subjects could actually extinguish native title.

In Blackburn's opinion the authorities showed that the law relating to the application of English law to the overseas possessions of the Crown was, in principle, well settled by 1788 at least since the publication of William Blackstone's *Commentaries* in 1765. Blackstone himself distinguished between settled colonies, where the land, being desert and uncultivated (including territory in which live so-called uncivilized inhabitants in an allegedly primitive state of society), is claimed by right of occupancy, and conquered or ceded colonies. The difference between them is that in those of the former sort all the English laws, applicable to the colony, are immediately in force there upon its foundation. In those of the latter type, the colony already having its own law, that law remains in force until altered. Blackstone himself famously distinguished between written and unwritten laws or as he put it *lex scripta* and *lex non scripta*. What does it mean for a primarily literal society to divide the law between written and unwritten? In my view this maps onto that fecundity of nothing whereby unwritten law can be read as the absence of law and therefore used to justify actions that would otherwise have no foundation whatsoever apart from their mere factual existence.

The line of this succession is clear. The pedigree of the idea refers back to biblical themes and arrives at the shores of Australia through papal bulls, royal commissions and charters to writings of theologian jurists like Vattel and Vittoria all the way to Blackstone and the scores of legal cases citing him with approval. Its effects are not only still apparent to see in the marginalized and dispossessed status of indigenous Australians but also in an irrepressibly theological register which persistently structures argumentation and response. Even in these contemporary secularized times a barely disguised Christian legacy still silently holds sway.[6] As Agamben points out even though modernity has banished God from the world, it not only has not exited theology, but also has only in a certain sense brought to completion the project of a providential economy (Agamben, Chiesa and Mandarini 2011: 287). 'Economy' here refers to relating specific immanent means to certain transcendental ends based upon necessity (Agamben, Chiesa and Mandarini 2011: 141). The late litigant Eddie Mabo himself both reviled and

6 See for instance: 'Ours is, and always has been, a Christian State. The English family is built on Christian ideals, and if the national law is not Christian there is none. English law may well be called a Christian law …' *Bowman v Secular Society Ltd* [1917] AC 406. Lord Finlay, the then Lord Chancellor, also agreed that 'there is abundant authority for saying that Christianity is part and parcel of the laws of the land' ([1917] AC, 425.

revered cuts a messianic figure. He was exiled for a long time from his home in the Merriam Islands and his people but nevertheless devoted himself to their collective cause. What is more, he did not live to see the fruits of his labour but his self-sacrifice opened the door to redeeming the entire Australian community. The judicial decision role here serves as legitimation of governmental power via the glory of law.

A concise statement of the *Mabo* legacy is that there is a clear and meaningful separation between sovereignty and its exercise. That distinction differentiates between the Crown (permanent, completely good) and government (temporary, of necessity sometimes has ill effects). It strikes some notes on the political-theological register, such as a mysterious grounding of a 'bare sovereignty' that confers jurisdiction and jurisdiction that provides legitimacy and legitimacy that in turn justifies sovereignty. Finally it depends on a mystical origin and foundation of the contemporary legal order where regrettable and transient 'evil' is explained away as collateral to the desirable and temporary 'good'.

The Australian decision is in spite of its legality fairly theological in terms of its theodicy, that is to say, justifying the existence of evil (indigenous dispossession) in the face of a supposedly all-powerful god (the sovereign). The case does this through the notion of a providential economy that is the necessary accompaniment of freedom. The basic message is that occasional evil is the price we pay for being entirely free in our choices. This is the sacrifice offered for our well-being as humanity. As is demonstrated below, international legality and globalization now means that globally everyone is caught up in an endless cycle of sacrificial redemption. It is not essentially or even primarily racial although it always begins with the most vulnerable in society in order to order all of the rest of society. The points made regarding the *Mabo* case in principle apply as well to the Kenyan case with some points of difference in application. In both cases similar challenges to sovereign acts were ruled as non-justiciable in the courts (*Ol Ole Njogo and Others v The Attorney General Civil Case No. 91 of 1912* (E.A.P. 1914), 5 E.A.L.R. 70).

Secession Threats in Kenya

Kenya has persistent religious, cultural and economic flashpoints. Among the most immediate is the threat of secession and communal mass violence mixed up with the global war on terror along the Kenyan coast, a predominantly Muslim area of the majority Christian nation (BBC 2012a and BBC2012b). In the Kenyan situation historically the mainland was broadly considered terra nullius for all intents and purposes while the coast was nominally a British Protectorate under the Sultan of Zanzibar (*Municipality of Mombasa v Nyali Limited* [1963] E.A. 371). Abdallah Mwahima, a coastal Member of Parliament, in a public meeting with the highest provincial government official, referred to the Kenyan state's presence as a 'government of fetishes and idols' as he pointed out that most of the meeting's attendants were supporters of a secessionist movement the Mombasa Republican Council known as the MRC (Goldsmith 2011: 43).

In *Randu Nzai Ruwa & 2 Others v Internal Security Minister & Another* [2012] eKLR a judgment delivered on 25th July 2012, the High Court looked into whether or not the action of the Government of Kenya in proscribing the MRC for advocating the secession of the Kenyan coast from the rest of the republic was unconstitutional. The substantive question arising was whether the Kenyan nation, striving to be open and democratic, should accept the ban as reasonable and justifiable.

The court concluded secession was a political agenda and the MRC was a political movement. The court went on to say that democracy was not a licence to disorder or lawlessness. The court granted MRC members the opportunity to fully enjoy their rights in a context that was formal, orderly and permitted by law. The court strongly suggested organizing and registering as a political party. In the court's view secession was only possible by far-reaching amendments to the Constitution by a referendum (Article 255 of the Constitution of Kenya). One interesting point about the ruling was its navigation not just of the legal-political divide but also of the law-violence divide. The decision clearly strove to extend the rule of law even to the most bitter of disputes and discounted violence of both the state the secessionists as having a place in a democratic state guided by the rule of law.

With regard to the human rights of MRC members and sympathisers, the Kenya Police have evidently internalized international and domestic use-of-force accountability mechanisms (Kiarie 2012, NTV Kenya 2012). In that sense the ICC has already been effective to some extent in discouraging indiscriminate use of force by governmental organs in Kenya. That much is reasonably clear. The relevant law domestically is the *National Police Service Act* (2011). In section 61(2) and in its sixth schedule it is provided that force may only employed when non-violent means are ineffective and the force used should only be to the extent necessary and proportional in the circumstances. The Act further provides for the Cabinet Secretary responsible for Internal Security and the Inspector-General of Police to make regulations on the lawful use of force, include listing the lawful means to use force as well as stipulating the training requirements allowing use of those means. Neither of these has yet been done which gives the police pause for thought as well as the courage to publicly decline to use force to quell the political violence even while discounting the use of the military as an alternative (Kisia 2012). Here the matter would have perhaps rested except that the MRC rejected the court's recommendation to register as a political party. Consequently, the government declared it an unlawful society and started rounding up its leaders (Oketch 2012). If the physical state of the suspected leaders making court appearances is any guide, the police have significantly overcome their initial reticence to use force (Daily Nation 2012). Therefore the riddle of how to overcome violence by law still persists in the Kenyan context despite the best efforts of the courts. The paradoxical cost of getting a hearing before a court is the recognition of the sovereignty that is being challenged.

Emergency and Law/Lawlessness

Thomas Hobbes' view was that a world without law existed as *bellum omnium contra omnes*, 'the war of all against all'. In this state, any person has the natural right to do anything to preserve his or her own liberty or safety. People in a state of nature ceded their individual rights in a social contract to create sovereignty, retained by the state, in return for their protection and a more functional society. A human sovereign becomes a god to humans, *homo homini deus*, as distinct from the state of nature where humans were wolves to human, *homo homini lupus*.

One thesis drawn from Hobbes's work is that the original political relation is the ban (interesting Kenyan connection) that incorporates a state of exception, which renders outside and inside, exclusion and inclusion, indistinct (Agamben 1998: 181). Roberto Esposito traces the linguistic difference between *homo* for human and *persona* for person to make much the same point that human beings are excluded from the polis by only including persons (Esposito 2012). The explanatory power of the concept of a state of nature as an *ex post facto* justification of the law should not be underestimated. The state of nature is in essence a thought experiment that imagines a world without law. This means that it begins with a law-shaped void that consequently requires the law in order to be complete. In this way it is both reflexive and recursive: of law and from law.

According to Gerry Simpson (2007: 133) 'the regulation and criminalization of war represents the culmination of the juridical project'. In a similar vein Giorgio Agamben (2005a: 48) argues that the state of emergency/exception is 'an emptiness and standstill of the law'. Noting this, Simon Chesterman states that in crises 'the Security Council does not invoke emergency powers in the sense of enhanced centralized authority; rather, the crisis (a threat to international peace and security) justifies a temporary suspension of the law (the non-intervention principle enshrined in Article 2(7) of the UN Charter) for a specific purpose (restoration of peace and security)' Chesterman (2009: 1518). Chesterman also quotes Lord Curzon's remark that the Persians would rather govern themselves badly than be governed well by others (Chesterman 2009: 1540). This succinct statement of a Faustian pact can be paraphrased easily in the words John Milton put in the mouth of the devil in *Paradise Lost*: 'better to reign in hell than to serve in heaven'. This heaven/hell theme too can be seen in a quote attributed to Dag Hammarskjöld, UN Secretary-General from 1953 to 1961: 'The UN was not created to take mankind to heaven, but to save humanity from hell'.

This is how even departure from law can be justified as a higher adherence to the law when packaged as compromise or pragmatism. Because the law is at both ends of the equation it is impossible to imagine the *absence* of law as anything other than as a *lack* therefore making it necessary to extend the rule of law to prevent resort to violence. All of this, however, is in a rhetorical or symbolic or expressive sense not in an actual material sense. The law is rendered infinitely more powerful when it is internalized throughout the community as part of society's continuous self-defining narratives. The expressive role of the law as we see below has a sacrificial logic.

Society's Sacrificial Economy

Hannah Arendt (2004) considered Joseph Conrad's *Heart of Darkness* 'the most illuminating work on actual race experience in Africa'. To what does the ellipsis at the beginning of this piece allude to in this deeply ironic work? Race and self-sacrificial redemption leap out of its pages. However, does it offer any contemporary insights regarding the acquisition of sovereignty over persons and territory, and legitimation of both? *Heart of Darkness* could have been just as easily titled darkness of the heart. In this work we encounter a faux Faustian papier-mâché Mephistopheles. The contrast between Christian Europe and the pagan Congo maps onto the motif of light versus darkness not just in the story and the story within a story but in the hearts of human beings as well. Without spoiling the book for those that may not have read it or read it too long ago to remember, central to the narrative is the quest for a Mr Kurtz who sits quite comfortably as the author of a report to the delightfully named 'Society for the Suppression of Savage Customs' and yet styles himself as a god presiding at sacrifices partaking of human sacrifice.

In shifting register for a moment to the literary from the philosophical we gain greater appreciation of Conrad's deeply ironic and profoundly ambiguous work. Chinua Achebe discounted irony in Conrad's part. Achebe's most famous work and probably the greatest African novel *Things Fall Apart* is in part a riposte to Conrad and explicitly deals with sacrificial themes. Ikemefuna is the scapegoated victim given over as a peace sacrifice by Okonkwo his surrogate father (Achebe 1971: 8). Ikemefuna was originally from a neighbouring clan and was given up by his natural family as compensation for the death on Umofia person. He grows close to Okonkwo's family but nevertheless meets his death at the hands of Okonkwo and others. Okonkwo later commits suicide fated to end up as a single paragraph of one chapter in a book titled 'The Pacification of the Primitive Tribes of the Lower Niger', plainly a nod to Conrad (Achebe 1971: 183).

In Conrad, foreshadowing Agamben, the usually well-policed boundaries between civilized and savage, enemies and criminals, inside and outside and centre and periphery are problematized. Indeed consistent across Agamben (when highlighting social, historical and political taboos) is his characteristic move of ferreting out 'zones of indistinction' which is to say the ambivalent point at which two non-binary but opposed poles acting in tension nevertheless become indistinguishable. Such is how contingency and necessity can be problematized through sacrificial practices. Such practices merely exist to link an idea and its realization through embodiment by substituting actual bodily vitality for metaphorical but no less real artificial bodies of which the state as a political community is exemplary.

The Faustian pact problematizes necessity by showing its contingency and problematizes contingency by linking it to contingency in the following ways. The common elements of a Faustian pact are desire and offer, acceptance and delivery then either doom and damnation or forgiveness and redemption. Also the devil usually appears in a pleasing shape (for example a poodle in Goethe's version or Franciscan Friar in Marlowe's), offering good in exchange for evil. The generic form of a deal with the devil involves a contract for a soul in return for the object of desire. As Conrad puts in the mouth of Marlowe: 'I take it, no fool ever made a bargain for his soul with the devil: the fool is too much of a fool, or the devil too much of a devil – I don't know which'. Because the devil is a deceiver it is immaterial whether you have a soul to sell or not in regard to achieving the sought after aim. There is therefore no necessary causal link between that deal and the realization of the desire. In other words the person supposedly trading away their soul could have achieved it without the deal in the first place. However, given their faith in the transaction their heart's desire also could not have been achieved without making the deal.

According to René Girard (2011: 27) 'The miracle of sacrifice is the formidable "economy" of violence that it realizes'. That is, 'the invention of ritual sacrifice must be the first properly human initiative, the point of departure for religious culture, which is to say, the point of departure for human culture itself' (Girard 2011: 31–2). 'Sacrifice is not then merely an instrument of peace; it sets in motion a process of repetition that engenders, no doubt very gradually, what we call our social and political institutions. The more sacrifices are repeated, the more they tend to become what we call funerals. Marriages, rites of passage, initiations of all sorts, and likewise royalty – political power- is always suffused with the sacred – all the institutions in short, of our culture' (Girard 2011: 32). Sacrifice being mythic is 'neither entirely fictive nor entirely real' (Girard 2011: 50).

According to Agamben the gesture of sacrifice and the morality of prayer present a theurgical aspect in that humans act ritually on the gods in order to effectively create them. This glorification is itself what produces glory, which glory is the very substance of God and the true sense of his economy (Agamben, Chiesa and Mandarini 2011: 226). Agamben states 'glory' is 'the uncertain zone in which acclamations, ceremonies, liturgies, and insignia operate' (Agamben, Chiesa and Mandarini 2011: 188). For Giorgio Agamben sacrifice provides a mythical foundation for society rather than the fact of mere action without any actual grounding (Murray and Whyte 2011: 173). It supplies the fiction of a beginning for a community, which beginning by a simultaneous exclusion and inclusion excludes what in reality, is the entire foundation of communal life (Agamben 1991: xiii, 111 and 105). Which is to say 'all human action' … 'inasmuch as it is not naturally grounded but must construct its own foundation, is according to the sacrificial mythologeme, violence' (Agamben 1991: xiii, 111 and 105). Agamben claims a close and intimate connection between the sacrificial function and political power secularization notwithstanding.

In *Kingdom and the Glory*, Agamben explores the concept of *oikonomia* (Agamben, Chiesa and Mandarini 2011: xi). Agamben argues that whereas in the Christian tradition it was conceived as the government of the immanent world, currently it has shifted meaning to refer to a transcendental 'economy'. In this work Agamben makes several points regarding the relationship between theology and economy while examining the term 'providence'. His conclusion is that: 'The central mystery of politics is not sovereignty, but government. Yet the government is not God: it is the Angel, the minister; it is not law, but the police. That is, the governmental machine that they form and keep functioning' (Agamben, Chiesa and Mandarini 2011: 276).

Agamben establishes two paradigms derived from Christian theology: political theology, which founds in the one God the transcendence of sovereign power, and economic theology, which substitutes for this God the notion of an *oikonomia*, conceived as an immanent ordering of the divine as well as the human. The first provides political philosophy and the modern theory of sovereignty while the second engenders modern biopolitics and the triumph of economy and government. *Oikonomia* is etymologically and conceptually linked to 'dispositive' through the Latin *dispositio* and *dispensatio*, and as Agamben also notes to 'exception' (Agamben, Chiesa and Mandarini 2011: 49–50). Here *oikonomia* signifies not only the mysterious incarnation of the *Logos*, but also the 'occasional restriction or suspension of the effective rigor of the law and the introduction of attenuations which "economize" the command of the law' (Agamben, Chiesa and Mandarini 2011: 49–50) These exegeses of *oikonomia* links Agamben, to Michel Foucault and Carl Schmitt (Bussolini 2010: 108–43). Agamben subverts Carl Schmitt's thesis that all key concepts of modern state theory are nothing other than secularized theological concepts, and argues, instead, that secularization shows that theology persists in the immanent world (Minca 2009: 177–82). Any ambiguity generated in the state of exception is only resolvable by action that is to say by Schmittian decisionism, which is ultimately not through force of reason but by reason of force, not by political philosophy but by political theology.

But is it necessary or unnecessary? Conrad wrote 'I take it, no fool ever made a bargain for his soul with the devil: the fool is too much of a fool, or the devil too much of a devil – I don't know which' (Conrad, Matin and Stade 2003: 110). The passage demonstrates how the Faustian pact is profoundly ambiguous and ambivalent. It creates its own reality by retroactively positing the preconditions to its own existence. This is why legality of the sort described by Thomas Hobbes' social contract resembles a Faustian bargain in that it renders it impossible to distinguish whether it was necessary or not. It is further quite reminiscent of the extortionist's movie trope simply transposed to: 'Nice community you have there. Shame if something were to happen'. As a testament to its fecundity, adaptability and endurance Faust's legend has gone through different iterations including a roll call of German greats from Goethe to Richard Wagner and Friedrich Nietzsche from Baruch Spinoza (Seung 2006: i). Even *Thus Spoke Zarathustra* is supposedly a parody of Wagner's *Ring*, which itself is arguably a parody of *Faust* (Seung 2006: xiv). All these though make it clear to see that it is not the ring (which ring for our purposes stands in for the law) that gives power but that power gets the ring (Seung 2006: 324).

Is there a way out of this Faustian bargain? According to Mikhail Bakhtin the image of Faust originated in the atmosphere of carnival legends (Bakhtin 1973: vii, 249 and 109). Agamben (2005a: 71) explicitly identifies the carnival as the state of suspended law exception. Agamben teases out a possible solution. We are like humans in limbo abandoned in the absence of God. This means we have no destiny and are therefore indifferent to redemption and as such embody that life that is merely human and not sacred which can survive the end of the politico-theological machine (Agamben 1993: 5–7). Agamben's model for this is the messianic vocation that he considers the revocation of every vocation (Agamben 2005b: 95).It does not destroy or annihilate the factual existence of the world but rather suspends it 'as if it were not'. This does not have a negative connotation, does not constitute a new identity but rendered inoperative and thereby fulfilled in being opened up to its true use (Agamben 2005b: 95). Agamben often calls for profanation. Profanation itself is a species of carnivalization given both its ambivalence and its turning of concepts into their opposites. In Dostoevsky's *The Idiot* Prince Myshkin does not occupy any position in life that might define his behaviour and limit his pure humanity (Bakhtin 1973: vii, 145 and 249). This as such makes him a fairly Agambenian figure. We can render inoperative any activity directed towards a Faustian pact in order to open it to a new use. A new use does not abolish the old but only exposes and disarms it (Murray and Whyte 2011: 107).

We do well to remember that the essential ingredient of Faustian pacts is renunciation of love in exchange of power (Carnegy 1973: 97). In sum such a pact is more about shaping present reality by after the fact justifications for law's existence. Where does this leave us in the here and now? Exactly where we were before of course with freedom and responsibility of action. Mephistopheles is Faust's alter ego (Seung 2006: 139). They both reside in the human heart. We all are both Faust and Mephistopheles. The pact is not an external drama but an internal dialogue.

Chapter 4
Global Law: From Force and Law to Aggression and Legality

Introduction

This chapter is intended to bring to light a dynamic between spaces devoid of rules and humans stripped of their rights. This dynamic explored here is achieved through calibrating the relationship between law and force. The theme examined relates certain textual practices associated with the law to demonstrate the law (being a system of enforceable rules) functioning as a social link between persons (being bearers of rights and duties within a legal system) and social practices, and how these are either fostered or undermined by the relationship between law, force and violence.

It is a fact that force is used in the social context. The argument presented below is that it is then politicized in society by being divided into a binary of social/anti-social. The former is permitted if not encouraged and the latter is abhorred if not confronted. Afterwards, force develops to recognize and be recognized by law. What is therefore value-neutral in a mythical state of nature becomes decried in society (partially) and exalted (partially) depending on whether it is characterized as social or anti-social. Ordinarily, therefore, a specific factual context of the use of force is assessed through a legal text concealing or sublimating a political subtext. However, originally the political subtext has produced the legal text brought to bear in the general social context.

What this is intended to demonstrate is that law is the appropriate regulatory medium for force. It attempts this by indicating that any claim that a certain use of force, while admittedly contrary to erstwhile laid-down texts, is in fact an exception to or a change in the law, results in violence that is not just *contrary* to law but also *against* the law. That is, it is simultaneously a crime of aggression and an abuse of the legal process and undermines the global order. This is therefore violence against the notion of law itself, not only against its provisions but actually against the very order or normality that makes the law intelligible. As St Augustine had it, it is an attempt to reconstruct violently the present 'normal' to a state of a new 'normal' more congenial to the ends of the aggressor.[1] There is, therefore, a line to be drawn separating self-defence from taking the law into one's own hands.

1 'For every man is in quest for peace, even when waging war, whereas no one is in quest of war when making peace. In fact, even when men wish a present state of peace to be

This study separates force from violence by initially uniting them in the value-neutral concept of coercion. It subsequently distinguishes them as force being coercion used for social ends (for example, law enforcement or self-defence) while violence is coercion used for anti-social ends (here the crime of aggression). With reference to human society writ large, the distinction social/anti-social is congruent with friend/enemy in the political sphere and lawful/unlawful in the legal system.[2] The resolution suggested here therefore to increase clarity is more legalization that embeds deeper the use of force in society for social ends and either blackens or whitens the current grey areas that are still rhetorically insisted upon as a matter for politics.

The Alchemy of Law and Violence

In classical international law, the direct relationship between territory and the ability to project force was most clearly present in the notion of territorial sea. Thus, according to the Dutch jurist Cornelius van Bynkershoek, sovereignty could be claimed over the seas to the extent it could be protected from shore (Brownlie 2002: 179, Schmitt 2003: 183). Thus at the time, cannon ball range, or three nautical miles, served as good title to what would otherwise be no man's land. It followed on that ordering of territory through domestic laws on citizenship, disabilities of aliens and so forth created persons linked to concrete territories by spatio-temporal practices. This is the boundary linking and separating international and domestic law.

With reference to human rights, at least since AD 1215 with the Magna Carta, the law struggled to stabilize the future expectations of English subjects by normatively (and not descriptively) 'binding time' within the defined space of England. That is, an enforceable text (wrung out by force) inculcated a relative security of life, liberty and property as 'individual rights'. These elements were thus protected within the strictures of the law from being taken by the sovereign, who was also charged with protecting such rights of their subjects from internal or external dangers. However, given exceptions relating to conflicts between the rights themselves and in cases of emergency, exercising power was related to movement toward and away from text but always linked to text in the sense that no powers over human beings were conceived of as without limit because an absolute sovereign cannot be spoken of in relation to any law. Indeed absolute sovereignty is the antithesis of law not merely its negation or absence.

---

disturbed they do so not because they hate peace, but because they desire the present peace to be exchanged for one that suits their wishes'. Saint Augustine 2003: 866.

2 The binary coding of Luhmann's Sociological Systems theory is especially useful in this regard, together with the insights of Carl Schmitt. For the affinities and differences between Niklas Luhmann's and Carl Schmitt's thoughts (examined later herein) see Chris Thornhill 2007: 499.

In relation to the global sphere, since the Nuremberg trials, the Magna Carta (or its principle of only taking life, liberty or property via due process) was in a sense de-territorialized. The London Conference setting up the tribunal was figuratively a Magna Carta for humankind, with the spectre of Hitler standing in for all would-be-scourges of humanity. In other words, the Magna Carta in the United Kingdom, the French Revolution in France, the American Revolution in the United States and the Bolshevik Revolution in the USSR all could neither jointly nor singly project their application to protect human rights onto the actions of the Axis Powers in Axis or occupied territory without recourse to the notion of a 'humanity' over and above nation states and individual humans.

It transpired that, after being a space of conflict following two world wars, the entire globe was transformed to a place of peace (normatively not factually) governed by a law anchored on human rights that was enforceable through individual criminal responsibility in the extremities of aggression and other crimes against humanity. This was the new 'normal' and all law had to conform when read in this context.

This fallout from war was probably the strongest single impetus to the new regime of human rights, decolonization, (Louis 2006: 639, Heinlein 2002: 183)[3] and rewriting of the law of armed conflict. For the first time in history, legal discourse was concretely developed on a global social scale, right down to individual human beings; that is, universally, without the inside/outside dichotomy and generally without the opposition self/other.

As the two studies below show, cases from a lone 'terrorist' to so-called 'wars of national liberation', which are ostensibly as different as night and day, nevertheless display the same phenomenon at the core. This phenomenon broadly encompasses spatio-temporal practices involving force and violence. These practices are wielded with life as the object through manipulating the link between law and the force ordinarily associated with the law. In this manner human personality may be conjured up (through for example grant of citizenship and the appurtenant rights thereto) or conjured away (through reduction to the status of an alien). Specifically, where law is viewed as 'enforceable rules', fidelity to the rules is reduced and discretion to apply force (now unbound and therefore violence) is increased.

The chapter ends with the observation that now the whole world is in the process of a new upheaval where it is in danger of sleepwalking into a space of violent political struggle instead of a place of mutual peaceful existence sanctioned by laws. That is, the crime of aggression now coincides with the abuse of legal process on a global scale. The difference with the past is that now the law is imminently reducible to the status of a plaything and is no longer a guide to conduct. Therefore in regulating force, global law has conceptually shifted from

3 For American official hostility to colonialism see William Roger Louis 2006: 639, and Frank Heinlein 2002: 183.

a passive force and law (immanent in and regulating an identifiable place) to an active aggression and legal process (effective in and ordering a given space).

By controlling the legality of the use of force, one may not only legitimately impose legal order on chaos initially but also subsequently wreak disorder upon legal order by creating spaces open to violence out of places erstwhile governed by rules (Frazer and Hutchings 2007: 180, 191–2). This renders the resisting enemy a criminal, by definition killable in combat and punishable outside combat. This is to say that absence of (law and) order can be either chaos or disorder dependent on whether it is 'natural' or willed by human agency. Further, both strong and weak states perceive order protected by law as overwhelmingly positive. Such order is desirable to strong states in order to maintain and consolidate their possessions and positions. Weak states espouse order as well to be secure from superior force.

To a certain extent, in terms of permissible and non-permissible manifestations, law from the local to the global context already governs force. In the local context, there are laws against treason and insurrections while in the international context there are regimes governing the lawful use of force via the United Nations Charter and customary international law.[4] Moreover, this distinction is not absolutely clear-cut and there are instances of internationalized domestic violent disputes (the Hague and Geneva Conventions encompass instances of parties in civil conflict being viewed as belligerents by external powers) or globalized local contexts. In this chapter, two global and local examples are used to make some of these points.

Law, Politics and Determining Aggression

This section endeavours to show that the fact that the texts forming the basis of both the Nuremberg International Military Tribunal (IMT) and Tokyo International Military Tribunal for the Far East (IMTFE) prosecutions affected only the Axis powers linked a social context to a political subtext, mediated through a legal text. That is, the trials after the Second World War coupled singular political events to a general legal structure. The intention is to showcase judges as riding legal text

4 See for instance *Prosecutor v Miroslav Deronjic* Sentencing Judgment, ICTY Case Number: IT-02–61-S 30–03–2004: Dissenting opinion of Judge Schomburg at para 7: 'The International Prosecutor is not controlled *de jure* or de facto by independent judges or a government in the selection of suspects to be indicted and in determining the scope of an indictment, as it would be on a domestic level. The state's and the international community's monopoly over the right to exercise force, however, urges the Prosecutor to act in a way that makes victims of crimes and their relatives understand that the Prosecutor is acting on their behalf. When it comes to prosecuting crimes against individuals, a Prosecutor acts with the goal to stop a never-ending circle of "private justice", meaning mutual violence and vengeance. This goal can only be achieved if the entire picture of a crime is presented to the judges'.

between the Scylla of subtext and the Charybdis of context with the law still fairly clear and coherent, or at least as clear and coherent as solemn words can ever be.

There are logically only two possible opposed points of entry to the debate regarding criminal aggression from that time to the text of the Rome Statute for the International Criminal Court (ICC). The first is that the crime of aggression exists but an adequate definition for the purposes of the ICC is yet to be arrived at, while the second is that the crime of aggression does not exist; however, the issue of its existence is still open.

The current legal precedent value of the trials after the Second World War thus involves a delicate balancing act between the social systems of law and politics as represented by the intentions of the framers of the relevant texts and facts that they grappled with and mediated through the texts produced. That is, future expectations of peace were guaranteed through the written word.

The text could be narrowly interpreted in politics as instrumental (only intended to apply to particular persons, at the places and times mentioned), or broadly construed in law as overarching (covering similar actions dispersed at different times involving diverse actors). The political subtext drives a narrow approach to the legal text but the social context demands a wider interpretation utilizing the political system to produce mutually binding decisions and the legal system to stabilize expectations in the face of disappointment in living up to those decisions.[5]

This part of the current work is intended to demonstrate a clear conceptual relation between the crime of aggression and the abuse of process. Using the political subtext-to legal text-onto social context narrative, I will endeavour to show that the fact that the texts at the basis of both the Nuremberg and Tokyo prosecutions affected only the Axis powers linked a social context to a political subtext, mediated through a legal text.

This context and subtext existed uneasily together. The trials after the Second World War represented both singular political events and a general legal structure. The legal text depended on the broad principle that a breach of the international peace was a breach of the international rule of law. The social context, however, was that although the Axis powers were not the first, nor would not be the last, to breach the principle, their acts were correctly considered too egregious to escape legal sanction of some form. Despite all legal protestations to the contrary, the political subtext was law as the continuation of politics by other means: woe to the conquered. For instance, Winston Churchill, Britain's wartime Prime Minister, strongly urged that the Nazi leaders be extra-judicially executed (Simons 2006). There was no intention of applying the same yardstick to the past or future acts of the Allied Powers.

5 It has been argued that all law is indeterminate because rules are only as important as their purposes which are by no means clear. See Martii Koskenniemi 2004a: 839 [Book review of Christian Joerges and Navraj Singh Ghaleigh (eds), 2003. *Darker Legacies of Law in Europe: The Shadow of National Socialism and Fascism over Europe and Its Legal Traditions*].

According to the American prosecutor at Nuremberg, Justice Robert Jackson, the most serious disagreement upon which the United States declined to recede, at the risk of failure of the London Conference setting up the Nuremberg tribunal, concerned the definition of crimes. The Soviet Delegation had proposed a definition that, in his view, effectively declared certain acts as crimes only when committed by the Nazis. The United States at the time correctly contended that the criminality of acts could not depend on who committed them. International crimes could only be defined in terms applicable to statespeople of any nation guilty of the proscribed conduct. As it happened, the Soviets later concurred (Yale Law School 2008b).[6]

The legal precedent value of the trials after the Second World War thus involves a delicate balancing act between the intentions of the framers of the relevant texts and facts that they grappled with, mediated through the text they produced. That is, the text could be narrowly interpreted as only intended to apply to particular persons, at the places and times mentioned, or broadly construed as covering similar actions dispersed at different times involving diverse actors.

The political subtext drives a narrow approach to the text but the social context demands a wider interpretation. Justice Jackson, to his credit, was certain that future efforts to codify international criminal law (or conduct trials, hearings or arbitrations) would find the origins, evolution and background of the Nuremberg process instructive (Yale Law School 2008a).

Political Subtext

Experiential evidence of a political subtext extends to court decisions on 'illegal war' from both the United States and the United Kingdom. These decisions faithfully regard the questions as less legal than political and decline jurisdiction over the subject matter or, at best, although accepting its international legal status, nevertheless exclude such matter from domestic law while readily admitting its relevance outside the national legal order.[7]

The social context is such that the political subtext drives the interpretation of the legal text. To the courts then, advancing a *political* dispute is abusing the *legal* process, utilizing the binary coding of one system (powerful/powerless) to attempt to directly influence the operations of another (legal/illegal). These cases include *Luftig v McNamara* 252 F. Supp. 819 (D.D.C. 1966), *Velvel v Johnson* 287 F. Supp. 846 (D. Kan. 1968), *Atlee v Laird* 339 F. Supp. 689 (E.D. Pa. 1972) and *Holtsman v Richardson* 484 F. 2d. 1307 (2d. Cir. 1973) from the United States and *R v Jones & Others* [2006] UKHL 16 from the United Kingdom. These cases will be examined more critically in Chapter 5 which references abuse of process.

---

6 See also Yale Law School 2008b.

7 See for instance Lord Mance's opinion in *R v Jones & Others* [2006] UKHL 16 para 99.

More evidence is in the creation of the United Nations Security Council's Chapter VII powers under the United Nations Charter, especially as read in Articles 25 (binding members to the decisions of the Security Council) and 103 (raising obligations to the charter above all other obligations).[8] Once again, despite all legal protestations to the contrary, these render the Security Council able to act outside the norm as a matter of law when utilizing its powers to keep the peace, as for instance when setting up various international criminal tribunals. This is the closest to a *Grundnorm* as the international community has developed.

Legal Text

It could thus be argued with some support that, upon a literal reading, the legal texts were only with reference to specific acts at specific times of specified actors, who indeed were explicitly referred to as 'criminals' even prior to trial. Such a reading militates against any general legislative intent or identification of a customary international law rule but only recognizes political might in trying the vanquished and does not enforce any legal right in the name of the international community.

Article 1 of the Nuremberg charter states:

> In pursuance of the Agreement signed on 8 August 1945 by the Government of the United States of America, the Provisional Government of the French Republic, the Government of the United Kingdom of Great Britain and Northern Ireland and the Government of the Union of Soviet Socialist Republics, there shall be established an International Military Tribunal (hereinafter called 'the Tribunal') *for the just and prompt trial and punishment of the major war criminals of the European Axis*. [Emphasis added]

Likewise, Article 1 of the Tokyo charter states:

> The International Military Tribunal for the Far East is hereby established *for the just and prompt trial and punishment of the major war criminals in the Far East*. The permanent seat of the Tribunal is in Tokyo. [Emphasis added]

Even though somewhat supportable against the literal wording of the extracts above, attribution of such a narrow meaning to the text cannot stand for reasons advanced below.

---

8 See for instance *Libyan Arab Jamahiriya v UK* (Lockerbie case) [1992] ICJ Rep 3.

Social Context

As illustrated in the following paragraphs, the means chosen, the negotiations preceding and succeeding the trials, and the trials themselves all expressed the social context supporting a reading of the text within a general rule of law framework as a one-off political expedient.

These facts supported the idea that prosecuting the Axis powers would provide an example to the rest of the world that the use of military force was no longer a legally viable means of pursuing national policy. This view has shown resilience, from the dawn of the League of Nations, to the birth of the United Nations and to the Rome conference for the ICC, against the political subtext of might trumps right. In the light of this, Justice Radhabinod Pal's dissent at the International Military Tribunal for the Far East, where he stated 'when the conduct of nations is taken into account the law will perhaps be found to be that only a lost cause is a crime' (Chomsky 1993: 239), rings hollow.

Justice Jackson's (Yale Law School 2008c) words at the closing of the Nuremberg trial hardly need elaboration to establish the generality and universality of the law produced at Nuremberg:

> We charge unlawful aggression but we are not trying the motives, hopes, or frustrations which may have led Germany to resort to aggressive war as an instrument of policy. The law, unlike politics, does not concern itself with the good or evil in the status quo, nor with the merits of grievances against it. It merely requires that the status quo be not attacked by violent means and that policies be not advanced by war … We may admit too that the world had failed to provide political or legal remedies which would be honorable and acceptable alternatives to war. We do not underwrite either the ethics or the wisdom of any country, including my own, in the face of these problems. But we do say that it is now, as it was for sometime prior to 1939, illegal and criminal for Germany or any other nation to redress grievances or seek expansion by resort to aggressive war.

From a purely criminal law perspective excluding motive, taking the prevalent social pecking order as a normative given and restricting inquiry to the conduct of the accused, though in and of themselves problematic, was hardly a novelty. Extending this to international law with criminal liability for individuals was the bold development. Here was the first instance of international law being globalized in its presumption to traverse and even transcend the nation state and directly apply to individuals. That is, for the first time outside the nation state, force was brought to bear both in enforcing law and judging the very use of force itself. Whether the use of force being judged was a general one or specifically that of the vanquished is today an open political debate but a closed legal one (that is, any claims of customary international law not prohibiting the illegal use of force are arguably a mere political pretext).

Discretion to Apply or Not Apply the Law to Force

Explicitly disregarding the politics of both sides of the matter, whatever their purported merit or otherwise, is to clear the decision-making space for law in a place hitherto occupied by politics. This is despite the fact that keeping within the bounds of law is, from the political perspective, sometimes seen as fighting with one arm tied behind the back. The distinction maintained here between space and place, therefore, is between zones or localities open and closed to violence respectively.

Declaring a given group 'terrorist' as a matter of law means the force of law is freed from the law it is usually coupled with, and group members' lives are declared open to death without legal consequence (Agamben 2005a). Superior force very effectively creates spaces (of struggle) out of places (of order) and subsequently the reverse: that is, places out of spaces by instituting rules of law backed by force. In terms of illegitimacy, which is crucial here, what matters is not the act (judged from the victim's perspective) but the actor (or victimizer).

Aggression, Abuse of Political Power and Abuse of Legal Process

Justice Radhabinod Pal (*United States v Araki*, 105 The Tokyo Major War Crimes Trial at 36–7) articulated a cogent argument against the criminalization of the use of force as aggression and assimilated it to the abuse of political power by abuse of the legal process.

> The so-called trial held according to the definition of crime now given by the victors obliterates the centuries of civilization which stretch between us and the summary slaying of the defeated in war. A trial with law thus prescribed will only be a sham employment of legal process for the satisfaction of a thirst for revenge. It does not correspond to any idea of justice. Such a trial may justly create the feeling that the setting up of a tribunal is much more a political than a legal affair, an essentially political objective having thus been cloaked by a juridical appearance.[9]

As demonstrated above, the fact that all persons have the right not to have their lives or liberty taken away unless by due process of law is, legally speaking, trite. Due process is the proper use of law and procedure while abuse of process is its improper use. They are therefore two sides of applying the same distinction of legal/illegal. The uniqueness is in self-referentiality. That is, the law refers to itself to determine by itself whether it should be utilized, or whether it is utilized for proper reasons, in the proper manner and form. Further, because force and law are so intimately connected in terms of enforceability, then the legality or illegality of the use of force is again decided by the law determining the terms of its own use.

Following the form of the law but eschewing the substance – that is, taking life or liberty under the guise or colour of the law but contrary to its purpose – would

9 *United States v Araki*, Dissenting Opinion of Justice Pal, *in* 105 The Tokyo Major War Crimes Trial 36–7 (R. John Pritchard, ed.) (1998) at 37.

be an abuse of the process of the law (in French law, this is referred to as *abus de droit*, the use of legal right for the sole purpose of injuring another). In common law, this doctrine originated in civil proceedings. It dates from the earliest times (*Metropolitan Bank v Pooley* (1885) 10 App. Cases 210. Per Lord Blackburn 220, 221) where all courts had inherent power (*Metropolitan Bank v Pooley* Per Lord Selbourne 214) to see to it that their processes were not abused so as to be vexatious and harassing.

As mentioned before, Giorgio Agamben considers due process the earliest documentary recording of bare human life as a juridical subject (Agamben 1998: 123). Abuse of process is therefore, again, at the outer limits of where law becomes politics and vice versa (that is, where force and law coincide). Again, Julius Stone also reached a structurally similar conclusion via a different path of argumentation and in another context (Stone 1958: 87).

Mr Richardson, speaking for the United States of America at the United Nations Diplomatic Conference of Plenipotentiaries on the Establishment of an ICC, succinctly stated the arguments against the criminalization of aggression. He said that acts not clearly criminalized under international law should be excluded from the definition of aggression. It was, therefore, premature to attempt to define it in terms of individual criminal responsibility.[10] American academic commentators too (Walker 2004: 245) have weighed into the criticisms by adding that acts of aggression by non-state actors are excluded and both pragmatic considerations and the role of the Security Council's have been overlooked.

The two examples presented below stand in for processes operating from the global to the local, international to national or macro to micro levels. They both illustrate the difference between what Walter Benjamin identified as law creating and law destroying violence (Benjamin 1978: 277–300, 281). The connection between the two goes beyond the fact that there have been calls both for (Arquilla as cited in Hersh 2005) and against (Chin 2007: 21) the Americans to adopt British tactics, as used in colonial Kenya, to the situation in Iraq. In both instances, the legatee of a legal system created by its predecessor conflicts with that same system. That is to say, the Mau-Mau in setting up a national constitutional order in Kenya approximates the United States Government in instituting a global legal order with the United Nations Organization at the centre. Meanwhile Mungiki is in a position analogous to the current administration of the United States vis-à-vis the attempted overturning of the existing order that makes law intelligible and able to distinguish between force and violence. Arguably, this shows an inbuilt objectivity to the law that is distinct from its creators and enables it to distinguish between the violence that endangers the law and the force that engenders the law.

10 *United Nations Diplomatic Conference of Plenipotentiaries on the Establishment of an International Criminal Court Rome, 15 June – 17 July 1998: Official Records Volume II Summary records of the Plenary Meetings and of the Meetings of the Committee of the Whole* Document No. A/CONF.183/13 (vol. II) para 51.

John Locke once remarked 'In the beginning the whole world was America' (Locke as cited in Schmitt 2003: 97). As what follows shows, in a different yet related sense, this is even truer today. At the time, Locke meant that the state of nature once prevailed upon the whole world. What this section claims is that American force-of-law is at present projected outside its territorial boundaries with scarcely any limits recognized.

This is exemplified by the case of David Hicks, who was an Australian citizen under the custody of the United States Government at Guantanamo Bay, Cuba (Bikundo 2007: 494). He was alleged to have served with the Taliban and al-Qaeda in Afghanistan. This led to his detention for more than five years as an 'unlawful combatant'. This category is claimed to be outside the normal protections of United States Constitution due process and criminal law and outside relevant provisions of international law, especially the Geneva Conventions.

Hicks' trial was essentially for making war against the United States, despite his lowly position in the overall hierarchy and lack of allegiance to the United States. This section proposes to show that Hicks was held extra-legally, tried and punished on his own guilty plea on allegations that touch on the propriety or legality of the use of force. It suggests that the United States authorities both tore up and made up legal categories arbitrarily in a legally inappropriate but politically expedient manner. To counter this linguistic strategy, this chapter argues for the restoration of the appropriate legal characterizations and rejection of novel nomenclature in order to maintain the functional separation between law and politics.

Hicks' initial charges covered conspiracy, attempted murder by an unprivileged belligerent, and aiding the enemy. His trial before a United States military commission was due to begin in November 2005. These proceedings were cancelled following the Supreme Court ruling in *Hamdan v Rumsfeld*[11] that declared the military commission process unconstitutional and illegal.

The response of the United States Government was then to pass the Military Commissions Act of 2006 (Pub. L. No. 109–366, 120 Stat. 2600 (17 October 2006)) and press new charges. However, the Attorney General for the United Kingdom (which along with Australia is a principal ally of the United States) deemed the changes as too little and too late to be of much significance.[12] Nevertheless, the subsequent charges encompassed providing material support for terrorism and attempted murder in violation of the law of war (US Department of Defence 2007). This study focuses on the legality as opposed to the expediency or propriety of the facts allegedly surrounding the capture and incarceration of Hicks. Moreover, it deplores the overtly political nature of the process that has

11 On 29 June 2006, the Court issued a 5–3 decision holding that it (contrary to the federal government's arguments) had jurisdiction, that the federal government did not have authority to set up these particular military commissions, and that the military commissions were illegal under both the Uniform Code of Military Justice and the Geneva Conventions.126 S. Ct. 2749 (2006).

12 <http://www.miami.com/mld/miamiherald/16682688.htm> at 21 February 2007.

displaced the considered discernment of legality. Legality is what enables the proper distinctions and characterizations to be made.

The so-called 'war against terror' raises numerous issues fraught with distinctions having far-reaching implications (Mégret 2002: 361–99, 377). For example, the distinctions between war (a state of armed conflict) and peace (the absence of armed conflict), combatant (those who engage in armed hostilities) and non-combatant (those who do not, or no longer, engage in armed hostilities), extraterritorial domestic criminal law enforcement and armed conflict (Schmitt 2004: 6), and so forth, are all consciously effaced to the detriment of David Hicks.

The legal basis for Hicks' trial is partly in the case of *Ex parte Quirin* 317 U.S. 1 (1942)1. Here the Supreme Court of the United States upheld the jurisdiction of a United States military tribunal over unlawful enemy combatants and approved their being sentenced to death. The court stated that: 'Lawful combatants are subject to capture and detention as prisoners of war by opposing military forces. Unlawful combatants are likewise subject to capture and detention, but in addition they are subject to trial and punishment by military tribunals for acts which render their belligerency unlawful' (*Ex parte Quirin* para. 30–31).

This decision only covers conduct of hostilities. It in no way refers to the reasons for engaging in hostilities or the capacity to engage in armed conflict and is therefore (as explained below) of limited utility in Hicks' specific circumstances.

To start with, the term 'war against terror' is itself a misnomer in that it is neither a war nor is it even against terror.[13] To be sure, there *are* wars against the States of Afghanistan and Iraq that can be located in both space and time. This is unlike the rhetorical action against the improper noun 'terror' that essentially references a tactic of political violence unrestricted in actors, time and space. The point is that the *figurative* rubric of a war against terror makes all these *literal* wars actually possible in the political and physical realms (Mégret 2002). However, Realpolitik never makes good law, nor does it make bad law. It is simply not the law.

Crucially, international law distinguishes between *why* and *how* one fights as governed by separate areas of the law. Reasons permissible to fight for fall under the law on the use of force (principally the United Nations Charter and customary international law), while how one fights is governed by the law of armed conflict/international humanitarian law (codified in The Hague and Geneva Conventions). So for example, deliberately targeting civilians is a breach of the latter, while taking up arms in self-defence is well in keeping with the former. In the 'war against terror', this basic distinction is finessed for political capital. The cause that the terrorists fight for (in the rare occasion it is even investigated) is discredited by the methods that they use (deliberately targeting civilians), while the methods

13 The Director of Public Prosecutions in England and Wales, Sir Ken Macdonald, had occasion to say: 'We need to be very clear about this. On the streets of London, there is no such thing as a "war on terror", just as there can be no such thing as a "war on drugs"'. Dyer 2007.

that the authorities use (re-defining torture, domestic surveillance, invasion of countries, etc.) are absolved by the cause (security) that the authorities fight for.

The new regime is an odd fit with the rest of the law because not all of the law can be erased at the same time. Therefore, such a strategy must run aground at one time or the other if only out of systemic inertia. The central example here is in human rights, specifically the related rights to liberty and due process. Further, because the law will have to be manipulated in one way or the other, issues of abuse of power by illegitimate use of legal processes arise. Ousting the jurisdiction of regular courts and unilaterally suspending the operation of entire chunks of law relating to armed conflict, human rights, extradition and torture are by now familiar tactics.

The legality of the entire anti-terrorism process is thus wide open to question. The relevant authorities stated that it was well within their power to free Hicks at any time, presumably even without trial (Coorey and Banham 2007). They instead elected to ask the United States to speed up Hicks' proposed trial (ABC 2006). This was a perhaps unwitting but nonetheless unmistakeable admission of the political calculations and complete lack of due process in the affair. It resulted in a deliberately concocted semantic legal vacuum distinguishing the law 'then' from the facts 'now'. This privileged a present day emergency redeemable only by political power and discretion from which recourse to objective adjudication was substantially blocked. All this was at the expense of legitimate expectations worldwide that the laid-down international law would be obeyed.

In contrast to Australia, the British demanded and got their citizens repatriated home from Guantanamo Bay. In fact, in terms of legal personality, David Hicks sought and obtained British citizenship to avail himself of similar protections, only to have the citizenship duly granted and promptly stripped in a matter of hours to deny him the remedy (Crabb 2006). This is another instance of executive discretion employed at the expense of rights in the name of enforcing those same rights.

The reasons for such extraordinary treatment of a more or less ordinary citizen of Australia are not hard to seek. David Hicks had his freedom taken away from him not for what he did per se but for what he represented. He was seen (rightly or wrongly) as representing persons willing to take up arms against the United States and possibly its allies as well (US Department of Defence 2007). The wisdom and patriotic filial feeling of such a choice aside, he had made an aggressive, highly threatening and deeply unpopular political decision. However, is this in itself a crime? If it is such, then it has to be a breach of the international law on the use of force, which the United States could then perhaps enforce on behalf of the international community by criminal sanctions, possibly based in part on the only legal precedents available, that of the Nuremberg and Tokyo tribunals after the Second World War. Interestingly however, the exact opposite is what seems to be happening, as shown in the following section.

The war on terror has given rise to a grim state of affairs in general circumstances with devastating particular effects to David Hicks. While the United States excludes its own use of force from any legal purview whatsoever, whether domestic or international, it progressively criminalizes other states' and even individuals' resort to armed force against itself. Such use of force is then characterized as a breach of United States domestic criminal law, rather than international criminal law.

At the Rome conference for the establishment of the ICC, the United States opposed development on the law on the use of force by international codification of a crime of aggression.[14] Notwithstanding this stance, the Military Commissions Act of 2006 in section 948 defines *lawful* enemy combatants as members of regular forces, militia or volunteer corps of a state, or members of a regular armed force professing allegiance to a government not recognized by the United States, who engage in hostilities against the United States.

This drafting explicitly distinguishes them from *unlawful* enemy combatants, who are persons that include members of the Taliban and al-Qaeda and who engage in or support hostilities against the United States and are not lawful enemy combatants. The legal consequence of such classification is that the Taliban and al-Qaeda affiliates are by definition unlawful enemy combatants *for the mere fact of taking part in hostilities* against the United States. However, under international law, if they belong to a belligerent side engaged in armed conflict they are therefore privileged combatants entitled to take part in hostilities without penalty. The war on terrorism and the crime of aggression appear to be two sides of the same coin that was flipped and landed on its edge.

Here the United States conflates the distinction between recognizing a government and recognizing a state. It did not recognize the Taliban as the lawful government of Afghanistan even when it was in control of 70 per cent of the country's territory, but recognized instead the Northern Alliance which controlled only 30 per cent and for good reasons enjoyed greater international goodwill. Therefore, it withheld from members of the Taliban the privilege of being lawful combatants. However, Afghanistan is and was a state party to the Geneva Conventions. This did not change whether or not its government was recognized. Such a situation also applies to the al-Qaeda members captured in Afghanistan while engaging in hostilities on behalf of the Taliban government. It is not possible to make war against a non-state actor outside your territory without invitation from the state it is operating in (or from) unless you make war on that state and

14 Mr Bill Richardson, for the United States: 'The Court must have a clear, precise and well-established understanding of what conduct constituted a crime. At the same time, acts not clearly criminalized under international law should be excluded from the definition. It was, therefore, premature to attempt to define a crime of aggression in terms of individual criminal responsibility. Vague formulas that left the Court to decide on the fundamental parameters of crimes should be avoided'. See United Nations Document *United Nations Diplomatic Conference of Plenipotentiaries on the Establishment of an International Criminal Court Rome, 15 June – 17 July 1998: Official Records Volume II Summary Records of the Plenary Meetings and of the Meetings of the Committee of the Whole* Document No. A/CONF.183/13 (vol. II) 95 para 61.

conduct hostilities on that basis. Therefore the criminalizing of unlawful resort to political violence is laudable and to be supported by reference to all states in international law and not just a single state through its domestic law.

In sum, Hicks was charged not just with targeting non-combatants as it were, but also with the very use of force itself. In any event, it is precisely the allegations of the unlawful use of force that provide the basis for the charges pertaining to attacking civilians and combatants unlawfully. Whether this force was brought to bear upon combatants or non-combatants is rendered immaterial by the arguments founding jurisdiction.

It is said that Hicks was an unlawful combatant, which deprives him of the protections of the law applicable in both war and peace but without waiving his own obligation to obey them. He was in a double bind, having all the obligations under both United States domestic criminal law and international law but none of the entitlements under the same laws. Meanwhile his accusers had all of the entitlements (to prosecute breaches of domestic criminal law and wars on other countries) but none of the obligations (to respect human rights and the international rule of law).

Analogically, it would have been absurd had the Iraqis declared, prior to the Second Gulf War, that they did not recognize the United States Republican administration due to the controversial 2000 presidential election and that therefore all American soldiers in Iraq were unlawful combatants and liable for prosecution under the death penalty. The interplay of law and force in this case is that Australian law abandoned Hicks, while international law was banished and American force-of-law took its place, leaving Hicks open to any action, including death, without legal consequence.

This study takes up where the previous left off by considering another example of the law on the use of force in effect upon the position of 'wars of national liberation' and would-be insurgencies post Nuremberg. It concretizes some of the spatio-temporal practices already mentioned in constructing personality and demonstrates that, where legal text can be relied on, the entire basis and effect of political violence can legitimated. Without such a textual basis, mere violence is inadequate to engender new political spaces.

The *Mungiki* is the appellation given to an amorphous tribal association in Kenya. The name itself roughly translates into mob, multitude or even 'the people'. This secret society has been variously described as a movement, sect and militia but, from its characteristics, it is possibly all these in general and none of them in particular. It draws its members exclusively from the Kikuyu tribe who at 7.4 million in number make up almost 22 per cent of Kenya's total population and are the largest of 42 other ethnic groups in the country.

Mungiki has made lurid headlines due to a spate of gruesome killings of civilians and unbridled violence targeting police and government functionaries. A typical incident involved the beheading of at least seven individuals and the subsequent impaling of the heads on telephone and gate posts strategically placed at or near government premises. Given the targets, this appears to be not random criminality but political violence with a calculated message deliberately sent (Nyamboga 2007).

The group's membership is difficult to estimate with any reliability. Members themselves boast of a membership beyond the psychologically important million mark. This is probably grossly exaggerated but membership is estimated at the very least to be in the thousands. Some of the people alleged to be sect sponsors, members or beneficiaries, and thus under investigation, include a substantial bloc of the most prominent Kikuyu politicians, including former and sitting members of the national parliament and even cabinet (Nyamboga 2007). Some members of the security forces have also been suspected of having sympathies with the group's avowed aims and even of infiltrating state security organs to this end (Nyamboga 2007).

The movement purportedly traces its lineage back to the far reaches of Kikuyu history and society and both sees and describes itself as the successor, if not contemporary manifestation, of the Mau-Mau guerrillas that fought the British in colonial times (Nyamboga 2007). The movement engages in extortion rackets affecting public transport and provision of utilities, like water and electricity in slum areas, and collects membership fees from affiliated persons.

Given this scenario, the police have been quoted as saying 'Mungiki is not a police problem it is a political problem' (Nyamboga 2007). I propose to frame the phenomenon not primarily or even essentially as a group, collection or coordination of individuals but *as a self-sustaining violent strategy of acquiring and maintaining power*. This is a more fruitful way than the current polarized debate futilely seeking to bracket it into either a law and order issue or a socioeconomic issue. It is both and neither because it is a political issue.

Mungiki has extended its tentacles first to the control of people, second to spaces and third to things. With reference to persons, Mungiki initially only affected young, willing and disgruntled Kikuyu men that yearned for a return to the old tribal ways and customs as a means of improving their worldly lot. After the hold on this constituency was accomplished and consolidated, Mungiki moved to controlling the actual geographical areas where the Kikuyu tribe was numerically dominant. Having secured that position, it has now finally involved itself in activities where it seeks to rival the state's monopoly on violence in promoting its influence to the wider Kenyan body-politic. That is, Mungiki has extended its reach just as the state has neglected, or retreated from, places and things it is expected to control as the legitimate authority. Mungiki has turned places of nominal governance into spaces of struggle for supremacy with the formal State apparatus.

Predictably, there have been vociferous calls for the government to ruthlessly deal with the menace once and for all. A blame game has ensued, with the cabinet minister in charge of internal security blaming the judiciary for not appreciating the gravity of the situation by setting free suspected members for inadequate evidence. In turn, the judiciary blames the police for shoddy investigations, while the police allege political involvement with Mungiki, if not outright interference with their investigations (Nyamboga 2007).

Exceptional circumstances seem to call for extraordinary measures in the 'war on Mungiki' (Nyamboga 2007).[15] The stage is therefore set for tragedy recurring as farce via implementing a novel legislative regime to deal with this phenomenon. The lawyers' professional body, the Law Society of Kenya, has, true to type, even called for a state of emergency to be declared in the affected areas to re-establish the rule of law. The government's response has been brutal, with the Kenyan Human Rights Commission (a government body) reporting 500 extra-judicial deaths (Allen 2007). This is, of course, highly reminiscent of the colonial administration when the Governor declared a state of emergency and promulgated a whole new legal regime that enable wholesale detentions, herding into camps, new capital offences and separate courts, and facilitated numerous abuses such as murder, rape and torture that disproportionately affected the Kikuyu community (Gregory 2005: 367).

The approach utilized below is to examine how force affects and is affected by the law in order to avoid conflict and engender peace. Giorgio Agamben's (1998) notion of *homo sacer*, Michel Foucault's (1975) panopticism and Carl Schmitt's (1985) sovereign exception and friend-enemy distinction (1996) are used as tools to this end. By this, it is hoped to conceptually retrace the steps leading to this phenomenon and demonstrate the threat it poses, as well as to sharply distinguish between violence as perpetrated by the Mau-Mau and that of Mungiki through the legitimacy accorded the former and denied the latter. The argument is made for disputes to be channelled through the municipal and, if need be, international legal system.

The stock historical narrative in Kenya has two closely related prongs that are ultimately in tension if not outright contradiction. Firstly, the Kikuyu (and closely linguistically related allied tribes) play the role of independence heroes, who in 1952 took on the might of the British Empire with little more than machetes and homemade guns and by their valiant efforts achieved independence for Kenya in 1963. On the other hand, they were also the victims of harsh repression and vicious counterinsurgency violence for which they still bear scars both social and bodily. In fact, representatives of the victims affected have since sued the British Government for these abuses (McGreal 2006). Most importantly, with this privileged identity as both victors and victims, the Kikuyu are deemed entitled to an enhanced social, political and economic position from the rest of the tribes. This in practical terms means that supremacy within the Kikuyu community is a springboard to national preponderance.

A key to open up understanding in this matter is Michel Foucault's notion of 'disciplinary power' (Elkins 2005: 101).[16] Disciplinary power has a gaze

15 Kenya government accused of using murderous sect <http://www.religionnewsblog.com/20318/mungiki-37 at 14June 2007; 'Brain, not brawn, will win war on Mungiki' <http://www.nationmedia.com/dailynation/nmgcontententry.asp?category_id=24&newsid=99710> at 14 June 2007.

16 See this phrase mentioned without elaboration in Caroline Elkins 2005: 101.

incorporating three elements: hierarchical observation, normalizing judgement and manipulative examination (Foucault 1975). The opposition between whose disciplinary powers were to be applied initially pitted Western civilization to African traditions as modernity versus atavism. Aspects of this struggle survive to the very day in both the Kenyan psyche and society. In this example, through discipline Mungiki individuals are created out of the Kikuyu masses in a series of steps as outlined below.

Agamben (1998) defines *homo sacer* as human life included in the juridical order solely in the form of its exclusion. *Homo sacer* is therefore a figure *excluded* from law itself, while being *included* at the same time. What the British did during the Emergency period in Kenya's history with concentration camps, Mungiki accomplish by ritual means. That is, they transform their tribe into potential *homo sacer* or 'sacred men' who may be killed without being sacrificed. These are lives expendable without legal consequence as they are abandoned by law and left outside its protections yet paradoxically still under the spell of the force that ordinarily accompanies law. The British did this as a mode of control but Mungiki do it with the calculated intention of extending this paradigm over the entire country's population.[17] Crucially, this figure is the exact mirror image of the sovereign who stands both *within* law (exercising constitutional and statutory powers) and *outside* the law (exercising prerogative power including suspending law itself) (Agamben 1998). By reserving the very worst excesses for 'defectors' from its ranks, the sect reveals them as *homo sacer* and constructs inner bonds by instituting an us/them dichotomy through rituals to sharply distinguish them from the broader society. These rituals include such radically anti-social artifices as initiates drinking human blood while partaking of illegal oaths binding themselves internally and distinguishing them externally.[18]

Carl Schmitt (1996a) described the political struggle as first constituted by the clash of groups distinguished by a friends/enemies criterion.[19] What is here at stake is not some personal animosity pitting one individual against another, but rather the division between a given community and the public enemy. The sovereign's decision to describe an enemy as such is then the foundational decision in which politics expresses its essence.

Seen through the prism of political struggle, control of bodies and their products – that is, over people, spaces and things – is what is at stake. This is essentially a will to hold power over bodies (from female circumcision to life and death)

17 Where the British utilized the concentration camp, Mungiki use appeals to tribal solidarity. For the camp as the original paradigm of power, see Giorgio Agamben 2004.

18 'Police attack stronghold of blood-drinking sect in Nairobi slums' <http://news.scotsman.com/international.cfm?id=888902007> at 12 June 2007.

19 '[t]he friend and enemy concepts are to be understood in their concrete and existential sense, not as symbols or metaphors, not mixed and weakened by economic, moral, and other conceptions, least of all in a private-individualistic sense as a psychological expression of private emotions and tendencies'. Schmitt, 1996a 27–8.

and their labour (extortion, etc.) within a very narrow segment of Kenyan society projected outwards toward a national platform. It is therefore not so much who they *are* but what they *do*. That is, Mungiki is not so much a noun referring to an objective group as such but a verb denoting a particular set of political practices.

Insight is gained by examining why female circumcision was a rallying point for both the Mau-Mau and Mungiki. This was a matter of deep division among the Kikuyu community and went right to the core of their self-identity. Mungiki openly promote Kikuyu supremacy over the territory of Kenya and the handing over of power to themselves as its younger generation (Nyamboga 2007). Like the Mau-Mau before them, the sets of practices instituted are more towards this end than an expression of 'atavistic' (Pakenham 1992: 677) African barbarousness (Anderson 2005: 41). It is therefore a ruthless but quite effective, if somewhat unsophisticated, politics of violence.

This characterization opens up a far more fruitful space for inquiry to gain insight as to whether and how far the force they bring to bear for political purposes may be regulated by law (Derrida 1989–90: 920). That is, the general question to be answered in this instance investigates force in political discourse being countered by legal means such as strategies of special regimes through emergency legislation incorporating parallel courts, novel definitions of crimes, enhanced policing tactics and so forth. These legal means paradoxically free up the use of force by those authorities whose legitimacy is directly under challenge by a greater or lesser armed force.

The historical case of *Regina v Dedan Kimathi* S/o Wachiuri [1956] eKLR makes these points remarkably well. Dedan Kimathi was tried and hanged for fighting against British colonization. The strategy utilizing unusual or exceptional means produced the desired result at the time. However, the convicted 'criminal' now has a statue cast in his honour prominently mounted in the city of Nairobi. This distinguishes the Mau-Mau as a movement leading to national independence from its ersatz successor, which mainstream accounts consider a criminal organization because they cannot point to any legal basis for their violence within the current concrete spatial and legal order to which it, after all, profoundly stands in opposition.

The factual studies above were intended to demonstrate similar dynamics in diverse circumstances where the relationship of force and law is problematized and brought to the fore. The purpose was to put the Nuremberg and Tokyo trials in context as being creative of a certain order and demonstrate their achievement of emergent differentiation between law and politics in the global society that is in peril today.

Justice Pal's dissent in the IMTFE essentially was that the international order then prevalent was unjust and outlawing force meant that unjust privileges were not only sanctioned *by* law but sanctioned *as* law. However, his characterization of this as an abuse of legal process was significantly weakened by the mere fact that he could dissent. This meant that the trial was not for mere show but was a site for substantive, albeit imperfect, justice. The upshot was that, in terms of the distinction between law and politics in the context of the use of force, law looks at the act sought to be criminalized while politics considers the actor as central.

The process described above, as begun at Nuremberg, can be conceptually recast with the social trying to capture what is outside itself (the unsocial). This is done by perceiving society as the norm (or rule) trying to govern the exception and, in this way, capture it. Following this, peace which is now the norm (as a value not as a fact) is sought to be generalized and thereby capture war as the exception. As illustrated above, by means of progressively developing rules, law is applied to re-ordering the world. It tries to capture facts and change them. In terms of application, it is the textual that tries to capture the non-textual by interpretation or through construction as elaborated in Chapter 3. This process of conceptual development is further explained below.

The most general distinction applicable here as per Luhmann's Sociological Jurisprudence is between society and its environment. This can be further broken down and recast as between social/non-social as fact and social/anti-social as norm. Politics draws a distinction between social/anti-social as friend/enemy commensurate with force and violence as positive and negative attributes of power respectively.

The positive value is sociability and the negative value anti-sociability. For example, only humans can be inhuman. Again, in criminal law, a plausible if unconvincing argument exists that society itself is responsible for the anti-social criminal. This is a clear instance of the social trying to capture the unsocial inside it with all the attendant paradoxes.

Because global society is all encompassing, it is unable (and does not have to) look outwards to an invader to unite but must look inwards to itself to determine what pressures within sustain it (and are therefore to be reinforced) and what forces tear it apart (and are therefore to be resisted). To impose criminal liability in the name of society it is necessary to link all of society to each individual by making an injury to be a wrong to both simultaneously. The public wrong is one done to global society while the private wrong is that which is done to the immediate victim. In fact, a breach of the peace is only inherent in society as there is no 'right to peace' traceable to an individual outside of society, only a 'right to violence' or at any rate no disability to apply violence except greater violence. The victim of violence therefore has two bodies: the private body immediately affected and the public body socially affected.

The next dynamic to emerge as society strengthens and views itself as the rule is that it tries to capture what is outside itself by deeming it the exception that it gradually whittles it down as society expands. That is, promotion of social values such as overall harmony is defined against and poised to overcome the counterpoint of disharmony or unsociability.

The ultimate social breakdown is war, and all-out war is only considered 'normal' prior to society. On the advent of society, war becomes less and less the norm and more and more the exception, just as peace becomes less and less the exception and more and more the norm; so much so that one may quite plausibly claim to be warring for peace. The only question is who is to judge this claim and by reference to what standards.

The capture of war by peace is only possible if 'facts', such as 'human beings murder each other', are not taken for granted. This is to say that law as a social means to ordering society is not merely descriptive of the ways of society but progressively normative as to which ways are desired and which are not. Given this stance, facts are seen as subject to law and not vice versa. Therefore, the breaking of law is not an argument against the law but an argument for more, or more vigorous, application of the law to the facts of its breach. Further, changing notions of fact into notions of law (for example, by having a list of terrorist groups declared as such by executive fiat and not being declared so by court of law) renders fair trial in a sense illusory by turning what should be sought to be proved into what the court must take as given. The separation of powers is undermined by stealth adjudication in the guise of legislation, yet another abuse of the legal process.

Given the problems of clarity and application inherent in the textuality of the law, individual clauses have to be applied not literally in the abstract but creatively in the light of the facts that were not envisaged at the time of legislation. The most appropriate present example is the so-called Martens clause[20] which prescribed that in cases not covered by the treaties 'civilians and combatants remain under the protection of authority of the principles of international law derived from established custom, from the principles of humanity and from the dictates of public conscience'. By dint of this provision, the Hague Conventions sought to implicitly cover what was not literally covered in the Hague Conventions by declaring the parties were still bound by laws not necessarily reproduced in text.

The process described above is not in itself necessarily a good thing as the success of each may be simultaneously their failure.[21] Nietzsche's admonition comes to mind: 'He who fights with monsters should look to it that he himself does not become a monster. And when you gaze long into an abyss, the abyss gazes also into you' (Nietzsche 1886: 146). At the present a stage approaches where the categories so painstakingly delineated blur into each other and become virtually indistinguishable by being politicized in order to reduce social conflict into a gigantic test of strength.

As the political processes of consolidating hitherto differentiated heads of power intensify, the social and unsocial collapse into each other as in the case

---

20 First introduced based on a compromise proposal by the Russian delegate at the 1899 Hague Peace Conference into the preamble of the 1899 Hague Convention II and appears now in the preambles of Hague IV of 1907 and the 1980 UN Weapons Convention and in Articles 63/62/142/158 respectively of the four Geneva Conventions.

21 See for example: 'The risk is not merely the development of a clandestine complicity of opponents but that the hunt for security leads to a worldwide civil war which destroys all civil coexistence. In the new situation – created by the end of the classical form of war between sovereign states – security finds its end in globalisation: it implies the idea of a new planetary order which is, in fact, the worst of all disorders'. Agamben 2001b para. 5.

of social responsibility for the criminal already mentioned above. The rule and the exception gradually approach equilibrium becoming distinctions without difference. Peace captures war at the price of war being assimilated into peace (as police actions, low intensity conflicts, etc.) (Žižek 2002). Law captures fact by being treated as fact itself by the rule of law getting substituted with rule-by-law (as just another arrow in the political quiver or grist for the mills of those with the will) and the textual captures the non-textual, but only by undermining social consensus and popular will with technocratic skill.

Examined in this light, the arguments against the jurisdiction of the ICC over criminal aggression are revealed as being more of a power discourse than a rights discourse; that is, they are an attempt to bring might to bear onto right by making arguments based on power in legal contexts, thus politicizing law and legalizing politics. These arguments are reminiscent in subject matter, scope, structure and intent of those of the 'war against "terror"', where the non-state adversary's methods discount their motivations while paradoxically the State's unorthodox methods are themselves absolved by the State's motivation.

To counter this, it is noteworthy that global society optimally functions when its social subsystems have exclusive overall control of their programmes, especially here in being independent of political intervention. With law specifically in mind, the next chapter further develops the theme delineating the proper sphere of the law and what lies at its margins, highlighting the institutional and conceptual limitations of the law and exposing the reliance on and vulnerability to force (or violence) embedded in the notion of the law as a set of enforceable rules.

Chapter 5
The Deficiencies of Law before Overwhelming Violence

This chapter elaborates on a theme developed in the previous chapters speaking of some normative and descriptive links between the use, misuse and abuse of law and how these relate directly to law and violence. Principally, the argument is that extreme violence shows up certain inadequacies in the law that go beyond mere systemic lack (of law and order resources) to conceptual befuddlement (given a monopoly on violence, when is might not right?). Is there a meaningful or consequential distinction between a *monopoly* on the legitimate use of force and a *legitimate* monopoly on the use of force? This refers back to the original and central question of the entire inquiry: *Must a judicial entity decline to entertain a prosecution for criminal aggression as,* ipso facto, *an abuse or misuse of its procedure?*

Essentially, this project is a thought experiment intended to help construct a normative model to reduce the risk of political violence by providing penal sanctions against it. This calls for initially delineating the proper sphere of the law and what lies at its margins, highlighting the institutional and conceptual limitations of the law and exposing the reliance on and vulnerability to force (or violence) embedded in the notion of the law as a set of enforceable rules.

Global Law and Local Politics

Currently, according to Ulrich Beck (2002: 42), there is dialectic between global and local questions that calls for cosmopolitan world politics. Moreover, these so-called cosmopolitan politics apparently involve in one way or the other promoting a neo-Weberian global monopoly on the legitimate use of force that erstwhile reposed on each and every nation state. Even though, or perhaps because, nation states are weakening, all kinds of cultural, political and religious movements are enjoying a new lease of life. There is an 'ethnic globalization paradox' where the world is growing more cosmopolitan and yet ethnic identities and divisions are strengthening, with numerous ethnic groups fighting for the 'right to self-determination' as a result (Beck 2002: 38). These groups violently pursue varying degrees of self-determination while justifying themselves both below and above the state. Invariably, there is a conflict not merely of arms but also of claimed rights that the law is tasked to resolve if recourse to violence is to be discouraged. The claim to legitimacy here is transforming through a triumph of function over form.

That is to say, the state's monopoly on violence is presently being displaced by the use of force for humanitarian and/or security ends. This process is not without its critics and the law in itself is not above reproach; indeed, it has been identified as being part of the problem.

The example below, drawn from the hypothetical, is proffered both as exemplary of this and a general theme. As Mark Findlay (2008: xiv) cautiously notes, studying global crime and control reveals contexts in which international criminal justice is politically co-opted to advance a monolithic global order against the sometimes legitimate local communal resistance.

For Findlay, there is much more than the curtailed freedom of a few perpetrators at stake. The 'issue is who should and does have legitimate access to the legitimate provision of violence for governance sake' (Findlay 2008: 88). He explicitly links the monopoly on legitimate violence to the monopoly of criminalization in the world-political context: 'The monopoly possessed by criminal justice to award and impose violent discrimination on those it deems liable is an all too attractive capacity for dominant political alliances' (Findlay 2008: xv). Legal instruments are therefore utilized for political ends. Is this illegal or merely to be expected?

The essential challenge sought to be overcome by the law was expressed by Foucault (1977: 151) as follows: 'Humanity does not gradually progress from combat to combat until it arrives at universal reciprocity, where the rule of law finally replaces warfare; humanity installs each of its violences in a system of rules and thus proceeds from domination to domination'. Taken descriptively this statement seems fairly well grounded in history. However, the law is such a phenomenon that it does not take things as they are, but rather seeks to modify them. That is, because the law relies on a coincidence between power and authority (Higgins 1963: 15), or principle (United Nations 2004), a crisis appears when these are asunder which is not caused by an excess of law but a manipulation of its instruments. In other words, a proposed solution to the violent domination of others via imposed rules is to expose the links between the violence and the rules in order to transform the violence without necessarily dissolving the rules. This allows for peaceful reform of the rules in a more equitable albeit imperfect fashion. The rules are transformed by being better grounded in either communal consent or linked to transcendent or objective values, and not mere efficacy. Thus to draw out the sting without being stung is the task set out in this chapter.

The role of the law here would be to anticipate and thereby discourage political violence. This introduces the notion of risk to international criminal law. International criminal law has been the widest generality (humanity as sovereign) brought to bear upon the narrowest specificity (the individual as subject). Risk intensifies this movement by deepening the narrowness and widening the generality by reaching into the individual's own undesirable qualities or acts and relating these to communally sanctioned qualities and acts in the global community. The individual is the glue that binds human qualities to the global community through being punishable.

Ideally speaking, respect for personal autonomy raises the individual to sovereign. A community of individuals that allows each to participate meaningfully in decision-making wields legitimate and hence moral authority over the sovereign individuals upon whom power, supposedly, ultimately resides. This allows a tripartite distinction between power, authority and legitimacy, which are unified in sovereignty and thereby the fountain and origin of all law. This study argues that we should move from a reactive stance to a reduction of risk approach in dealing with political violence in order to enhance stability and promote peaceful change by disincentivizing political violence via penal sanction of leading perpetrators.

This chapter has three parts. This introduction of the argument is followed by an outline of the limitations of the relevant domestic and international legal provisions, with an explanation, drawn from the hypothetical case study's legal and political issues, containing some theoretical discussion. The final part suggests penal disincentives to engaging in political violence as a palliative measure, as the violence witnessed has an almost clockwork recurrence coinciding with the general elections every five years (Cheboi 2008).

Juridical Paralysis

A survey of the relevant law, both local and international indicates how extreme violence limits and therefore guides its application. Chaos and disorder tend to separate the law from its enforceability by neutralizing its epistemological basis of legal/illegal. In this way, they dissolve elemental distinctions between law and fact, legitimacy and legality, and force and violence.

Violence, Force, Force of Law and Legal Force

Revolution can be provisionally defined as the situation where radical social or political change is sought without exclusively peaceful means. In this context, Georges Sorel sought to distinguish violence from force. According to him, violence rightly referred only to acts of revolt because force was intended to impose a certain social order that violence sought to destroy (Sorel 1915: 195). This notion of order threatened by violence was present during the American Civil War. Abraham Lincoln believed he had no choice but to employ the war power of the United States Government in order 'to resist force employed for its destruction by force for its preservation'. His justificatory rhetorical question in opposing force by greater force eschewing law was: 'Are all the laws but one [the right to habeas corpus] to go unexecuted, and the Government itself go to pieces lest that one be violated?' (Agamben 2005a: 20). By this, it was possible to justify departure from strict legality, the derogation of basic human rights and freeing up the application of force in the name of order and the protection of human rights.

It would seem then that when order in certain extremes is threatened by force, it sets the law to one side (in the name of the law) and applies force in its place to the detriment of human rights that it seeks to protect. With regard to Western legal traditions, Agamben (2005a: 9) distinguishes between those that regulate the state of exception in the text of the constitution or by a law and those that do not regulate the problem explicitly. However, how is one to distinguish between forces applied by different parties without the law as a standard? Can the law be the standard?

Luhmann (2004: 357–8) points out that the law was already extant when the state appeared. Moreover, one could not separate *iurisdictio* and *imperium* politically (although this is possible conceptually) without opening up a lawless *imperium* and an unenforceable jurisdiction. This divide was bridged by the concept of *potestas* and the same is applicable to contemporary understandings of 'sovereignty' (Luhmann 2004). This concept of sovereign power (*potestas*) contained the notion of a capacity to secure obedience to commands through legal force, meaning in a form specified prior to its exercise (Luhmann 2004: 359).

Critique of Violence

Walter Benjamin addressed his mind to the relationship of violence, law and justice. His work has subsequently been expanded and commented upon by writers as diverse as Carl Schmitt, Jacques Derrida and Giorgio Agamben, among others.

In his *Critique of Violence* Walter Benjamin (1978: 277) sets out his purpose as explicating the relationships between violence, law and justice:

> The task of a critique of violence can be summarized as that of expounding its relation to law and justice. For a cause, however effective, becomes violent, in the precise sense of the word, only when it bears on moral issues. The sphere of these issues is defined by the concepts of law and justice. With regard to the first of these, it is clear that the most elementary relationship within any legal system is that of ends to means, and, further, that violence can first be sought only in the realm of means, not of ends.

The primary distinction Benjamin utilizes is thus that of means and ends. This teleological approach taken to violence meant that his criterion of judgment was the intention of the violence. Therefore, violence without intention did not fall under his critique. However, from the perspective of criminal law, a crime is either an unlawful act or a lawful act done by unlawful means. This means that both means and ends are criminalized and the rationale for commission of crime is not an excuse. Using the foregoing as a springboard, Benjamin (1978: 287) advanced the view that '[a]ll violence as a means is either lawmaking or law-preserving', thereby irreducibly linking violence with legal process.

If justice is the criterion of ends, legality is that of means. Natural law attempts, by the justness of ends, to 'justify' the means, positive law to 'guarantee' the justness of the ends through the justification of the means. For if positive law is blind to the absoluteness of ends, natural law is equally so to the contingency of means. On the other hand, the positive theory of law is acceptable as a hypothetical basis at the outset of this study, because it undertakes a fundamental distinction between kinds of violence independently of cases of their application. This distinction is between historically acknowledged, so-called sanctioned violence, and unsanctioned violence (Benjamin 1978: 278–9).

In his deconstruction of the *Critique of Violence*, Derrida (1989–90: 920 and 983) explains:

> [T]o ask ourselves if violence can be a means *with a view* towards ends (just or unjust) is to prohibit ourselves from judging violence *itself*. The criteriology would then concern only the application of violence, not the violence itself. We would not be able to tell if the latter, as means, is in *itself* just or not, moral or not. The critical question remains open, the question of an evaluation and a justification of violence in itself, whether it be a simple means and whatever its end may be.

Elsewhere in his work, Derrida (2002: 242) says that in its founding law can rest on nothing but itself and is therefore 'a violence without ground' that is neither legal nor illegal nor even illegitimate or unjust.

He posits the state of nature as drawing no meaningful distinction between law and fact and displays how this leads up to a freedom to use violence:

> If, according to the theory of state of natural law, people give up all their violence for the sake of the state, this is done on the assumption (which Spinoza, for example states explicitly in his *Tractatus Theologico-Politicus*) that the individual, before the conclusion of this rational contract, has *de jure* the right to use at will the violence that is de facto at his disposal. (Benjamin 1978: 278)

Derrida (1989–90: 1001) notes the double-edged nature of this description:

> On the one hand, it appears *easier* to criticize the violence that founds [the law or legal system] since it cannot be justified by any pre-existing legality and so appears savage. But on the other hand, and this reversal is more the whole point of this reflection, it is *more difficult*, more illegitimate to criticize this same violence since one cannot summon it to appear before the institution of any pre-existing law: it does not recognize existing law in the moment it founds another.

Benjamin also set justice against legality and described violent justice as a danger to the legal system itself and not mere laws. This then exposes the true horror of violence to the legal system:

> It can be formulated as a general maxim of present-day European legislation that all the natural ends of individuals must collide with legal ends if pursued with a greater or lesser degree of violence. From this maxim it follows that law sees violence in the hands of individuals as a danger undermining the legal system. (Benjamin 1978: 280)

Derrida summarizes this as: 'At its most fundamental level, European law tends to prohibit individual violence and to condemn it not because it poses a threat to this or that law but because it threatens the juridical order itself' (Derrida 1989–90: 987). Further, he states: 'Law has an interest in a monopoly of violence to protect neither justice nor legality but law as such' (Derrida 1989–90).

It must be stressed that the monopoly on violence is in terms of *legitimacy* and not merely occurrence. Max Weber even defines the state as 'the rule of men over men based on the means of legitimate, that is allegedly legitimate, violence' (Arendt 1969: 35). Similarly, Hannah Arendt (1969: 42) writes the 'extreme form of power is All against One, the extreme form of violence is One against All', thus linking violence to anti-sociability and power to communitarian ends. She goes on to say that violence is a last resort to protect the power structure from the foreign enemy and the native criminal (Arendt 1969: 47). Further, she is of the opinion that:

> Power is indeed the essence of all government, but violence is not. Violence is by nature instrumental; like all means, it always stands in need of guidance and justification through the ends it pursues. And what needs justification by something else cannot be the essence of anything. (Arendt 1969: 51)

Arendt (1969: 51) also believes that the end of war is peace, while peace is an absolute and like power an 'end in itself' that enables the conceptualization of the means/end dichotomy. Further, she is of the opinion that ruling by sheer violence only comes into play where power is being lost (Arendt 1969: 53).

Benjamin's own view is instructive:

> It will be argued that a system of legal ends cannot be maintained if natural ends are everywhere still pursued violently. In the first place, however, this is a mere dogma. To counter it one might perhaps consider the surprising possibility that the law's interest in a monopoly of violence vis-à-vis individuals is not explained by the intention of preserving legal ends but, rather, by that of preserving the law itself; that violence, when not in the hands of the law, threatens it not by the ends that it may pursue but by it mere existence outside the law. (Benjamin 1978: 280–81)

However, Benjamin was also of the view that violence could be used for legal ends as well. He defined militarism as the compulsory, universal use of violence as a means to the ends of the state (Benjamin 1978: 284). In it, violence is not simply applied to natural ends but for legal ends (Benjamin 1978). Benjamin called the first function of violence the law-making function, and the second the law-preserving function (Benjamin 1978). He concluded that military violence, as well as being primordial and paradigmatic of all violence used for natural ends, also has an inherent law-making character (Benjamin 1978: 280–81).

For Benjamin (1978: 286), the crucial function of power over life was how law ultimately reaffirmed itself above any other legal act. This led him to ask whether there were any non-violent means for regulating human conflict. His rueful conclusion was that totally non-violent resolution of conflicts could never lead to a legal contract (Benjamin 1978: 287–8). Although conflicts could be sorted outside the legal system, through the fear of mutual disadvantages from confrontation, regardless of outcome (Benjamin 1978: 290), 'from the point of view of violence, which alone could guarantee law, there [is] no equality, but at the most equally great violence' (Benjamin 1978: 296).

Providing guidelines and outlining criteria make possible the taking of life while seeming to prohibit it:

> Those who base a condemnation of all violent killing of one person by another on the commandment [Thou shalt not kill] are therefore mistaken. It exists not as a criterion of judgment, but as a guideline for the actions of persons or communities who have to wrestle with it in solitude and, in exceptional cases, to take on themselves the responsibility of ignoring it. (Benjamin 1978: 298)

This linking of decisionism to life and death by Benjamin is strongly related to Agamben (1998: 57) when he says that at the two extremes of order are the sovereign and *homo sacer* who are correlative. The 'sovereign is the one with respect to whom all men are potentially *homines sacri*, and *homo sacer* is the one with respect to whom all men act as sovereigns' (Agamben 1998). Derrida (1989–90: 1005) explains this thus: 'If the origin of law is a violent positioning, the latter manifests itself in the purest fashion when violence is absolute, that is to say when it touches on the right to life and to death'.

During the French revolution, Louis XVI was deemed to have forfeited the right to due process and was thus an outlaw (Edelstein 2007: 86). Robespierre considered him to be placed in a 'state of nature' (Edelstein 2007). Couthon declared that the King, like other 'enemies of humanity' (that is, the *hostis humani generis*), had transgressed the very laws of nature and was not entitled to a trial but only deserving of speedy execution (Edelstein 2007).

It would seem that faith in the law, even when coupled with violence as the exclusive means, has its limits:

> A gaze directed only at what is close at hand can at most perceive a dialectical rising and falling in the lawmaking and law-preserving violence formations of violence. The law governing their oscillation rests on the circumstance that all law-preserving violence, in its duration, indirectly weakens the lawmaking

> violence represented by it, through the suppression of hostile counterviolence. (Benjamin 1978: 300)

At the very end, Benjamin (1978: 300) supports neither law-making nor law-preserving violence but instead looks to a so-called sovereign violence that does neither:

> But all mythical, lawmaking violence, which we may call executive, is pernicious. Pernicious too is the law-preserving, administrative violence that serves it. Divine violence which is the sign and the seal but never the means of sacred execution, may be called sovereign violence.

More recent work in this area is not as shy of prescription as this. In *State of Exception*, Giorgio Agamben lucidly speculates on a behind-the-scenes and covert engagement between Walter Benjamin and Carl Schmitt that concerns a battle of these prominent intellectuals over the void that is the state of exception, where nothing is forbidden and the law is neutralized. Carl Schmitt famously wrote that '[s]overeign is he who decides the exception'. This was a 'borderline concept' that pertained to 'the outermost sphere', was not routine, referred to a general concept, and was not 'a construct applied to any emergency decree or state of siege' (Schmitt 1985: 5). Further, Schmitt (1985: 36) stated that all 'significant concepts of the modern theory of the state' are secularized theological concepts because of the 'historical development' and 'systematic structure'. The exception was therefore analogous to the miracle in theology (Schmitt 1985).

What Agamben overlooks or underplays is that the state of exception's structure reveals a fatal self-contradiction (Kisner 2007: 222 and 239–40). By definition it is exceptional and hence cannot be generalized on its own terms. Further, whatever choices may be made within the boundless freedom to choose can only be taken from externally given and, of necessity, limited options (Kisner 2007). In essence, therefore, freedom appears to be the right to choose one's own limitations or the right of self-determination (Kisner 2007).

Political Monopoly on the Legal Use of Force versus a Legal Monopoly on the Political Use of Force

Is there a meaningful or consequential distinction between a *monopoly* on the legitimate use of force and a *legitimate* monopoly on the use of force? The latter involves questioning the monopoly bearer's *right* to use force regardless of their *ability* to use it. Anthony Giddens, who along with Ulrich Beck is a leading light in the notion of risk, has recognized that the relationship between force and violence invariably calls the political into question. Giddens notes that Weber defined both the state and indeed the sphere of the political in terms of control of the means of violence. Further, as per Weber, politics simply cannot be specified in relation to the ends to which it is devoted but only the means it employs towards whatever ends it chooses: namely, the use of force (Giddens 1987: 19). Weber's view appears to be that not only does politics utilize violence as a means without specific ends but also that everything is either politicized or amenable to becoming politicized (that is, politics seamlessly links actuality and potentiality). This brings his work into the constellation of the other names that have toiled in the law and violence like Schmitt, Benjamin, Derrida, Agamben and Luhmann.[1]

In *Politics as a Vocation*, Weber (1991: 77–8) sets out to sociologically define a political association:

> But what is a 'political' association from the sociological point of view? What is a 'state'? Sociologically, the state cannot be defined in terms of its ends. There is scarcely any task that some political association has not taken in hand, and there is no task that one could say has always been exclusive and peculiar to those associations which are designated as political ones: today the state, or historically, those associations which have been the predecessors of the modern state. Ultimately, one can define the modern state sociologically only in terms of the specific means peculiar to it, as to every political association, namely, the use of physical force.

His conclusion is that given the varied ends of the state it can only be defined by the means peculiar to it, which is force as distinct from violence. Intriguingly enough, Weber links this force to violence without specifying their difference (if any) and indeed further links this to the law itself, arguing that anarchy follows lack of violence:

> 'Every state is founded on force,' said Trotsky at Brest-Litovsk. That is indeed right. If no social institutions existed which knew the use of violence, then the concept of 'state' would be eliminated, and a condition would emerge that could be designated as 'anarchy', in the specific sense of this word. (Weber 1991: 77–8)

Weber concedes that force is neither normal nor the exclusive means to the state. He nevertheless holds that the relationship is an intimate one:

> Of course, force is certainly not the normal or the only means of the state – nobody says that – but force is a means specific to the state. Today the relation between the state and violence is an especially intimate one. (Weber 1991: 77–8)

However, Weber distinguishes the use of force as normal before the modern state and goes on to give his famous and influential definition of the state:

1 Affinities between Luhmann and Schmitt in what constitutes the political can be traced back to Weber. See William Rasch 2000: 162.

> In the past, the most varied institutions – beginning with the sib – have known the use of physical force as quite normal. Today, however, we have to say that a state is a human community that (successfully) claims the monopoly of the legitimate use of physical force within a given territory. Note that 'territory' is one of the characteristics of the state. Specifically, at the present time, the right to use physical force is ascribed to other institutions or to individuals only to the extent to which the state permits it. The state is considered the sole source of the 'right' to use violence. Hence, 'politics' for us means striving to share power or striving to influence the distribution of power, either among states or among groups within a state. (Weber 1991: 77–8)

Whatever else that may be said about this definition, its sole referent is a state in control of territory. This in itself tends to sound a bit dated to current readers. With globalization, the state is increasingly marginalized and the monopoly on the use *of* force is becoming a monopoly on the use *for* force. That is, humanitarian and security concerns increasingly underpin resorts to force and claims to sovereignty in justifying resorts to force are no longer legitimate.

Because the humanitarian and security justifications are rhetorically powerful and seemingly unassailable in political discourse, reducing them to principles and rules would help check their abuse. Juridification seems to be the way forward.

War, Law and Crime

Gerry Simpson has a body of recent work related to these issues that is both contemporaneous and precisely on the debate concerning the present inquiry. His work explores and reveals the links between law and politics mediated through violence and displays law's profound challenges in this context. Over the period 11–14 June 2007, the Special Working Group on the Crime of Aggression, a committee mandated by the Assembly of State Parties (ASP) of the International Criminal Court (ICC) (2007), had an informal inter-sessional meeting at Princeton University in the United States. This was part of the effort to consolidate the codification process that began after the Second World War with the trials of the leaders of Nazi Germany and Imperial Japan for international crimes. They discussed various proposals pertaining to a legal definition of criminal aggression under the ICC Statute. The issues they looked at in codifying the crime of aggression under the statute included defining the blameworthy conduct of the individual and the state, and conditions for the exercise of jurisdiction.

Although these diplomats may readily concede that they were engaged in a political process to produce a legal text, it would be more difficult for a scholar to sustain the claim that their activity was in actuality 'politics in a different key' (Simpson 2007: 1). However, this is precisely what Professor Gerry Simpson seeks to defend in his book, *Law, War and Crime*, which is a closely reasoned analysis of the legal project of criminalizing war itself, as well as aspects of its conduct.

As the title seems to suggest, the theoretical standpoint of this enterprise encompasses (at least conceptually) issues of law, war and crime. First, Simpson renders these issues on the border of politics and law as comparable, and then distinguishes them from each other formally and substantively. The inquiry calls for, as it were, to render to politics what belongs to politics and to law what belongs to law.

Given this requirement, a sociological standpoint in unravelling the similarities and differences would be key in simultaneously integrating politics and law within a single gaze. This would not only provide a common basis for comparison but also subsequently enunciate the telling differences that distinguish law from politics. In fact, Simpson approaches the law as a 'field' (Simpson 2007: 2), in a manner rather redolent of the form of sociological analysis that Pierre Bourdieu developed. However, this methodological issue is not particularly developed and, given the specific focus and argument of the work, this is probably just as well; it is not, in any case, a fundamental flaw.

The upshot of this is that, although the book seems and is articulated as a work on law, about law and by a legal academic, its central claim is that its subject is politics (Simpson 2007: 12). However, how would this stand up to Bourdieu's (1977: 814 and 831) claim that entry into the juridical field tautologically implies acceptance of the field's fundamental law that 'within the field, conflicts can only be resolved *juridically* – that is, according to the rules and conventions of the field itself'; in other words, that a legal problem is only legally soluble? Even further, the 'constitution of the juridical field is inseparable from the institution of a professional monopoly over the production and sale of the particular category of product's legal services' (Bourdieu 1987: 834–5). Simply put, lawyers have the monopoly on law once it is law. How then can law be politics?

The beginnings of such an inquiry are, intriguingly enough, traceable at the end of Simpson's book. In chapter 8 entitled 'Law's Fate', he asks: 'What sort of wars are we now waging? And how should we respond to them? With Law? Or with fatalism and irony?' (Simpson 2007: 179).

These starting points bring into question the very utility of the law itself with reference to war and in the alternative suggest resigning oneself to the problem of war with sophisticated ambivalence. This review attempts to examine how Simpson ended up with these questions and aims to identify possible trajectories for future investigation.

These arguably could include whether there is a distinction between just and unjust force, who decides this, how, and with reference to what. Couched like this, these questions are more amenable to processing within the legal system from legislation to adjudication and enforcement and not by a preponderance of force.

In chapter 1, entitled 'Law's Politics: War Crimes Trials and Political Trials', Simpson (2007: 4) formulates a dialectic between the legal and the political to disentangle the meanings and demarcate the spaces occupied by these. He argues that 'war crimes law is a place where politics happen' (Simpson 2007: 12), positing that the 'political' is understandable through four images that frame or distort war crimes trials, as follows:

1. *Deformed legalism* (the idea that war crimes trials represent a form of flawed or deformed legal practice);
2. *Transcendental legalism* (the idea that war crimes law promises the application of uncontaminated legal categories to the problem of war and mass atrocity);
3. *Utopian politics* (the idea that war crimes trials are a form of bad or imprudent or insufficiently retributive politics);
4. *Legalistic politics* (the idea that war crimes trials can achieve defensible or indefensible results depending on the political arrangements that define them) (Simpson 2007: 28).

However, as per the preceding discussion, given a conflict between law and politics, the question of regulating force presents itself as no longer a distinction of law/non-law distinguishable under the proposition that a politician, through some alleged and allegedly overwhelming compulsion, should decide. It is a differentiation between normal law (during peace) and exceptional law (during armed conflict) and accordingly amenable to adjudication via reference to rules.

Although Simpson (2007: 11) concedes that ideally 'the trial is a place liberated from politics and the contamination politics threatens', he challenges this as 'orthodoxy' by arguing that war crimes trials are political trials (2007: 11) because 'war crimes law is saturated with conversations about what it means to engage in politics or law'. He goes to say that these politics are thinkable as a set of relationships. He relates the cosmopolitan to the local (chapter 2); the collective to the individual (chapter 3); the didactic to the juridical (chapter 4); show trials to legitimate proceedings (chapter 5); law in war to law of war (chapter 6) and legal sanction to extra-legal action (chapter 7). Apparently, these '*are* international criminal law' (Simpson 2007: 29).

Simpson provides the case of Ramush Haradinaj in the International Criminal Tribunal for the Former Yugoslavia (ICTY) to bolster up his argument. In that case, the court was engaged 'in a dispute about the limits of the law and the boundaries of the political' (2007: 25):

> The result of this was that Haradinaj's activities were to be overseen, jointly, by both UNMIK (a political body) and the ICTY (a judicial organ). This form of rather delicate decision-making could be viewed, though, as simply politics by other means or legalistic politics: the court applying legal standards as honestly as it could while at the same time, remaining aware of the political effect of its judgment (but allowing none to trump the other). (Simpson 2007: 26)

It is not at all clear that this example can *only* be read as politics triumphing over law rather than vice versa. The legal process is by its very nature more objective e status of a plaything and is no longer a guide to conduct. It is now something f a stalking horse underneath which one shoots one's missiles. Rule *by* law upplants the rule *of* law. That is, the crime of aggression now coincides with the ouse of legal process on a global scale. Therefore in regulating force, global law as conceptually shifted from a passive force and law (immanent in and regulating identifiable place) to an active aggression and legal process (effective in and dering a given space). How does this rather abstract process connect with ersons within these places and spaces?

Chapter 3 of Simpson's book, entitled 'Law's Subjects: Individual Responsibility d Collective Guilt', is structured around the dialectic of social and individual. also addresses the following conundrum: when the state is itself criminal, how n it then be the judge of criminality? Simpson (2007: 56) rightly points out at 'international law is largely auto-interpretative and states are beholden to no per-sovereign'. In connection with this, 'personalization of international law rough international criminal law is linked to the emergence of human rights as a ld' (Simpson 2007: 57). International criminal law evinces 'a perpetual tension tween the collective and the individual' (Simpson 2007: 58). Within it, 'there is an escapable tendency to see mass criminality as uniquely individualized expression criminal psychopathology, a matter of socio-political joint responsibility, historical vitability or national temperament' (Simpson 2007: 78). These tendencies reflected 'in the institutional oscillations between state crime and individual ponsibility, in the doctrinal ambiguities of a juridical order concerned with sonal agency and collective conspiracies, and in the way the field is structured und the problem of moral responsibility of groups and persons' (Simpson 2007). sum, international criminal law is the widest generality (humanity as sovereign) ught to bear upon the narrowest specificity (the individual as subject).

Giorgio Agamben contributes here (Minca 2007: 78 and 80–81) the notion of *no sacer* or 'sacred man', defined as human life included in the juridical order ely in the form of its exclusion (Agamben 1998: 83–5). *Homo sacer* is therefore gure *excluded* from law itself, while being *included* at the same time. Crucially, figure is the exact mirror image of the sovereign who stands both *within* law ercising constitutional and statutory powers) and *outside* the law (exercising ogative power including suspending law itself) (Agamben 1998).

This brings to the foreground certain practices wielded with life itself as object. Specifically, where law is viewed as 'enforceable rules', fidelity to rules is reduced and discretion to apply force (now unbound and therefore ence) is increased. This is through manipulating the link between law and force ordinarily associated with the law. In this manner, human personality rson' as a bearer of rights and duties within a legal system) may be conjured through for example grant of citizenship and its pertinent rights) or conjured y (through reduction to the status of an alien or non-person). The global war nst terror is exemplary but not unique in this regard. In contrast to Australia, British demanded and got their citizens repatriated from Guantanamo Bay. In in terms of legal personality, the Australian David Hicks sought and obtained than mere ad hoc decision-making within society. It transf irresoluble conflicts into technical legal questions constructed t within and by its procedural and conceptual means (Teubner 2 Consequently, a legal question may on its face have very little or to do directly with the social conflict in issue (Teubner 2001). Th fictions about the outside world but has to treat them as thoug realities (Teubner 2001). Therefore, it takes legal competence to legal process is appropriate or appropriately utilized to bring a co purview of the law.

According to Simpson (2007: 64 and 133), 'the regulation ar of war represents the culmination of the juridical project'. This nevertheless essentially correct. chapter 2 of Simpson's book, ti Internationalism and Localism', considers 'the place of plac Simpson attempts to show that the question of space or locatio in both the choice of place (domestic or international) and t (provincial or cosmopolitan). This chapter, then, is about the *pl* criminal law (Simpson 2007: 30). Simpson (2007: 5) pits internationalists and teases out 'what it means to act in the na opposed to more particular politics'. The conclusion is that int law is idiosyncratic being neither international nor national bu doing law.

One peculiarity often overlooked is that, by controlling use of force (relying on social contractarian theory), one r legitimately impose legal order on chaos upon initiating a so may also subsequently wreak disorder upon 'illegitimate' lega spaces open to violence out of places erstwhile governed by the resisting enemy a criminal, who is thus by definition kil punishable outside combat. That is to say, the absence of (la either chaos or disorder dependent on whether it is 'natural' agency. Further, both strong and weak states perceive order overwhelmingly positive. According to Simpson (2007: 45), 'i law is galvanized by the idea of humanity as a category to international justice involves perpetually negotiating betwe (incipient hegemony) and the local (privileged parochialism that international criminal law is made out of this negotiation

Such negotiation is desirable to strong states in orc consolidate their possessions and positions. Weak states esp be secure from superior force through inclusion in the large (the international community/humanity/humankind) in w is not eradicated but the next best thing is achieved (that i legitimate use of force is imposed).

By primarily relying on force without law, we refashion space of violent political struggle instead of a place of mut sanctioned by laws. In contrast to the past, the law now is in than mere ad hoc decision-making within society. It transforms politically irresoluble conflicts into technical legal questions constructed to be answerable within and by its procedural and conceptual means (Teubner 2001: 21 and 23). Consequently, a legal question may on its face have very little or virtually nothing to do directly with the social conflict in issue (Teubner 2001). The law thus creates fictions about the outside world but has to treat them as though they were hard realities (Teubner 2001). Therefore, it takes legal competence to *decide* when the legal process is appropriate or appropriately utilized to bring a construct within the purview of the law.

According to Simpson (2007: 64 and 133), 'the regulation and criminalization of war represents the culmination of the juridical project'. This bold statement is nevertheless essentially correct. chapter 2 of Simpson's book, titled 'Law's Place: Internationalism and Localism', considers 'the place of place'. In the chapter, Simpson attempts to show that the question of space or location is always in play in both the choice of place (domestic or international) and the choice of style (provincial or cosmopolitan). This chapter, then, is about the *place* of international criminal law (Simpson 2007: 30). Simpson (2007: 5) pits nationalists versus internationalists and teases out 'what it means to act in the name of humanity as opposed to more particular politics'. The conclusion is that international criminal law is idiosyncratic being neither international nor national but a peculiar way of doing law.

One peculiarity often overlooked is that, by controlling the legality of the use of force (relying on social contractarian theory), one may not only quite legitimately impose legal order on chaos upon initiating a society under law but may also subsequently wreak disorder upon 'illegitimate' legal orders by creating spaces open to violence out of places erstwhile governed by rules. This renders the resisting enemy a criminal, who is thus by definition killable in combat and punishable outside combat. That is to say, the absence of (law and) order can be either chaos or disorder dependent on whether it is 'natural' or willed by human agency. Further, both strong and weak states perceive order protected by law as overwhelmingly positive. According to Simpson (2007: 45), 'international criminal law is galvanized by the idea of humanity as a category to be protected'. Thus international justice involves perpetually negotiating between the cosmopolitan (incipient hegemony) and the local (privileged parochialism); the chapter argues that international criminal law is made out of this negotiation (Simpson 2007: 53).

Such negotiation is desirable to strong states in order to maintain and consolidate their possessions and positions. Weak states espouse order as well to be secure from superior force through inclusion in the largest possible collective (the international community/humanity/humankind) in whose name violence is not eradicated but the next best thing is achieved (that is, a monopoly on the legitimate use of force is imposed).

By primarily relying on force without law, we refashion the entire globe into a space of violent political struggle instead of a place of mutual peaceful existence sanctioned by laws. In contrast to the past, the law now is imminently reducible to the status of a plaything and is no longer a guide to conduct. It is now something of a stalking horse underneath which one shoots one's missiles. Rule *by* law supplants the rule *of* law. That is, the crime of aggression now coincides with the abuse of legal process on a global scale. Therefore in regulating force, global law has conceptually shifted from a passive force and law (immanent in and regulating an identifiable place) to an active aggression and legal process (effective in and ordering a given space). How does this rather abstract process connect with persons within these places and spaces?

Chapter 3 of Simpson's book, entitled 'Law's Subjects: Individual Responsibility and Collective Guilt', is structured around the dialectic of social and individual. It also addresses the following conundrum: when the state is itself criminal, how can it then be the judge of criminality? Simpson (2007: 56) rightly points out that 'international law is largely auto-interpretative and states are beholden to no super-sovereign'. In connection with this, 'personalization of international law through international criminal law is linked to the emergence of human rights as a field' (Simpson 2007: 57). International criminal law evinces 'a perpetual tension between the collective and the individual' (Simpson 2007: 58). Within it, 'there is an inescapable tendency to see mass criminality as uniquely individualized expression of criminal psychopathology, a matter of socio-political joint responsibility, historical inevitability or national temperament' (Simpson 2007: 78). These tendencies are reflected 'in the institutional oscillations between state crime and individual responsibility, in the doctrinal ambiguities of a juridical order concerned with personal agency and collective conspiracies, and in the way the field is structured around the problem of moral responsibility of groups and persons' (Simpson 2007). In sum, international criminal law is the widest generality (humanity as sovereign) brought to bear upon the narrowest specificity (the individual as subject).

Giorgio Agamben contributes here (Minca 2007: 78 and 80–81) the notion of *homo sacer* or 'sacred man', defined as human life included in the juridical order solely in the form of its exclusion (Agamben 1998: 83–5). *Homo sacer* is therefore a figure *excluded* from law itself, while being *included* at the same time. Crucially, this figure is the exact mirror image of the sovereign who stands both *within* law (exercising constitutional and statutory powers) and *outside* the law (exercising prerogative power including suspending law itself) (Agamben 1998).

This brings to the foreground certain practices wielded with life itself as the object. Specifically, where law is viewed as 'enforceable rules', fidelity to the rules is reduced and discretion to apply force (now unbound and therefore violence) is increased. This is through manipulating the link between law and the force ordinarily associated with the law. In this manner, human personality ('person' as a bearer of rights and duties within a legal system) may be conjured up (through for example grant of citizenship and its pertinent rights) or conjured away (through reduction to the status of an alien or non-person). The global war against terror is exemplary but not unique in this regard. In contrast to Australia, the British demanded and got their citizens repatriated from Guantanamo Bay. In fact, in terms of legal personality, the Australian David Hicks sought and obtained

British citizenship to avail himself of protections similar to British citizens, only to have the citizenship duly granted but promptly stripped in a matter of hours to deny him the remedy (Crabb 2006). This is a clear instance of executive discretion employed at the expense of rights in the name of enforcing those same rights. This internally contradictory process has to be legitimated and granted a patina of procedural objectivity in which the instrumentality of law's narrative style is indispensable. How is the law, or more accurately its process, captured?

Chapter 4 of Simpson's (2007: 79) book, entitled 'Law's Promise: Punishment, Memory and Dissent', is about the didactic and dissident functions of war crimes trials and the tensions between these and other effects and imperatives. This chapter discusses the didactic function of law in telling a compelling story and sets this off against the limits of the law in the light of legitimation in terms of both ideological innocence and facilitating erasure of memory (Simpson 2007).

The law itself is both a terrain of, and a weapon in, the struggle. In the Justice Trial, the Nuremberg Trials process charged legal practitioners for participation in an organized system of injustice that violated the laws of war and humanity, yet was perpetrated in the name of law through the instrumentality of the courts (*United States of America v Alstötter* et al. ('The Justice Case') 3 T.W.C. 1 (1948), 6 L.R.T.W.C. 1 (1948), 14 Ann. Dig. 278 (1948) 290). That is, functionaries of the Nazi state captured the legal process for their ends. However, upon losing the war, they were tried, convicted and punished by the Allied powers for grossly abusing the legal process.

Under the section titled 'Discordant notes', Simpson discusses what could well be the kernel of the matter. Firstly, trials 'retain at their core a symmetry that can never quite be dissolved by the political elites who convene the trial' (Simpson 2007: 93). Secondly, the 'politics' in such trials is 'a contest between authorized and bastard versions of history, law and politics' (Simpson 2007: 93). Law and, in particular, trials allow for usually forbidden forms of political engagement. Thirdly, law's adversarialism, its commitment to equality of participation, and openness create space for dissenting judgments that challenge the legitimacy of the law itself (Simpson 2007: 93). This may even take the form of challenges to the use of legality in judging political acts (Simpson 2007: 94). That is to say, the law procedurally entertains within itself the possibility of its own substantive negation (Simpson 2007: 93). It is exactly this projected negation that makes it law (Simpson 2007). What then distinguishes international criminal law?

In chapter 5, entitled 'Laws Anxieties: Show Trials', Simpson (2007: 131) claims that war crimes law is the application of legal categories to the problem of war where the defeated deserve defeat and punishment because they did wrong. He identifies certain resemblances between war crimes trials and show trials in terms of procedure. He argues that the notion of objective guilt and subjective innocence brings to light that both sorts of trials transform hitherto political acts into crimes (Simpson 2007: 123–4).

The first similarity between the two is 'the idea that individuals can be punished because they pose a danger to some new configuration of political forces or some contested notion of community' (Simpson 2007: 128). Both types of trials also involve 'the same setting aside of existing legal rules (as with preventative war) in order to remove threats to the revolution (Moscow), national security (Guantanamo Bay), the international system (Iraq) or peace in Europe (Serbia)' (Simpson 2007: 129). There is also the same 'disposability of human beings in the name of political projects' and the 'shared appeal to intuition over legality' (Simpson 2007). The crucial difference, however, identified by Simpson is the 'degree of risk' that is present in war crimes trials but negligible or non-existent in show trials (Simpson 2007: 130). According to this characterization, show trials are political projects under the guise of law as distinct from war crimes trials, which are legal projects albeit heavily influenced by politics. This distinction, though fine, is telling; war crimes trials are lawful while political trials are politics. Besides that, objective guilt and subjective innocence is a feature of the criminal law generally in the privileging of the objective (intention) over the subjective (motive) in discerning criminality. It is not only restricted to international criminal law. The high stakes international politics involved only make it more apparent.

Through distinguishing law from politics and privileging the former in disputes concerning the regulation of force in society, one is better able to counter their conflation. Simpson grapples with this aspect in chapter 6, entitled 'Law's Hegemony: The Juridification of War'. This chapter investigates the conduct of politics in the courtroom by a transmutation of politics into law. According to Simpson (2007: 132), war crimes trials belong to 'juridified diplomacy', which is but a genre of international politics. He argues that this juridified diplomacy translates political conflict into legal doctrine and then resolves these conflicts in legal institutions. Essentially, the whole book is about just this tendency.

In this particular chapter's first section, Simpson discusses recent examples of law's preponderance in areas of international conflict and then links this to the juridification of politics generally. In the second section, he considers war the sharpest and most visible instance of juridification of the problem of law and crime (Simpson 2007). He cites Carl Schmitt, who said once the international community wages war, then 'pest control' displaces war (Simpson 2007: 142). Simpson (2007: 143) disputes this by claiming 'another constituent relationship in international criminal law is formed around the tension between the project to criminalize war and a counter-project that denies the applicability of criminal categories to decisions about war and peace'. He mentions Justice Pal who, in his dissentient judgment at the International Military Tribunal for the Far East at Tokyo (IMTFE), regarded international law as a project for stabilizing and securing inequitable power distributions within international society. For him, criminalizing aggression was stabilizing an unequal status quo (Simpson 2007: 147).

The chapter also argues that the juridification of war through the criminalization of aggression has been so hugely controversial that 'the idea of individual responsibility for war ought to give us pause' (Simpson 2007: 156–7). This is principally because 'the juridification of war has been fixated on questions of individual agency' (Simpson 2007: 157). Second, juridification, in processing atrocity or war through law, may create unjust equivalences or rely on 'idiot's rules' that are oblivious to the nature of war or character of different wars; thus 'criminalizing 'aggression may be too blunt a mechanism for the problem of force in international relations' (Simpson 2007). Third, crimes against peace supplant prudent judgment by sharply distinguishing between what is and what is not acceptable (Simpson 2007: 158). Rather counter-intuitively, Simpson (2007: 158) goes on to summarize the problem as that, in the absence of clear standards or shared values in international society, we tend to 'criminalize our enemies *because* they are our enemies'. Provision of clear standards, earlier disparaged as supplanting prudent judgment, surely would be the ready antidote, rather than the devaluing of law or condoning of war.

Notwithstanding this, Simpson's own view is that, given the foregoing, aggression as a legal category will be consigned to the category of a 'crime to come' because it can neither be defined thickly enough, nor applied universally to include the Great Powers. However, it will remain in the international agenda to describe disfavoured states and their leaders as aggressors (Simpson 2007: 158). By first assigning criminal aggression to represent 'the culmination of the juridical project' (Simpson 2007: 133), then confining it to perpetual potentiality, Simpson gives it a decidedly shape-shifting quality by making it permanently imminent for Great Powers but immanently permanent for the not so great or not so powerful states. How is this different from what has gone on before?

In chapter 7, entitled 'Law's Origins: Pirates', Simpson demonstrates international law seamlessly joining ostensibly extra-legal politics. This is through the conferment of outlaw or pariah status, which takes piracy as the paradigm instance of extra-legalism. Pivotally, individual international criminal responsibility began with pirates who were outside the international order and yet were the only natural persons directly subject to the legal order's control (Simpson 2007: 162). This deserves extensive direct quotation:

> This chapter turns to the war on terror: a war on a figure who is neither a criminal (entitled to the protection of the criminal law, subject to war crimes trials) nor an enemy (afforded certain protections under the law of war). In the case of the war on terror, then, we have a transition from law back to politics (and war).
>
> In this chapter, I argue that a central figure in this war on terror is the 'enemy of mankind'. The original enemy of mankind is the pirate: an originating presence who is, at the same time, a harbinger of law's fate, a construct of war and peace, and an object of both legal regulation and unregulated violence. Piracy inaugurates international criminal law (pirates are the first enemies of mankind) and the pirate figure is reinvented in order to renew (or radically transform) the idea of international community that underpins this legal order (terrorists are the latest enemies of mankind). Paradoxically, though, the re-emergence of the pirate-terrorist, essential to the remaking of the international community through the war on terror, also threatens that community's prior legal

> commitments (frequently the treatment of the pirate terrorist is unconstrained by law). (Simpson 2007: 159)

This characterization, echoing *homo sacer* above, yields entities of varying personality:

1. The peacetime outlaw – outside the law, unprotected and open to anything;
2. The peacetime criminal – inside the law and open to punishment;
3. The wartime terrorist – outside the law, unprotected and open to anything;
4. The wartime enemy – inside the law, open to killing and injury but not open to punishment.

The dazzlingly crucial point that Simpson almost intuitively makes is that, although pirates are conceived as enemies of 'mankind' [*sic*] or outsiders, they remain mankind or insiders by defining inside and outside. In fact, both Empire and the international community need pirates as agents and objects of imperial ambition (Simpson 2007: 177). Moreover, the category of 'enemies of mankind' ensures the continued purchase of 'mankind' as a category capable of waging perpetual war in the name of international justice (Simpson 2007: 177). The difference in movement from enemies to criminals (via legalization, as at Nuremberg) and from criminals to enemies (via politicization, as in the war on terror) (Simpson 2007: 159) is that once legalization is done in the first instance, a precedent is set and law is differentiated from politics. That is, when time-binding is factored in, a being that was an outlaw, and therefore open to anything (including legal process – essentially a non-person), becomes both a legally protected and legally responsible entity (a person) following the invocation of legal process. Action contrary to this is then not non-lawful but unlawful.

Perhaps if the questions Simpson asked were 'What kinds of war are being waged *on* (as well as by) us and how is the law relevant to these?' or 'Is there an a priori conceptual bar to legalizing resort to force?', it would indicate that the law is indeed presently indispensable in judging the use of force in a world of increasing complexity and interconnectedness. The role of politics in this instance would be to provide the forum and enabling environment for binding decisions to be made, embedding the international use of force in an international regime through a global law in the name of humanity that covers both victims and aggressors, leaving none outside either the protection or penalties of the law.

Targeting leaders and instigators then, not mere perpetrators, is the necessary approach both at legal and conceptual registers, as, following the Nuremberg judgment, the crime of aggression contains within itself the accumulated evil of the consequences of resort to force. This ties in with the current international legal architecture in important ways.

Both criminologists and philosophers have noted the global trend of the utility of violence on governance. Through the prism of international criminology, Findlay (2008: 105) writes:

> [I]t is through terrorist violence and the violent *justice* responses that the democratic state and *deep state* contest. It is where the *deep state* employs terrorist violence (its infrastructure and foot soldiers) as a precursor to manipulating the justice response to confuse and violently undermine democracy as the functional authority for apparent state governance.

In the same vein, but from a theoretical perspective, Agamben (2001a: 6) writes that 'power no longer has today any form of legitimation other than emergency, and ... power everywhere and continuously refers and appeals to emergency as well as labouring secretly to produce it'. Thus 'in Western states it not only appears increasingly as a technique of government rather than an exceptional measure, but it also lets its own nature as the constitutive paradigm of the juridical order come to light' (Agamben 2005a: 6–7). Protection of democracy through violence is the new norm (Agamben 2005a: 16).

This though is not a reason to despair of the law and legal means but a call to adapt to new realities and ameliorate them through legal means. Findlay (2008: xxiii) suggests very sensibly that, in this regard, legitimacy for international criminal justice may be founded upon 'community engagement rather than political allegiance'. This is perhaps the most viable way forward.

Chapter 6

A Possible Methodology of Judicial Discourse in Marshalling, Interpreting, and Construing Aggression Clauses

Assuming jurisdiction was conferred to a court could a definition of criminal aggression necessarily entail an abuse of legality? This chapter canvasses as to how the court could approach an answer that would be in keeping with the law as well as mindful if not persuaded by the politics inherent it the case.

The aim is to establish interpretation/construction as a ubiquitously evolving procedure of the legal system in extracting legal meaning and applying it practically to facts; that is, indicating any discernible customary international law methodology in applying texts to contexts. This methodology is in theory expressed in legal traditions and operates in systems dispersed both historically and geographically. This process is intended to reflect the limitations upon how rules are applied in practice and the alternation between the security in following a rule and freedom in departing from it.

This chapter therefore interrogates the dialectical techniques of interpretation and construction in legalism. It weaves them into a specific methodology depicting their present utility in the social evolutionary aspect of legal oversight over the use of force as a form of social capital in a global societal sense.[1] This is attempted by using the self-descriptive social contract narratives of the law. These narratives (variedly in detail but identically in import) posit the use of force as initially actualized in fact, then politicized through force of necessity by vesting in a sovereign and afterwards being legalized for reason of legitimacy by subjection to validating processes.

This is because the current international legal system, during both war and peace, constructs its principal actors in the form of an institutionalized state possessing certain attributes as the basis for participation in international politics (Teubner 2001: 21 and 31). This war/peace dichotomy and the resultant differentiation of applicable legal regime are exemplary of an exception/rule scheme. Peace is the rule and war (armed conflict) the exception. This is why, for example, United Nations Security Council Resolutions authorizing the use of force do not do so explicitly but instead use the wording 'by all necessary means' to achieve their object. Such wording is deemed sufficient to permit the

1 Social capital here is the sum of resources linked to a network of institutionalized relationships of social recognition, as per Bourdieu 1986: 241–58.

use force without specifically recommending it.[2] In international law, therefore, armed conflict is the most radical state of affairs (being literally out of the norm where all that is necessary is permissible) in the most inclusive human society (the international community representative of universality).

The interlocutors in international law must therefore situate themselves in relation to the law by making themselves amenable to its claims. Arguments in declaring exceptions to the established law on war and peace are even then irretrievably imbued (or perhaps tainted) with issues of legality.[3] The law is thus on both sides of the question, neither external nor adjacent nor even contingent; in other words, the question of whether the law is applicable or not is a *legal* question.[4] If it were that a zone of a legality was being claimed politically, outside and beyond the formal system of domestic and international law (if such a radically ahistorical state of affairs were to come to pass even hypothetically), then executive orders and even presidential decrees would lose all meaning. This is because they too are essentially legal-juridical concepts, not factual-physical phenomena. Strictly speaking then, there is no question of 'all bets being off *ergo* no holds barred'.

In a conflict between law and politics, the question of regulating force therefore is no longer a distinction of law/non-law distinguishable under the proposition that a politician should decide. Rather, it is a distinction between normal law (during peace) and exceptional law (during armed conflict) and is accordingly amenable to adjudication via strict reference to rules.

The legal process is by its very nature more objective than ad hoc decision-making within society. It transforms socially, morally, politically and economically irresolvable conflicts into technical legal questions, which are constructed to be answerable within and by its procedural and conceptual means (Teubner 2001: 23). Consequently the legal question may on its face have very little or virtually nothing to do directly with the social conflict in issue (Teubner 2001: 23). The law thus creates fictions about the outside world but has to treat them as though they were hard-core realities (Teubner 2001: 23). These include the indispensable (for many theorists) construct of the social contract, which can of course only be empirically located in legal narrative, not objective reality. The same is true, of course, of other fictions. That is, only metaphorically or at the legal level of abstraction can the notions of social contract or rule/exception be 'objective reality' or 'empirically defined'. Therefore, it takes legal competence to decide when the legal process is appropriate or appropriately utilized to bring a construct within the purview of the law. This boundary riding is merely to determine any instance where the legal system is utilized for a purpose other than that for which it was designed or intended. The making of this decision (and its maker) it is what

2 See generally Freudenschuß 1994: 492, and Baker 1995: 304–5.

3 See Johns 2005: 613.

4 'The exception remains, nevertheless, accessible to jurisprudence because both elements, the norm as well as the decision, remain within the framework of the juristic'. Schmitt 1985: 12.

is actually at issue. More crudely speaking, this is located in a contest between might and right.

If we take a characterization of abuse of process as an indication of the wrongful utilization of law, then my thesis would indicate that the abuse of process discretion is an adequate safeguard to politically motivated prosecutions of criminal aggression. The argument underpinning this is that (as the narrative goes) force is first actualized, then politicized and finally legalized. The theoretical assumption making the argument and thesis possible is that the law is an inexorable process with irrepressible logic, unique and separate within society.

It is an inexorable process in the sense that objective laws procedurally followed and substantively applied by neutral observers are indispensable in resolving disputes. This process is at its core applicable to past texts with reference to future events within a given society. It has an irrepressible logic in that it divides the world into black and white; black letter law on a white page world. That is, a strictly binary code (law/fact, lawful/non-lawful, legal/illegal, etc., is applicable in classifying, selecting, distinguishing, applying and deciding: in a word, judging. These assumptions are supportable within Niklas Luhmann's systems theory's circular explanation of the law as a self-referential process. This process is further operationally concerned with internal validity, not external legitimacy. The law thus has the last word on legal issues and cannot be adequately conceptualized otherwise. The approach chosen is thus simultaneously self-referential, empirical and theoretical. It should therefore fit well within the systems theory adopted while retaining the capacity to supply an answer acceptable in legal doctrine.

Modelling Three Stages of Force: Factual Violence, Political Struggle and Legal Enforcement

The relationship of (or between) force and law is a problematic one. Although force is not necessarily linked to law, the opposite is demonstrably false. Law and force are intimately connected through the notion of *enforceability* (Derrida 1989–90: 920). Clearly while force may exist in the absence of law, law cannot exist in a meaningful sense absent from force to back it up *as a last resort*. This is one sense in which force *precedes* law.

In domestic law, force used within the law's bounds (for instance in self-defence and while apprehending criminals) is considered legitimate. However, the use of force outside the law is considered illegal (for example run-of-the-mill criminal or contrary to law activities, all the way to actions that are highly treasonous or against the legal order itself). Force outside the law is repressed as violence as long as it remains repressible, unless it is of such a magnitude that it successfully overthrows the legal system itself and is therefore transformed into a matter of extra-juridical or even meta-juridical pure fact with certain legal consequences.[5] Thus in a sense force also *succeeds* law.

The order of precession and succession of force and law is vital because violence of a magnitude to overthrow the legal system is, of necessity, not a legal question but a factual one belatedly recognized by law. What was hitherto a legal question is transformed into a factual one by the process of politicization through force. Therefore, the cyclical order in which force precedes and succeeds law is through politics. Both politics and law are in the final analysis expressed by (and may also be interchangeable modes of expressing) force.

A conundrum arises where the notion of force itself is rendered a question to be handled within the legal system, to be coded as either legal or illegal regardless of magnitude or effect; that is, when force is legalized by being subjected to the law and not being merely treated as a matter of fact. The particular instance here is codifying a crime of aggression that prohibits the unlawful use of force by imposing individual criminal liability in international law.

The argument made here is that there is a necessary order and occurrence in play that creates a ratcheting effect. The only order the process can go through and remain lawful is as described above: force once actualized by application is politicized in establishing a pecking order, then legalized by restriction in application and so on, *ad nauseam*. The contrary order where legalized force is politicized then actualized is unlawful as it upsets the basis for order itself. There is a certain direction and order in the development of raw force or violence to political struggle, which if successful engenders a social order then a legal system. That is, the movement is from violence to force through politics and law.

The particular situation giving rise to this exercise is aggression or, less judgmentally, the use of force, and in particular, its characterization as either legal

---

5 See Cox 2001: 5 – discussing *Republic of Fiji v Prasad* (Unreported, Court of Appeal of Fiji, 1 March 2001, Civil Appeal No. ABU0078/2000S), and *Madzimbamuto v Lardner-Burke* [1969] AC 645 (PC)) per Lord Reid at 723–4: 'It is an historical fact that in many countries – and indeed in many countries which are or have been under British Sovereignty – there are now regimes which are universally recognized as lawful but which derive their origins from revolutions or coups d'état. The law must take account of that fact. So there may be a question how or at what stage the new regime became lawful' ; *Uganda v Commissioner of Prisons, Ex parte Matovu* [1966] EA 514 per Sir Udo Udoma C J at 539 said: '... our deliberate and considered view is that the 1966 Constitution is a legally valid constitution and the supreme law of Uganda; and that the 1962 Constitution having been abolished as a result of a victorious revolution in law does no longer exist nor does it now form part of the Laws of Uganda, it having been deprived of its de facto and de jure validity' ; *In The State v Dosso* [1958] 2 PSCR 180 per Muhammed Munir C J said at 184: 'It sometimes happens, however, that a Constitution and the national legal order under it is disrupted by an abrupt political change not within the contemplation of the Constitution. Any such change is called a revolution, and its legal effect is not only the destruction of the existing Constitution but also the validity of the national legal order'.

or illegal, rather than its factual appearance. Whether such characterization may lead to imposition of individual criminal liability or otherwise is the debate.

During the negotiations leading to the adoption of the Rome Statute for the Permanent International Criminal Court (the Rome Statute), Philippe Kirsch, the Canadian diplomatic representative (as he then was; he later became the first President of the International Criminal Court (ICC)), chaired a session where consensus of sorts was brought onto two erstwhile irreconcilable factions.[6] One, the overwhelming majority, wanted inclusion of the crime of aggression in the statute. The minority, but by no means inconsequential for that fact, would not hear of this, with both antagonists viewing the issue as all-important.

The temporary solution crafted was to duly include aggression but then postpone the court exercising jurisdiction until a definition was found according to the terms of the statute. This thereby put off the disagreement for at least seven years until the next conference of state parties. The reasons proffered were that a definition of the crime and proper role for the United Nations Security Council within the Rome Statute were beyond reach at the conference. Both camps were thereby satisfied enough to append their signatures to the same text. Despite mutually opposed positions they found satisfaction in identical words. A minor miracle? Or was it? How does one then interpret the meaning of the clause in a court given all manner of plausible, if irreconcilable, authorial intents and infinite scenarios for application?

There exist at least two possible opposed points of entry to the debate. The first is that the crime of aggression exists but an adequate definition for the purposes of the ICC is yet to be arrived at; that is, juridical inclusion and political exclusion of subject matter. The second is that the crime of aggression does not exist; however, the issue of its creation through the political process is still open to the state parties. The controversy may thereby be reduced to the intense dialectic of whether the subject matter of force is excluded from law by politics or excluded from politics by law, which is insipid and does not take the debate sufficiently forward. This author's view is that society has separated law from politics by imposing rules on force and thereby separating power from authority; that is, mere ability from legitimacy. Therefore, in pondering the applicability of legality (the effect of rules) versus inapplicability of legality (the freeing up from rules), judges look to society in general through the prism of text.

There are two methodological approaches to reach a solution to this impasse. For convenience, I refer to them as interpretation (or hermeneutics) and construction

---

6 Regional blocs including the European Union, Group of African States, Group of Arab States and the Non-Aligned Movement supported inclusion of aggression. Brazil, Israel, Morocco, Pakistan, Turkey and the United States of America opposed inclusion. See UN Diplomatic Conference of Plenipotentiaries on the Establishment of an International Criminal Court Rome 15 June – 17 July 1998. Official Records Volume II Summary Records of the Plenary Meetings and of the Meetings of the Committee of the Whole. Document No. A/CONF.183/13 (vol. II).

(or exegesis). Here hermeneutics is the art or science of interpretation, commonly distinguished from exegesis or practical exposition. Exegesis itself is the explanation or construction of a sentence or word, for example, or an explanatory note or gloss.

For example, where the law is silent on the particular point before the court, whether the legislator 'saw fit not to include' (which would be exclusion of the point in issue by hermeneutics) or 'did not see fit to include' (which would be non-inclusion that thereby may be supplied by exegesis) is a subjective value judgement.[7] Such a judgement is arguably based more on the factual circumstances of the case than the law as embodied in mere words.

The Order, Interpretation and Construction of the UN and ICC Aggression Clauses

In public international law, the central provision relevant to criminal aggression is the United Nations Charter's Article 39. It was drafted before, and therefore without reference to, the relevant ICC provisions:[8]

> The Security Council shall determine the existence of any threat to the peace, breach of the peace, or act of aggression and shall make recommendations, or decide what measures shall be taken in accordance with Articles 41 and 42, to maintain or restore international peace and security.

Historically, the origin of the Article as reflected in the framer's intent was to give as free a hand as possible to the Security Council for freedom of action. Importantly, there is no link to criminality. What is more, no a priori definition of what constituted aggression was accepted at its inception.[9] With reference to international criminal law, it and related articles were expansively construed in the *Tadić* case.[10] More

7 Deconstructionists would probably call this an 'aporia'. See 'The undecidable is not simply a matter of vacillation between two determinate decisions in the application of a rule, but marks the infinite irreducible "idea of justice" that haunts every decision and necessarily haunts it in order for it to be a decision and not merely the application of a rule'. Mills 2004: 42 and 54.

8 See the debates recorded in United Nations document *United Nations Diplomatic Conference of Plenipotentiaries on the Establishment of an International Criminal Court Rome, 15 June – 17 July 1998: Official Records Volume II Summary records of the Plenary Meetings and of the Meetings of the Committee of the Whole* Document No. A/CONF.183/13 (vol. II). UN Diplomatic Conference of Plenipotentiaries on the Establishment of an International Criminal Court Rome 15 June – 17 July 1998. Official Records Volume II Summary Records of the Plenary Meetings and of the Meetings of the Committee of the Whole. Document No. A/CONF.183/13 (vol. II).

9 See Simma 2002: 718–19.

10 *Prosecutor v Tadić*, Case No. IT-94–1 (Appeals Chamber), Decision on the Defence Motion for Interlocutory Appeal on Jurisdiction, 2 October 1995.

recently, it was considered to be closely related to the ICC Statute's Article 5,[11] which was drafted in contemplation of the United Nations Charter. It reads:

> 1. The jurisdiction of the Court shall be limited to the most serious crimes of concern to the international community as a whole. The Court has jurisdiction in accordance with this Statute with respect to the following crimes … (d) The crime of aggression.
>
> 2. The Court shall exercise jurisdiction over the crime of aggression once a provision is adopted in accordance with articles 121 and 123 defining the crime and setting out the conditions under which the Court shall exercise jurisdiction with respect to this crime. Such a provision shall be consistent with the relevant provisions of the Charter of the United Nations.

However, the literal meaning of clause 2 is too simplistic. How about what it does not *say* but could perhaps *mean* within the realms of disputed possibility? Either interpreting it as a rule or constructing it as a principle and then proceeding accordingly is the basis for inquiry here. If exegesis looks at what the text means to the readers, hermeneutics observes what the text meant to the author. First, contrast it with the example below, augmented with a handily placed 'only' as the narrowest possible hermeneutical interpretation of authorial intent in the circumstances. This was the approach favoured by the then Chief Prosecutor of the ICC, Luis Moreno-Ocampo:[12]

> 2. The Court shall *only* exercise jurisdiction over the crime of aggression once a provision is adopted in accordance with articles 121 and 123 defining the crime and setting out the conditions under which the Court shall exercise jurisdiction with respect to this crime. Such a provision shall be consistent with the relevant provisions of the Charter of the United Nations.

Alternatively, a purposely placed 'also' may be considered as the basis for the widest possible exegetical construction dependent on factual circumstances; an approach that we may call the Nuremberg method:[13]

---

11 See UN Diplomatic Conference of Plenipotentiaries on the Establishment of an International Criminal Court Rome 15 June – 17 July 1998. Official Records Volume II Summary Records of the Plenary Meetings and of the Meetings of the Committee of the Whole. Document No. A/CONF.183/13 (vol. II).

12 '[T]he Court may not exercise jurisdiction over the crime until a provision has been adopted which defines the crime and sets out the conditions under which the Court may exercise jurisdiction'. See ICC 2006a.

13 The tribunal got round the absence of sufficiently literal legal text by stating: 'Crimes against international law are committed by men, not by abstract entities, and only

> 2. The Court shall *also* exercise jurisdiction over the crime of aggression once a provision is adopted in accordance with articles 121 and 123 defining the crime and setting out the conditions under which the Court shall exercise jurisdiction with respect to this crime. Such a provision shall be consistent with the relevant provisions of the Charter of the United Nations.

This sets the stage to bring out a subtle but telling ambiguity; that the meaning of clause 2 above completely shifts in the examples given. As expected, they faithfully reflect the opposed States' interests as represented in the record of the Rome Conference, which upon scrutiny resulted in more or less ambiguous wording.

Interpretation

The addition of either 'only' or 'also' totally reverses the meaning attached to 'shall'. If Article 39 is the most important article in public international law (Simma 2002: 718–19), then its linkage to Article 5 makes the latter the most important article of the Rome Statute. 'Shall' becomes then the most important word in the most important articles and thus the principal battleground of meaning. In my opinion, this disagreement specifically focuses on competing meanings that centre on grammatical mood. Upon close reading (at least of the English authentic text),[14] it may roughly bear equally both the imperative and subjunctive mood. When imperative, it lays down a primary institutive rule of what is to be followed; that is, how it *must* be done. In the subjunctive mood, it refers to how it *may* or *could* be done. The first is mandatory, the second permissive.

However, it does not provide a legal remedy to the situation by a secondary enforcement rule where, as may occasionally occur, the primary rule is not followed. In the context of aggression, the minority States' exclusionary position supports the imperative meaning but the majority States' inclusionary position favours the subjunctive meaning. That is, a secondary rule is lacking either because States do not see fit to include it or see fit not to include it. These then are the outermost limits to which Articles 15 and 39 may be legally and logically extended.

This is where the controversy was frozen in 1998 and is thus where law meets politics and law either stands up to, or gives up on, politics. It may also be reformulated as where politics meets law and either stands in for law or gives in to law. This is proof of Luhmann's thesis of different codes in different systems. The change in grammatical mood involves a wholesale change in coding from the legal/illegal of the legal system to the powerful/powerless of the contemporary

---

by punishing individuals who commit such crimes can the provisions of international law be enforced'. See Judgment of German Major War Criminals. ICC 1947.

14 See Rome Statute Article 128 on equally authentic texts in Arabic, Chinese, English, French, Russian and Spanish. Whether the same situation occurs elsewhere therein is beyond my linguistic competence.

international political system. In the midst of evolutionary (as opposed to revolutionary) change, we know what the law was yesterday and can reasonably surmise what it will be tomorrow. The problem is what the law is today. Is force legalized enough to bear prosecution where it is misused?

Construction

Whichever reading is adopted, it is obvious that the Rome Statute lacks clarity with regard to the criminality of aggression (or otherwise). The position remains as it was in customary international law. This is not mere argument. The Rome Statute itself explicitly says so in Article 10:

> Nothing in this Part shall be interpreted as limiting or prejudicing in any way existing or developing rules of international law for purposes other than this Statute.

In short, the Rome Statute does not affect customary international law but customary international law decisively affects the Rome Statute (Article 21para 1 clause (b)). It follows then that the case law generated by the ICC as evidence of customary international law as enjoined by its statute may even go as far as supplementing the statute.

The connection between the identical word 'aggression' in public international law and international criminal law can therefore occasionally be overblown. They should not be viewed as identical and coextensive in meaning as well as appearance. The same word in the same language and discipline could nevertheless have vastly different semantic effect let alone tenor and import. Take 'maintenance', for example, in family law's separation and maintenance and tort law's maintenance and champerty. Conflating the two is absurd. However, structurally similar fallacies escape attention, as in *factual* aggression under the United Nations Charter[15] and *criminal* aggression in the Nuremberg Charter, Judgment and Principles. The former relates to law on the use of force by States under public international law, and the latter to individual criminal responsibility under international criminal law by natural persons.

The process of the two Articles' creation indicates that at most the texts can be interpreted to block, or construed to allow (or at any rate not disallow), the prosecution of aggression at the ICC. Neither is definitive. It crucially depends on

---

15 Even though the ICTR said 'neither the text nor the spirit of the Charter conceives of the Security Council as *legibus solutus* (unbound by law)', there is an *ipso custodiet custodes?* (who will guard the guardians?) element where any Permanent Security Council Member may vote down such a finding based on self-interest. See *Prosecutor v Tadić*, Case No. IT-94–1 (Appeals Chamber), Decision on the Defence Motion for Interlocutory Appeal on Jurisdiction, 2 October 1995 para 28.

the facts in question. If a case involves criminal aggression between two or more States that recognize it, then there is no absolute legal bar to adjudicating upon it.

For this, one must separate the product of the Rome conference (the statute) from its process (as contained in the record of proceedings). The statute itself is not codificatory of customary international law, either in law or in fact. The debates of the conference itself, however, are indicative and evidentiary of customary international law. From these debates, one may conclude that while criminal aggression is an international crime (a legal answer to a legal question), the venue for trial is still open to debate (a political question awaiting a political solution). A special working group on criminal aggression is currently at work at the behest of the Assembly of State Parties.[16]

This follows from the fact that only the law can say what is lawful and unlawful. In deciding this, it refers to previous decisions and the subsequent consequences of future decisions (King and Schutz 1994: 261 and 275). Legally and logically, 'illegal acts do not become legalized *because they are committed*'.[17] Even international relations, where conflict resolution and rule production have been separate for centuries, has undergone gradual juridification where court litigation and norm production regimes mutually attract (Teubner 2001: 28).

Consequently, when interpreting the ICC Statute, the whole and its constituent parts are inseparable. To understand the clauses on aggression, one must consider both the statute and its environment in totality. The crime of aggression is within the jurisdiction of the ICC. The court can exercise this jurisdiction once the crime is defined and conditions prescribed for jurisdiction.

With respect to criminal aggression, the statute says when jurisdiction *shall* be exercised, not when it shall *not*. However, the prosecutor for the ICC[18] has interpreted Article 5(2) as indicating 'the Court may not exercise jurisdiction over the crime until a provision has been adopted which defines the crime and sets out the conditions under which the Court may exercise jurisdiction'. This limits the prosecutor and the court's mandate to conduct during a conflict, but not the legality of armed conflict. As has been argued above, and will be demonstrated in Chapter 6, the record of negotiations leading up to the statute does not indisputably support the prosecutor's stance.

Despite war not being eradicated, most countries are peaceful most of the time. In sum, peace is the rule and the use of force is the exception. Now that force is legalized and international sovereignty diffused, judges are therefore sovereign in declaring exception to peace (the legality/illegality of aggression). Finding an abuse of the process of the law in prosecution of aggression is in the final analysis declaring the ultimate exception (non-application of lawful process) to the ultimate norm (peace). The question arising is, given the textual analysis of the text above, is prosecuting criminal aggression at the ICC an abuse of the process

16 For their current progress see ICC 2009c.

17 Emphasis in original. Ibid., 279.

18 ICC 2006.

of law? That is, is it utilizing the law for a process that is patently not meant for it? If the text is considered in an imperative sense, then the answer is probably yes; if considered in a subjunctive sense, then no. The decision is at the discretion of the decision-maker. How this is possible is illustrated below.

The method applied in proving the argument is comparative casuistry. Like cases from diverse legal traditions are treated alike in the context of Mauro Cappelletti's phased comparative law methodology.[19] The tool utilized is analogy rather than either deduction or induction.

The means of proof adopted are to seek universality in principle via the description of broad and unrelated legal traditions doing the same thing in similar situations and different international judges following analogous practice. This starts with historical examples from when law and religion were indistinguishable[20] (unless the present day liberal human rights position is broadly conceived of as derived from humanism being a secular religion), and moves onto the practice in domestic and international courts. The product of this exercise is to venture as tentative a prognosis upon the ICC's context and method as may be attempted if it ever comes to interpreting its own statute's aggression provisions.

Interpretation versus Construction

As argued above and demonstrated below, there is a certain isomorphism in (con) textual application's topology. This is demonstrated below in the investigation of four different traditions exhibiting similar characteristics yet widely dispersed in space and time. The common societal problem isolated is a decision-maker applying text to context. The juridical solution in all instances has been reasoned decision methodology. The reason for this similarity in diverse contexts is probably a common need driving a common solution. The likely possible trend across traditions appears to be greater formalization and a resultant increase in complexity. An evaluation of the differing juridical solutions indicates no substantial difference but rather broad similarity. Lastly, a prognostication of possible future developments overwhelmingly indicates that even novel textual-contextual regimes would nevertheless exhibit similar traits in similar straits of stability and change.

There are three basic points of reference in the strategic handling of reified documents: texts, facts and authors anchor the reader's extraction and wielding

---

19 This methodology has, in a nutshell, six stages: identification of common societal problem or need; identification of juridical solution(s) given; investigation of the reasons for similarities and divergence of juridical solutions; identification of possible trends across traditions; evaluation of the differing juridical solutions; and scientific prophesy or prognostication of possible future developments. See Cappelletti 1992.

20 See Tamanaha 2005.

of meaning. In early forms of law, when it is indistinguishable from religion,[21] what may be called interpretation is synonymous with hermeneutics, while what may be referred to as construction is coterminous to exegesis. An implication of this is that the ICC will be constrained to take a similar approach in construing its statute as well.

In Jewish legal doctrine, both hermeneutical practice and exegesis are important sources of law.[22] Using arcane and complex rules, the judges or Rabbis contribute to the body of law (or '*Halakhah*') via interpretation or '*Midrash*'. *Halakhah* means 'the way to go' and constitutes the practical application of the Torah or written law as developed through discussion and debate in the classical rabbinic literature, especially the Mishnah and the Talmud, or through oral law as codified in the *Shulkhan Arukh* or code of law. The method applied is by exegetical expression of text in application to concrete factual contexts in deciding novel cases. The boundaries of Jewish law are determined through the halakhic process, a religious-ethical system of legal reasoning. Some principles of Mishnah were derived from the written Torah by virtue of inference from contexts where strict interpretation would not suffice.

Islamic legal doctrine has no central authority. The dominant schools are divided along sources and authority but not method, with which we are presently concerned (Tamanaha 2006: 23). Disputes always take place within the Sharia, the law or literally 'the way'. The debate between traditionalists and modernists is not over whether the Sharia must be followed but whether old understandings or new interpretations address contemporary issues. The focus is on the majority Sunni schools to establish hierarchy and method by demographic if not democratic representation.

There are five legal sources in descending order of authority. First is the Qur'an which is deemed as self-explanatory and therefore applied in literal fashion. Second is the *Hadith* being the collected sayings and practices of the prophet Mohammed. Third are the *Ijma* being the reports of the *Sahaba*, or companions of Mohammed, wherever there is a consensus. Fourth are *Quiyas*, being rules derived through reason, and fifth is the *Ijtihad*, which is more a method than a formal or material source. It involves the use of reason by deductive logic and evaluation of arguments to expostulate Islamic law derived from the other sources by exegetical method.

---

21 Schmitt is quite frank about this: 'The decision becomes instantly independent of argumentative substantiation and receives an autonomous value' (n 61). In the end, 'The exception in jurisprudence is analogous to the miracle in theology' (n 62). 'All significant concepts of the modern theory of the state are secularized theological concepts', he continues, 'not only because of their historical development – in which they were transferred from theology to the theory of the state, whereby, for example, the omnipotent God became the omnipotent lawgiver – but also because of their systematic structure, the recognition of which is necessary for a sociological consideration of these concepts. The exception in jurisprudence is analogous to the miracle in theology'. See Schmitt 1985: 36.

22 The summary of Jewish law is from Elon 1994.

The Islamic jurists, *Ulema*, evade the literal text where it leads to an oppressive situation for believers (Goldziher 1981: 56). The revealed law, *Tafsir*, is the product of juridical exegesis and interpretation (Rahim 1911).

The function of the *Ulema* is therefore derivation; that is, reviewing the entire texts of the law for a clear statement of the ideal behaviour revealed to humans and required of humans (Rahim 1911: 12). The sum revealed is the Sharia. The ideal *Ulema* possesses *Fikh* or understanding of what is for and against human welfare (Rahim 1911: 48); the *non liquet* equivalent aphorism they live by is 'no problem will confront a member of the community of God to which an indication cannot be found in the book of God, pointing to a solution' (Rahim 1911: 11). The method of exegesis is *Ijtihad* while the product is *Naskh* (Burton 1990). However, the closest analogue to precedent in common law is in the *fatwa* opinions of the *mufti* (Messick 1986: 102–104).

Civil law doctrine has two separate historical influences: Justinian's and Napoleon's codes. The French Civil Code sets the stage in Article 4 by stating: 'A judge who refuses to decide a case on the pretext that the law is silent, obscure or insufficient, may be prosecuted as being guilty of a denial of justice'. This is the prohibition against a *non-liquet* and means that once jurisdiction is found a judge can no longer plead inability to find the law. This thus in effect not only permits but also actively encourages, under penalty, creativity in applying legal text.

In the civil law tradition, scholarly commentators have always held centre stage. Civil law has been described as 'a law of professors' and legal scholars as the real protagonists (Merryman 1985: 56). In the Roman era, juris consults were the architects of much of Justinian's *corpus juris civilis*, while during the Roman law revival in Italy glossators played much the same role. Interestingly enough, back-handed compliments acknowledging external influence include the emperor Justinian forbidding commentary, while Napoleon exclaimed his code was lost upon hearing of the first commentary on it (Merryman 1985: 57). '*Mon code est perdu!*' he is rumoured to have said (followed by Napoleonic tears) when he found out that his *Code Civil* had, upon litigation, been changed by the sophistry of advocates and judges (Teubner 2001: 27). So much for legislating for all time.

Broadly, common law doctrine differentiates between constitutional, statutory and case law interpretation, with written constitutions being viewed as codified principles that are interpreted exegetically. Statutes, which are less lofty and more circumscribed, are generally interpreted hermeneutically, while case law, given its non-specificity and open-ended drafting, is interpreted exegetically.

Literal construction is only defensible where the plain meaning coincides with reason and justice. However, this is only so by accident (D'Amato 1991: 529) as there is no way to anticipate the workings of the law. In the American Supreme Court Case of *Hamdan*,[23] normalizing the exception in applying the law of war was

23 See *Hamdan v Rumsfeld, Secretary of Defense, et al.* Certiorari to the United States Court of Appeals for The District of Columbia Circuit No. 05–184. Argued 28 March 2006 and decided 29 June 2006, especially the lively debate in footnotes 31 and 32.

held in the final analysis to be a court matter and, without legislation by Congress, the Executive could not independently suspend application of law even in wartime without explicit and adequate legal provisions.

In the United Kingdom, the House of Lords ruled upon crimes against peace and crimes of aggression (*R v Jones and others* [2006] UKHL 16: para. 5). The court held that the crime of aggression was a crime under customary international law and that its elements were clear enough for prosecution and conviction (*R v Jones and others* [2006]: para. 19). However, it also held that aggression was not part of the domestic law and that only Parliament could make it so (*R v Jones and others* [2006]: para. 26–30 and 60). This decision was only possible by citing (among other post-1945 legislation) the Criminal Law Act 1967. One may note in passing the limited relevance and utility of citing legislation ostensibly to prevent judicial creation of a 'new' crime where such crime pre-exists the proffered legislation (but not the case).

International law provides several legal and factual systems, four of which are examined below. The systems deal with varied areas of law, dissimilar factual situations and different disputes but, it is argued, follow similar strategies of textual application.

In the much-cited *Nicaragua* case (*Military and Paramilitary Activities in and against Nicaragua (Nicaragua v the United States of America)*, Decision on Jurisdiction and Admissibility (1984) ICJ REP. 392, 27 June 1986) the International Court of Justice demonstrated great facility in ameliorating the effect of literalism. The court exegetically interpreted Article 36 (2) of the United Nations Charter by recourse to an eclectic array of materials. These included their yearbook (*Nicaragua*: para. 19), a telegram from the Ministry of External Relations of Nicaragua to the Secretary General of the League of Nations (*Nicaragua*: para. 17), their (the ICJ's) (*Nicaragua*: para. 21) and the Secretary General's reports to the General Assembly (*Nicaragua*: para. 22), *travaux préparatoires* (*Nicaragua*: para. 30), its Case Law (*Nicaragua*: paras. 28, 29, 32 and 35) reports of a national delegation Chair to the San Francisco Conference (*Nicaragua*: para. 33), a letter from the United States Government (*Nicaragua*: para. 41) and even the silence of the Nicaraguan Government (*Nicaragua*: para. 39). The reason for this extraordinarily expansive method was simply that the plain meaning was undesirable (*Nicaragua*: para. 26). Where the decision conflicted with the law, this was deemed a 'formal defect' that did not therefore affect 'the essential validity' (*Nicaragua*: para. 43) of the decision; that is, simple justice trumped mere rules.

The European Court of Human Rights (ECHR) has displayed great facility when faced with patent or latent textual inconvenience. The court has held that a court legislating in criminal cases is both 'traditional and necessary provided it is consistent and foreseeable' (*C.R v C.R*, 22 November 1995, Case 48/1994/495/577). This seemingly innocuous and well-meaning, even pedestrian, statement nevertheless involves importing the common law notion of judges making law into international law, even to the extent of departing from written law. By interpretation, the judges 'have arrogated themselves power to reduce meaning to performance and convention to invention' (Dallmayr 1989–90: 1449).

Effectively, the court may choose at its discretion whether to take a strict and narrow or wide and relaxed approach to the meanings of words.

The dynamics of such judicial power are manifest in the profoundly opposed doctrines of 'Margin of Appreciation' and 'Autonomous Concept', which embody exegesis and hermeneutics respectively.

The notion of Margin of Appreciation in European Human Rights Jurisprudence (*Ireland v United Kingdom* judgement of 18 January 1978, Eur. Ct. H.R,. Series A, no. 25; *Greece v the United Kingdom* decision of 2 June 1956, 7; *Lawless v Ireland* judgment of 1 July 1961, Series A, no. 3) originated from the French *Conseil d'État*, equivalent Continental institutions and martial law. When applied in judicial review of due process it allows governments to exercise discretion by situational exigency (Yourow 1996). This means in effect that the ECHR will interpret the claimed discretion exegetically. The 'Autonomous Concept', however, refers to a term of the ECHR (Letsas 2004: 279) that cannot be construed by mere reference to the domestic law but rather is strictly interpreted independently (*Engel and Others v the Netherlands* (1976) Series A no. 22). This means in effect that the ECHR will interpret the term hermeneutically. The conclusion is that there is no single empirical correct interpretation in a general sense but possibly one in a particular sense.

In the *Tadić* case, the International Criminal Tribunal for the Former Yugoslavia (ICTY) gave an unusual and unusually important decision (*Prosecutor v Tadić*, Case No. IT-94–1 (Appeals Chamber), Decision on the Defence Motion for Interlocutory Appeal on Jurisdiction, 2 October 1995). The court affirmed its own legitimate existence by going beyond a literal application of the United Nations Charter. The court raised their statute document to normative parity with the United Nations Charter at the most coercive. This was despite it being a mere annex to a Security Council Resolution. This reasoning was achieved based on its 'inherent jurisdiction' while interpreting the Charter's clauses on breach of the peace and acts of aggression. Thereby the court invested its own actions with the authority to trump other rules of international and domestic law, especially of state sovereignty and constitutional supremacy respectively.

The court relied on the suppression of aggression and breaches of the peace as a purpose of the United Nations to view itself as a Security Council subsidiary organ in performing its functions. Because the General Assembly could receive an account of measures by the Security Council to maintain international peace and security on their behalf, and because United Nations members accepted and had to carry out these decisions, they were bound to obey the court's decisions. This was because the Security Council could call upon parties to comply with provisional measures without prejudicing their legal status and apply measures not involving the use of force, unless these were inadequate.

The claimed inherent jurisdiction of the court was described as inversely proportional to the textual discretion of the Security Council (*Tadić*: para. 22). Further, 'neither the text nor the spirit of the Charter conceived of the Security Council as *legibus solutus* (unbound by law)'; instead it was limited by the jurisdiction of and internal division of power within the United Nations (*Tadić*: para. 28). The court had to resort to the '*compétence de la compétence*' or *Kompetenz-Kompetenz* jurisdiction to examine the validity of its establishment (*Tadić*: para. 23) in order to avoid begging the question or *petitio principii* because its very own statute was in dispute. Further, the Charter gave no explicit mention of setting up judicial tribunals nor did its drafters conceive of any such thing.

The Charter was supplemented (or circumvented) by a variety of interpretation aids. These were 'the intent of the Security Council', 'logical and systematic interpretation' and 'customary international law'. The last was evinced in 'settled practice of the Security Council and the common understanding of the United Nations membership in general' (*Tadić*: para. 30). Therefore, to disregard whether it was an internal or an international armed conflict (*Tadić*: para. 137) was simple. Perhaps as an afterthought, 'a simple literal analysis' was applied to show that the mechanism of a court, even though not included, was not excluded (*Tadić*: para. 35). In the *Kanyabashi* case, the International Criminal Tribunal for Rwanda also had to rule on the legality of the resolutions through which it had been created. The ruling in *Kanyabashi* is almost similar to the ruling of the ICTY in *Tadić* (Werner 2001: 345 and 359).

In *Akayesu* (*Prosecutor v Akayesu* Case No. ICTR-96–4-A (Appeals Chamber), 1 June 2001. Decision of 2 September 1998), the International Criminal Tribunal for Rwanda (ICTR) defined genocide wider than in both its statute and Genocide Convention. This was done by adding a new category of protected persons to those hitherto provided for in law: that of 'stable groups'. This departure from the literal word of the law was necessitated by the unacceptable effect of the facts of the case when juxtaposed to the law as it was. The Tutsi would not be protected from genocide under a literal interpretation of the law.

Article 2 of the statute is a verbatim reproduction of Article 3 of the Convention on the Prevention and Punishment of the Crime of Genocide (Genocide Convention). Genocide therein is defined as killing; causing serious bodily or mental harm; inflicting conditions of life calculated to bring about physical destruction; imposing measures intended to prevent births and forcibly transferring children; committed with the special intent or *dolus specialis* to destroy, in whole or in part, a *national, ethnical, racial, or religious group*, as such.

The court inconsistently relied on the *travaux préparatoires* of the Genocide Convention to add a new category of 'stable groups, constituted in a permanent fashion and membership of which is determined by birth' to national, ethnical, racial or religious groups. This, while laudable, reflected the fact that in the Rwanda context Hutus and Tutsis spoke the same language, had similar culture, religion and customs and were more akin to different social classes than different nations, ethnicities, races or religions.

The comparative perspective brought to bear above was an analytical tool for orienting the field of study (Tamanaha 1993: 192 and 211–12). The intention was to bring out into the open how and why legal linguistic concepts are judicially malleable upon application of legal texts to factual contexts. That is, I contend judges can either interpret text by perspectively moving from the present to the past or construe text by moving from the present to a speculated future, with no a priori reason to choose one approach over the other.

If the law were applicable literally, then every literate person could be a lawyer. Thankfully for legal professionals finding and applying texts keeps them remunerated, if only tangentially (Luhmann 1995a: 285 and 287). Despite the presumption that knowledge of law is imputed upon everyone, three to seven years of training are ordinarily necessary to formally qualify as competent in beginning to apply the law. This training, which establishes a professional interpretative class, includes instruction on where to find the law and how to understand it once found.

Accepting this proposition, at the very least, involves conceding that the true meaning of textual legal provisions is inaccessible without employing a certain skill and context external to the actual words, which are in any event accessible to a layperson conversant with the primary language these words are embodied in. A central assumption of this study is therefore that the practice of law necessarily involves the correct application of relevant texts to a selected set of facts.

A trial is a highly stylized narrative with the judge posited as impartial, disinterested and objective to counsels who are partial, partisan and subjective, with both united in upholding the values of justice according to law. Such desirable attributes generally remain just that, desirable, as they are unattainable aspirations not practical targets.

The point of departure for this theoretical framework is that there are, ostensibly, two formally differentiated but substantively identical approaches to interpreting or construing legal texts whose meaning is in doubt or disputed: the writer-centric and reader-centric approaches to texts. The former is exoteric and the latter esoteric in method. Though ostensibly different, their object, purpose and effect are almost indistinguishable as they are mostly used as a rhetorical device to justify the court's own reasoning.

The explanation offered is that whenever textual meaning is in doubt, the doctrine of *non liquet* comes into play, demanding an answer for every question in dispute over which the court can exercise jurisdiction. Judges may opt for the two stylistic options available, the first being to seek meaning behind words through somehow divining the 'author's intent' (the so-called 'original meaning') and the second to give present-practical meaning to the words according to the reader's understanding (the 'evolutionary meaning' approach). Both purport to provide meaning, the former through interpretation, the latter by construction. The unity of two ostensibly divergent approaches is the effect and intention of placing the judge at the centre of the textual discourse while absolving them of superficial appearances of subjectivity.

Legal texts are sometimes only good in parts. Intuitively or instinctively, readers sometimes seek authorial clarification of intent and not esoteric understanding of meaning. The text is seen as the port of departure, not the port of entry. The difference is that interpretation takes the text as the point of arrival and reasons backwards to the author, while construction takes the text as the point of departure and reasons forwards to the reader's understanding. The difference does not precisely coincide with restrictive and expansive approaches to reading texts. Both approaches may efficaciously be utilized one way or the other, analogous as they are to the plain meaning and living document approach to interpretation.

All law is of necessity textual, including so-called 'unwritten law' which is still evidenced in written law reports and customary international law. The last is derived from state practice impelled by legal requirements and evinced in communiqués, speeches and other textual forms. This inquiry therefore centres on texts, their interpretation, construction of their terms and their application to disputes.

The application of rules is not strictly governed by rules (Dallmayr 1989–90: 63). Notwithstanding standardized curricula, agreement among lawyers as to meaning of the simplest legal texts is conspicuous by its absence. A safety valve is to provide discretion in the application of rules in practice to meet the 'known when seen' ends of justice. Law upon application is sometimes classified into principles with regard to the general but rules with regard to the particular. Distinctions may then be drawn between reading a rule, reading from a rule and reading into a rule. The first category is most common, occurring where no dispute arises as to the meaning of the rule. The second category may be seen as extending the application of a rule by treating it as a principle through employing 'intrinsic' aids to reasoning, while the third category involves importing meaning by 'extrinsic' aids to reasoning. To apply a rule unreservedly involves viewing it as mandatory, while applying a rule with reservations means viewing it to some extent as hortatory.

International legal instruments are most useful for procuring consent from a wide variety of States. However, this is at the price of the texts themselves being amenable to different interpretations of meaning and construction of effect upon application. The widest agreement in accession to an instrument therefore goes hand in hand with the widest disagreement as to its actual meaning.

In practice, the utility of agreement is inversely proportional to the utility of clarity. States are generally quite free to register understandings, reservations and in general interpret for themselves their obligations under instruments to which they are party.

This state of things, as though not complicated enough, is compounded in international criminal law (ICL) due to the texts routinely being interpreted by interlocutors other than State Party representatives. When the texts are drafted and agreed, it is with the object of making the provisions as expressive as possible of the drafter's intent and therefore to leave as little open to adverse interpretation as is semantically and grammatically possible.

When the interlocutors engage the text in application to a specific set of facts, it is brought to bear in relation to an unforeseeable circumstance where the specific textual words in the abstract have to be applied in concrete reality and therefore with as little fidelity to the words as is sustainable by the facts. The drafters put legalistic Houdini into a straitjacket in general that he strains every sinew to escape from in the particular.

In this chapter the argument developed is that, sometimes, in a dispute as to meaning, the instrumental text should be honoured more in the breach than in the observance; that is, honoured in the sense of being followed rather than departed from. An opposite example is Shakespeare's *Othello*. Following the playwright's original intent and meaning, Othello himself would ostensibly be the darkest of the cast. However if the immediate audience were taken into consideration then a production of the play, say, at the Kenya National Theatre would make better sense if Othello were the lightest in the cast so as to highlight the incipient tensions of the play to the predominant audience.[24] Otherwise, although one might understand that dark pigmentation may not have been fashionable in Venice at the time the play is set, to viscerally grasp the original raw emotional content one must view Othello as 'the other' and thereby not to be identified with. Apart from the casting difficulties that would make virtue out of necessity, Shakespeare had no original intention that his plays be staged in the distant and future Nairobi, so perhaps his purpose is better served by inverting his product. Meaning is therefore necessarily contextual. It varies across time; changing readings may show more fidelity than unchanged readings over time (Lessig 1995: 2249 and 2262).

Perhaps a more legally persuasive argument to abandon the author's *intention* in favour of their *purpose* as expressed in their text is derived from the 'rule of law' principle, as distinct from the 'rule of man' expedient (Dallmayr 1989–90). At its simplest, the 'rule of law' principle claims that, by dint of the separation of powers, interpretative application of law ought to be in hands separate from those writing the law. Historically, resort to legislature was permissible in inquiries as to meaning. In France this occurred via the *refere legislatif* introduced in 1790 (Elliot 1956), while in England the fourteenth-century Kings Bench took advice from Parliament (Campbell 1846: 274) on meaning. However, modern legislatures may not tell the judiciary what its words meant but must let the words speak for themselves.

To amplify: 'There is no such thing as a neutral, principled interpretation of any word or set of words; the only thing that counts is justice' (D'Amato 1991). Following Montesquieu, it is commonly accepted that writing down the law frees us from the whims of the writer of the law. However, an additional necessary consideration seen above is that the justice system is a process whereby the rule of law is a law of rules that paradoxically incorporates discretion to depart from those rules in the name of an ephemeral, single event and context-dependent justice. That is, exceptions from law are governed by law, not by facts (or if by facts, then facts as constructed in law which is of course the law by another name). The entire discourse is a legal discourse.

24 For the same point (somewhat inadvertently made) from an anthropological perspective but regarding Hamlet see the uproarious Bohannan 1966.

In a dispute as to meaning, fidelity to the author by recourse to the context (exegesis) does not provide all the answers. As a corollary, excessive fidelity to the meaning behind reified words (hermeneutics), even in the absence of misunderstanding, does not necessarily represent faithfulness to meaning.

Both hermeneutics and exegesis are the means by which texts are handled. Hermeneutics proceeds by interpreting text from the standpoint of the author to avoid its literal meaning, while exegesis involves construing the meaning of a text from its words to meet present circumstances. Where hermeneutics rigidly treats principles as rules, exegesis flexibly treats rules as principles. Thus the literal meaning is modified either by avoiding exclusion (that is, contriving inclusion) or avoiding inclusion (that is, contriving exclusion), as circumstances seem to dictate. This is the central thesis of this chapter.

The indispensable point of departure or arrival when applying law is therefore text. To derive an obscure, novel or disputed meaning, one either may go hermeneutically backwards (to the author's explicit or implicit view) or exegetically forwards (to the reader's view of the meaning of the words). Hermeneutics is a posteriori, while exegesis is a priori, in their orientation to text. Sometimes this strategic movement is presented as conflict between 'Positivists', who set great store by the actual words, and 'Naturalists', who read the same words within a transcendental framework. However, it is important to note the inherent incapability of legal theory to identify which particular party should win any given legal case (D'Amato 1991: 513). That plausible arguments are available on any side of a question is demonstrably a basic legal assumption.

This same division may also be cast as 'concrete contextual interpretation', where the circumstances of individual cases are the interpreter's reference point, and 'rule governance' (Dallmayr 1989–90), where the words themselves apply in the face of factual consequences. The notion of let 'justice be done even though the heavens fall' encapsulates the latter approach. In general terms therefore, hermeneutists derive rules from principles while exegetes derive principles from rules; rule here referring to ordained conduct, with a principle being the general reason behind a rule. A rule is therefore (dialectically speaking) a particular manifestation of a principle, while a principle is a general manifestation of a rule. The distinction is inherent and invariable when applying legal texts in factual contexts.

It has been intended to show with reference to aggression how (and how far) texts are flexible upon application. The immediate context is how law has, does and shall view force. This author's hypothesis is that the various modes of legal textual analysis can be roughly represented in three movements: the plain or literal meaning style, the originalist or author's intention approach, and the purposeful or living document or evolutionary method of interpretation. The argument is made here that these are all essentially creations of the reader and are in fact the same process, simply with different emphases.

The literal meaning approach is relatively easy to dispose of for the simple reason that it is impossible to legislate literally. The element of abstraction is inescapable. The following is an absurd example of literalness. Parliament cannot (for pragmatic not competence considerations) legislate that it is unlawful for one Winston Smith to travel at 89 kilometres per hour on Sunday 10 September 2007 on a highway with a 60 kilometre per hour speed limit while in a blue Mercedes Sedan, especially with a chortling infant strapped in the back, and so forth. In framing a more generic rule, precision is sacrificed for inclusion and particularity for generality. A literal meaning then, if not a figment of the imagination, is a mere rhetorical device for somewhat unimaginative fidelity to *reading* a *text*.

The originalist approach is another metaphorical stance masquerading as a theoretical standpoint. Putting oneself into the mind of the author of a text can only be a figurative function, especially so if the author is an abstraction from a legislature consisting of numerous characters with opposed interests and varying abilities. It represents an unsophisticated hermeneutic means of reading subtext *from* a text fairly narrowly under the guise of *interpretation*.

The living document approach is the most interesting and controversial because it makes it plain that reading is always a reader's action and not related to the author's intention. Instead of reading *from*, it reads *into* a text. This exegesis is justified by the circumstances obtained at the time as necessitating textual *construction*.

This bundle of techniques is variously emphasized by different actors in a single judicial strategy which this author refers to as 'reasoned decision methodology'. To sum up, literal practitioners claim to read a text, interpreters claim to read from a text, and constructionists tend to read into a text. As ever, the methodology is inseparable from the task at hand. An independent but accountable judge is constrained from proceeding on frolics of their own by a collection of texts. However, in turn, they are beholden to no one and nothing save the ends of justice in applying the text to the facts while selecting between the broadening or narrowing techniques used to establish meaning.

The cornerstones of this study are 'text', 'interpretation' and 'construction' or, taken together, texts, their originating subtexts and their factual contexts of application. The text is the median point from which either interpretation (utilizing subtext) or construction (following context) depart. There are neither inherent (in the words) nor transcendental (in the context) reasons to choose among them. Rather it is the reader's motives that give wide (constructive) or narrow (interpretive) effect to the text. This author's hypothesis is that a combination of these approaches is not only evident in judicial activity but inherent in the judicial function and inevitable in varied factual situations as well. This combination of approaches is required to match the imprecision of words themselves, coupled with the infinite variety of social actions. Somewhat precariously, this author extrapolates the finding to posit clearly discernible limits in reasonable flexing of texts beyond which it is impossible to transgress meaning both legally and logically. In relation to aggression, such limits mean that the prosecution of aggression cannot be presently characterized as illegal. It remains a crime under customary international law as a matter of *jus cogens*, with the only issue remaining being identification of an appropriate enforcement mechanism, not aggression's actual criminality or factual existence.

In addressing the jurisprudence on the legality or otherwise of prosecuting criminal aggression, one might expect to find an evolutionary dialectical tension between judges moving rhetorically backwards in time through texts (interpretation or hermeneutics) and forwards to contexts (construction or exegesis). This oscillation is premised on the varying requirements of 'justice' as a contingent and context-specific internal aspiration and external legitimation of the legal system.[25] The dynamism is what enables both systemic stability and gradual change.

To reiterate, the purpose of the chapter is to introduce the evolutionary aspect of international justice, whereby politicized force is being progressively legalized through the development of an inclusive process preceding the decision to use force rather than the substantive outcome of the use of force. That is, the factual reasons for which force is used matter less than if a communal method exemplified by the United Nations is applied in initiating the use of force.

The tentative conclusions are that rules are text governed while exceptions are fact governed and judges should therefore decide between rules and exceptions. This decision is, following Carl Schmitt, a function of sovereignty.[26] The only slight modification is in sovereignty's mobility to pass from legislation to adjudication and to execution. There is no fixed international sovereign, at least not yet.[27] Different actors at different times are divisible into active/passive or insiders/outsiders. For instance regarding the rule of law, the executive is active in enforcing the law, the judiciary passive in deciding on the law's application and the legislature proactive in laying down the law. However, when argument actually takes place about meaning and application of legal rules, the legal system with the judge at the centre, legislature on the periphery and executive at the extreme border operates according to the reader as a collection of texts referring to each other.[28]

Even though each text is contingent and liable to change at any time, not everything is simultaneously changeable, not even in the most far-reaching and radical social upheaval or revolution. Even though change is a given, stability is the premium value of any system, not just the legal system. Stability is inimical to change. In the international legal system, an actor dissatisfied with the state of affairs (that is, with the prevailing stability) is likely to consider the use of force.

25 Perhaps this unchanging and ever present attribute is what Luhmann refers to as an 'eigenvalue' ('a value that is constituted by the recursive performance of the system's own operations and one that *cannot be used any where else*') oscillating as it does through text between past and future or subtexts and contexts or in semiotic analysis through signs to signifiers and signifieds. See Luhmann 2004.

26 See for instance Agamben 2005a: 30.

27 See the argument that what is needed is a political philosophy not erected around sovereignty (i.e. 'we need to cut off the King's Head') in Neal 2004: 373.

28 See Luhmann 2004.

The majority States generally do not readily approve such use of force unless and until it is successful in outcome and thereby irresistible as a fait accompli.

Eugene Erhlich elucidated fundamental differences between rules of conduct on one hand and norms for decision on the other.[29] Building on this, this author's argument is that individuals act according to personal morality but are judged through textual legality. This judging is done with one eye to the past (interpretation) and the other to the future (construction). Therefore, in order for the legal system to specify its operations as legal, it has to establish either what it has done so far or what it will do in future (Luhmann 1995b: 81). For instance, a court will refer to legal texts preceding the case at hand to guide its decision.

In international criminal law, some legal norms have clearly been transplanted from domestic criminal law. These are invariably at variance with lived norms; otherwise, they would be of no transformative utility or reformative value. They would only exist on paper until invoked to justify or challenge the decisions and actions of the state legal apparatus (Tamanaha 1993: 210). Such invocation is selective in spatial, temporal and subject matter terms. For example, the spectre of armed force was an issue in both Yugoslavia and Rwanda. Both the International Criminal Tribunal for the Former Yugoslavia (ICTY) and the International Criminal Tribunal for Rwanda (ICTR) had no jurisdiction over aggression. This can only be for other than legal or factual reasons, as opposed to political ones.

The ICC has far more resilience to avoid politics and focus on legalities because it is a product of a widely negotiated and ratified treaty, not an annex to a United Nations Security Council Resolution. International justice is very much a work in progress. In situations of inadequate legal development, the legal system is best seen not as a mechanism of maintaining a just normative order but only as an instrument of power in society for the elites, who wield it in all sorts of ways pursuing parochial stakes (Tamanaha 1993: 211) rather than communal ends. However, this is precisely what the law is not supposed to be for. It is illegal on the face of it. Within the limitations of reasoned decision methodology, it is possible for a court to defer to the political system in both a legal and legally transparent manner through extraordinary jurisdiction of the abuse of process type.

The trials after the Second World War embedded individual criminal liability for aggression as legal principle. Presently its contours and content are in doubt for exact detail of action but not precise principle of identity. The debates at the 1998 Rome Conference for the ICC brought this fact into high relief. However, the existential international law dilemma of the realpolitik stance of might equals right versus the liberal stance of right equals might has impeded progress in adapting applicable legal elements from domestic criminal law. The reception of the aforementioned abuse of process discretion into the ICC would reflect an internationally diffused sovereign between the individual at the micro level and the community at the macro level or the essentially identical rights and power held by a functional, if informal, separation of powers.

29 See Tamanaha 1993: 209.

Legal counsel struggling with their duty to the court (to protect the collective interest) versus their duty to the client (to advance the individual's *qua* individual interests) could argue that since political disputes are best resolvable by political wisdom and legal ones by judicial process, judges are best placed to declare the difference. This gives rise to the argument under discussion that the abuse of process discretion is an adequate safeguard against political prosecutions of criminal aggression. There is no way to interpret existing law to decriminalize aggression but only to oust or delay jurisdiction of the ICC.

Where texts are silent, only the judicial role is left with the prohibition against *non-liquet*. Utilizing the abuse of process as self-observation for self-protection is justified by reference to both individual rights and elite excess. The point is that the courts are the best placed to consider challenges to legality including the utility of law over defining aggression. This sets the stage for answering the queries raised in the hypothetical scenario over the utility of law over violence and law's autonomy from politics. It is not mild insolence to power but at most gentle insouciance to attempted bullying. When faced with a profoundly ill-motivated prosecution, the judge may hold that even though they have the jurisdiction they would prefer not to proceed with the trial and thereby put the matter to rest without going into the actual merits or demerits of the charge itself. How and why this may be done is investigated in the next chapter.

Chapter 7
Exclusion and Inclusion: From Biopolitics to Biolegality

The major theme of this chapter is to introduce biolegality as outlined below. This chapter is an exercise in theorizing and represents neither policy formulation nor a descriptive overview. It aims to create a theoretical framework to illuminate some obscure connections between international crime and global governance. A major theme of the chapter is to introduce the shorthand term 'biolegality' as an active form of global governance. Two minor themes addressed are aggression and abuse of legality. The links between these themes are that biolegality connotes law with life as its referent and justification, while criminal aggression is the taking and degrading of life contrary to law in a scenario involving sustained armed force, and the abuse of legality is the taking or degrading of life under the colour of law nevertheless contrary to legality.

This chapter investigates where the themes of biolegality, aggression and abuse of legal process overlap and intersect as the ensuing global process of monopolizing force by criminalizing rival violence through the law becomes clearer as it gradually becomes entangled less in local particularities and parochial concerns. That is, when globalization utilizes criminalization as a technique of governance it lays bare the links constructed between law, life and death because it ignores cultural differences and erases political boundaries (Findlay 2008: 152–4). As outlined in the chapter's structure below, through criminalization, governing stretches from localized individuals below the state and within its territory all the way to the entire globe and all of humanity. Torture provides a sounding board to interrogate the issues arising when law is linked directly to life and death by excluding and including individual lives within its ambit and protection. This globally governing process is then examined as it operates upon people and places incidental with instituting a distinction between force and violence and thereby a legitimate monopoly that is mediated through and by the law.

Torture in the Global War on Terror

The narration below is taken verbatim from a report of the International Committee of the Red Cross (ICRC) chronicling treatment meted out to one Abu Zubaydah, a suspected high-level member of al-Qaeda (ICRC 2007: 30–31):

> After the beating I was then placed in the small box. They placed a cloth or cover over the box to cut out all light and restrict my air supply. As it was not high enough even to sit upright, I had to crouch down. It was very difficult because of my wounds. The stress on my legs held in this position meant my wounds both in the leg and stomach became very painful. I think this occurred about 3 months after my last operation. It was always cold in the room, but when the cover was placed over the box it made it hot and sweaty inside. …
>
> I was then dragged from the small box, unable to walk properly and put on what looked like a hospital bed, and strapped down very tightly with belts. A black cloth was then placed over my face and the interrogators used a mineral water bottle to pour water on the cloth so that I could not breathe. After a few minutes the cloth was removed and the bed was rotated into an upright position. The pressure of the straps on my wounds was very painful. I vomited. The bed was then again lowered to horizontal position and the same torture carried out again with the black cloth over my face and water poured on from a bottle. … I thought I was going to die. I lost control of my urine. Since then I still lose control of my urine when under stress.
>
> …
>
> I was then made to sit on the floor with a black hood over my head until the next session of torture began. The room was always kept very cold. This went on for approximately one week. During this time the whole procedure was repeated five times. On each occasion, apart from one, I was suffocated once or twice and was put in the vertical position on the bed in between. On one occasion the suffocation was repeated three times. I vomited each time I was put in the vertical position between the suffocation.
>
> …
>
> I was told during this period that I was one of the first to receive these interrogation techniques, so no rules applied. It felt like they were experimenting and trying out techniques to be used later on other people.

'Torture'. The very word invokes images of medieval bestiality and primitive cruelty. Yet this is precisely how the ICRC characterized the allegations of ill-treatment towards detainees held by the United States pursuant to the global war on terror (ICRC 2007: 26). The position of the United States was that, although the Torture Convention (UN General Assembly 1987) applied, it was only according to the United States' understanding of torture which did not include the kind of coercive interrogation described above.[1]

1 See Memorandum of 4 April 2003 entitled 'Working Group Report on Detainee Interrogations in the Global War on Terrorism: Assessment of Legal, Historical, Policy, and Operational Considerations'. In Greenberg and Dratel 2005: 288–90.

These allegations are currently before a Spanish court against six members of the Bush administration – all lawyers – who as lawyers are suspected of having given legal advice that justified, caused or led directly to torture (Horton 2009). Along with this, United States lawyers also provided legal advice recommending the inapplicability of the Geneva Conventions and claiming a presidential authority to suspend them.[2] In other words, their alleged 'offence' entails their manipulation or abuse of the law and legal process in order to 'legalize torture'. When put in that way, the question raised is: 'But is it "torture"? In the 'ICRC's view the victims were placed outside of the protections of law' (ICRC 2007: 24). This begs the question as to whether the perpetrators of these acts were also simultaneously placed outside the prohibitions of the law (which is their argument). But this exclusion and inclusion has another strand because the victims are included in regard to prohibition of their actions by law yet simultaneously excluded from the usual protections of the law. Essentially the United States has arrogated itself the power to make law and immunity from breaking it, while denying its adversaries from the protections of law yet holding them to legal accountability.

By omitting to address this, and merely citing provisions of the law, the ICRC tends to assume as proven precisely what is in dispute: that is, the applicability of the law itself as the standard of judging, distinguishing or discernment.

According to Article 1 of the United Nations Convention Against Torture, torture is:

> any act by which severe pain or suffering, whether physical or mental, is intentionally inflicted on a male or female person for such purposes as obtaining from him, or a third person, information or a confession, punishing him for an act he or a third person has committed or is suspected of having committed, or intimidating or coercing him or a third person, or for any reason based on discrimination of any kind, when such pain or suffering is inflicted by or at the instigation of or with the consent or acquiescence of a public official or other person acting in an official capacity. It does not include pain or suffering arising only from, inherent in, or incidental to, lawful sanctions.

For emphasis, according to the legal definition torture does not include pain or suffering arising *only* from, inherent in, or incidental to, *lawful* sanctions. The battleground then is the boundaries of lawfulness: that is, the characterization of such acts as lawful/unlawful and not their actual occurrence.

The 'global war on terror' is difficult to adequately characterize. It is at once an event, justification and specific set of techniques and tactics in accordance with a strategic plan and long-term objective. According to Julian Reid (2006), the war on terror is in reality not defending the integrity and security of human life against an enemy with a nihilistic will to destroy of human life but rather is fought

2 See Memorandum from G.W. Bush to Vice President and others dated 7 February 2002. In Greenberg and Dratel 2005:134.

over the political constitution of life pitting liberalism principally against Islam as an alternative belief system. Race, as David Hicks' beatings and other physical maltreatment showed, is not really the issue[3] and the idea that this could be an egregious example of 'a few bad eggs' is not borne out by the documentary record (Sands 2008: 13).

The United States' National Security Strategy of 2002 is a case in point. It regarded the war on terror as an 'opportunity to extend the benefits of freedom across the globe' and 'democracy, development, free markets, and free trade to every corner of the world' (2002: 4). This meant that weak states were as much a danger to United States national interests as strong states and poverty, weak institutions and corruption were linked directly to terrorist networks and even drug cartels (Chairman of the Joint Chiefs of Staff, Department of Defense 2002: 4). This is an explicit link to criminalization as a tool of global governance.

The United States Administration reorganized its government by creating a new Department of Homeland Security and a new unified military command ensuring 'the homeland encompasses every level of government and the cooperation of the public and the private sector' (Chairman of the Joint Chiefs of Staff, Department of Defense 2002: 6–7). This strategy meant that emergency management was to 'cope not just with terrorism but with all hazards', both 'bioterror' and 'all infectious diseases and mass-casualty dangers' (Chairman of the Joint Chiefs of Staff, Department of Defense 2002: 6–7). Here crime, war and disease are simultaneously the defined enemy in a war waged on the terrain of life itself.

Modernizing public health infrastructure means an enhanced ability to respond to pandemic public health threats and counter the threat of biological warfare (Chairman of the Joint Chiefs of Staff, Department of Defense 2006: 21–2). For instance, the Department of Health and Human Services received a thirtyfold increase in funding for bioterrorism research (Bush 2004: 3). The blueprint for the future biodefence program, 'Biodefense for the 21st Century', fully integrates national and homeland security and the 'medical, public health, intelligence, diplomatic, and law enforcement communities' (Bush 2004: 3).

For the United States, the 'war against global terrorism' appears ultimately to be about fighting for 'democratic values and way of life' (Chairman of the Joint Chiefs of Staff, Department of Defense 2002: 7). Furthermore, the campaign against terrorism forges new international relationships and redefines existing ones in a future-oriented manner(Chairman of the Joint Chiefs of Staff, Department of Defense 2002: 7). Violence is therefore being deployed to found new revolutionary legal orders.

Giorgio Agamben's (2005a) notion of the state of exception describes how sovereignty now paradoxically defends the law from outside the law in the name of security thereby blurring, distorting or erasing the lines between law and

3 See Affidavit of David Hicks dated 5 August 2004 in *S Rasul et al. v GW Bush et al.* Civil Action No. 02–299 (CKK) United Sates District Court of Columbia. In Greenberg and Dratel 2005: 1234.

lawlessness. Due to its efficacy in addressing extraordinary circumstances, this state of exception gradually becomes the rule. Governments increasingly rely on this seemingly bottomless source of power and legitimacy which, when coupling security and risk, means that even modern democratic societies are not exempt from a state domination that approaches the totalitarian.

What do we make of all this? Torture as a political issue encompasses both what Michel Foucault would call 'disciplinary' and 'regulatory' aspects of power. Foucault (1998: 145–6) demonstrated how sex could come to be at the forefront of wielding power because it 'was at the pivot of two axes along which developed the entire political technology of life' and 'was a means of access both to the life of the body and the life of the species'. Torture occupies an analogous position in the war on terror. It too is 'tied to the disciplines of the body but applied to the regulation of populations' (Foucault 1998: 145–6). It therefore fits both categories of power because it applies to 'man-as-body' and 'man-as-species' (Foucault 1998: 145–6). Whereas discipline orders a multiplicity of individualized persons by surveillance, training and punishment, regulation is addressed to a multiplicity of persons as 'a global mass' affected by the processes of birth, life, illness, death, and the like (Foucault 2003: 242–3). Thus torture links 'the anatomo-politics of the human body' to 'a "biopolitics" of the human race' (Foucault 2003: 242–3).

With regard to war that could be characterized as aggression, Melinda Cooper (2008: 80) has identified the issue as not only the securitization of human life (incorporating 'humanitarian warfare'), but that the United States' defence discourse is integrating:'*the whole of life*, from the micro- to the ecosystemic level, within its strategic vision'. This 'war is no longer waged in the defense of the state … but rather in *the name of life in its biospheric dimension, incorporating meteorology, epidemiology, and the evolution of all forms of life, from the microbe up*' (Cooper 2008: 98). Further, '[t]he extension of pre-emptive warfare to include the sphere of environmental [*sic*] and biopolitics conflates the externalization of war with the evolution of life on earth – as if permanent war were simply *a fact of life*, with no other end than its own crisis-driven perpetuation' (Cooper 2008).

When the ICRC report is juxtaposed with the National Security Strategy these points become clearer:

1. 'Torture' or 'coercive interrogation' is done at both bodily disciplinary and group-regulatory levels.
2. Biopolitics is operating at the level of the human species and confined to the species given the supersession of race by ideology.
3. Law is given as the justification for violence and violence is given as justification for the suspension of legal provisions.
4. We see the creeping development of 'biolegality' as law relating to exposing life to, and protecting it from, death.

Law, Life and Death

Friedrich Hegel (1983: 145), when speaking of 'Law, Life, and Death', said that the administration of penal justice was the force of law exerted over individual life. Foucault (2005: 143) in turn said 'For millennia, man remained what he was for Aristotle: a living animal with the additional capacity for a political existence; modern man is an animal whose politics places his existence as a living being in question' (Foucault 2005: 143, Orford 2006b: 183). This chapter builds on these notions and argues that the law not only regulates both the states of life and death but also defines the boundary between them. The law does this by assigning rights and duties among the living to create different forms of life. Law additionally abandons life to the exposure of conditions that lead to death by deciding which lives are worth living, which are not, and even when a person is as good as dead or deserves death. I refer to this process as biolegality.

The aim of the project is to explain partially law's relationship to violence in the context of criminalizing aggression in international law. This aspect of the argument works through examining the calibration of legal responses that alternately protect and expose persons and populations to degrees of violence. The argument is that law is the only practicable division and divisor between life and death.[4] Law is indeed the differentiator between life and death even as it regulates forms of life, distinguishes levels of death[5] and ultimately condemns to death. Extending this applicability directly from legal entitlement to life onto entitlement to take life legally seems logically implicit. The criminal law is just a narrow aspect of various possible approaches but it is the focus of this project.

In pursuing its object, this discussion concludes in the final section that law and violence are bound together so intimately that they cannot be viably distinguished without reference to each other. This leads to the enigmatic explanation that violence always defers to law except when it does not (because the state generally has both a factual preponderance of and normative monopoly of force over violence) and law never defers to violence except when it does (because there are exceptional circumstances such as successful revolutions and *coups d'*état where erstwhile governments are overthrown). The task set out is to broadly map out these shifts as they occur in legal contexts and examine their effect on human life and death as both protections and penalties are excluded and included principally through the wielding of the criminal law.

---

4 See '... in any ethical debate of topics involving life and death, one is forced to introduce cultural constructs such as, on the one hand, the concept of clinical death and, on the other, the concept of existence'. Boniolo and Di Fiore 2009: 609, 611, and '... or perhaps it is better to say that, in contemporary medicine, life and law have always been indistinguishable'. Bishop 2009: 538, 539.

5 See the following press reports: Medew 2008; 'Debate: When to Declare Donors Dead' <http://www.time.com/time/health/article/0,8599,1832688,00.html?iid=336x280_health2> at 18 August 2008.

Luhmann (1995b: 374–5) conceptualizes the legal system as the social system's immune system that seeks to avoid 'violent resolution of conflicts' by providing alternative means of communication for every conflict. Linking this characterization to force as the social system's ultimate sanction and violence as its greatest threat renders the malady (violence) and the remedy (force) identical. Thus, it makes force both a healing poison and a health-giving disease against violence, which are in any event each other's closest kin and worst adversary. To stretch the analogy to cover auto-immunity as well, terrorism (viewed as violence) and the military counter reaction (constructed as force), as Jacques Derrida noted, appear to be the effects of social auto-immunity on a global scale (Borradori 2004: 94, Esposito 2008: xvi–xvii). Within the context of a life and death struggle, some lives are necessarily valorized and protected while others are devalued and run the gamut of progressive privations running all the way to exposure to death through being excluded from legal protections while included in legal sanction.

Exclusion and Inclusion

The mechanism of inclusion and exclusion is generally how the law meaningfully applies force or allows violence. The law may either exclude persons and populations from or include them within the penalties or protection of the law and thereby violently expose or forcefully protect them. Frédéric Mégret (2006: 265) has identified the hyper-inclusivity of international humanitarian law that nevertheless contains the logic of exclusivity as well. Carl Schmitt too traced an exceptional zone that was excluded from law, which took the shape of a 'free and juridically empty space' in which sovereign power was no longer bound by the limits fixed by the rules governing the normal territorial order. In classical international law, this zone corresponded to the New World and European colonies, which were assimilated with the state of nature in which nothing was prohibited and therefore everything was permitted including unbridled violence. In domestic law, through declarations of emergencies or states of exception, the state frees up the restrictions on the use of force to meet immediate threats that are repressed as treason or mutiny and the like.

In constructing society's relationship to the human, both Luhmann and Agamben agree that any inclusion of aspects of humanity necessarily implies exclusion of others (Stäheli and Stichweh 2002: 5). This is so despite the fact that humanity is on both sides of the distinction, even and especially when using descriptors like inhuman or subhuman. The distinction used can make a re-entry and it then becomes impossible to distinguish between who are inside and who are outside when outside appears as inside and inside as outside (Stäheli and Stichweh 2002: 4–5). William Rasch (2002: 44–8) sees Agamben as indicating that Hobbes' sovereign saves us from the state of nature only for the self-same sovereign to plunge us into the analogous situation of the state of exception. To paraphrase this in systems theory terms, the initial distinction between society and a state of nature re-enters in society to produce the state of exception (as distinct from the state of normality) that for all intents and purposes mirrors the state of nature. Therefore the justification of the law in keeping the state of nature at bay as society's environment is fundamentally undermined by the society producing the state of exception at its core, even as it keeps the state of nature at its periphery.

What Agamben calls the political, Hobbes called the state of nature (Rasch 2002: 46). This is because Agamben (1998: 36–7) concludes from the above that the state of nature and state of exception are 'two sides of a single process in which what was presupposed as external (the state of nature) now reappears, in the inside (as the state of exception)'. For Agamben (1998: 1–12), life is what appears both inside and outside the law as 'bare life' and 'the good life'. The outside is viewed as the environment and conveyed as excluded yet this environment is produced by the society itself through its functional subsystems of law, politics, economics and so forth. The concrete manifestation of this for Agamben is Guantanamo Bay while for Luhmann it is Brazil's Favelas or shantytowns (Blake 2002: 27). Therefore, for both Luhmann and Agamben, all of humanity as such is initially and as a matter of default excluded until it is included in certain limited capacities such as customer or consumer, citizen or refugee, combatant or civilian and so forth. Thus forms of living are like statues carved out of the marble block of life.

In essence, this 'biolegality' has always been inscribed in law's reference to and protection of life because law has been organized around and upon life at least since the signing of the Magna Carta (Agamben 1998: 123). The protection of humanity is the protection of life itself and not individual lives (Douzinas 2006: 54). International criminal law is the epicentre of this development in at least two ways. First, genocide is the paradigm example of this in protecting whole groups against total or partial death against other groups. Conceptually speaking, condemnation of genocide cannot be grounded in each group individually but only on all groups collectively as an all-inclusive 'group of groups' that has purchase over everyone, not just within singular groupings. Second, crimes against humanity are by definition inhuman acts. The enemy of humanity is necessarily inhumane and their acts and standards inhuman. It follows that the total enemy of humanity is again necessarily a criminal and the worst of the category at that. These crimes are viewed as deserving the most extreme repression society can muster up as it acts in the name of supreme good against supreme evil. International criminal law is therefore at the forefront of this and the crime of aggression is the leading edge of the criminalizing sword because it monopolizes the means through which life is either protected or exposed to death. Genocide and crimes against humanity (among others) are what are sought to be repressed through suppressing aggression.

Grounding Legality in Life to Simultaneously Protect and Expose Lives

As outlined above, biolegality refers to the law active upon human life itself as a supreme principle. In seeking to ground fundamental human values and rights as all transcending, distinctions have long been sought to be drawn between the secular and the religious, with the secular being derived from the religious (Grbich 2006: 202).[6] For instance, in words attributed in the Bible to Jesus, he exhorted his followers to 'render unto Caesar what belonged to Caesar and to God what belonged to God'. Carl Schmitt (2005: 36) famously wrote that under sociological considerations '[a]ll significant concepts of the modern theory of the state are secularized theological concepts' because of their historical development and systematic structure. It follows then that life and death issues are simultaneously classifiable into biology, theology and law, to name but a few possible subject areas (Bellamy 2006: 4). While biology may define and describe these issues scientifically, theology provides a transcendental explanatory or ethical view, and law provides both a mechanism for decision and a regulatory framework. Following on from Schmitt's observation that the modern state has politicized *everything*, and therefore vastly expanded the range of the political (Schmitt 1996a: 22, Deuber-Mankowsky 2008: 135), it is only through the political process that law may gain its deserved prominence.

We can therefore perceive that the opposition between secular and religious originally derives from differentiating heavenly from secular on the one hand, and religious from earthly on the other. Thus the distinctions between the sacred and profane or religious and secular can be identifiable as 'nested oppositions', which are oppositions that 'involve a relation of dependence, similarity, or containment between the opposed concepts' (Balkin 1990: 3). This is not idle theorizing because it has definite implications when applied to social categories especially when comparing and contrasting theology and politics (Foucault 1993: 98, Agamben 2005a, Žižek 2001, Gray 2007). It opens up the space for a 'Biopolitics' that refers to techniques of power linked to life that are prevalent in society and utilized for subjugating bodies and controlling populations (Harris 1911: 10, Agamben 1998, Esposito, Foucault 1998.[7] This is accompanied by a concomitant 'Thanatopolitics', referring to the power to expose to death or kill that necessarily accompanies the power to foster life (Agamben 1998: 122, Rabinow and Rose 2006: 195).

Both systems theory and discourse analysis are post-foundational in that foundations are not abolished as such but are rendered radically contingent and contextual (Marchart 2002: 74). Anne Orford (2006a: 1 and 18) points out the placeholder Father/God/Market to who decision-makers are beholden. Foucault (2008: 87–8) too traced the shift of the organizing principle in the genealogy of government from God to the king to the people and then to the market. This process, whilst changing the overarching justification over time, leaves the underlying activities intact. The modern equivalent of this ultimate rationality and supreme benchmark is probably the democratic free market state that respects

6 See e.g. Grbich 2006: 202.

7 Biopolitics' as coined by Harris (1911: 197), and as developed by Rudolf Kjellén, extended by Michel Foucault and further developed by Agamben, above n 40, and Esposito, above n 34. See e.g. Foucault, above, 140.

human rights. Globalization then can readily export or replicate this model all over the world, even through force.

This supreme 'authority' over life and death retains a distinctly religious or quasi-theological air. Even the contemporary prevalence of atheism does not necessarily abolish the notion of God in disavowing belief in the existence of a supernatural being. Instead, it opens up possibilities for humans to play the role previously reserved for a god (Patel 1997). In addition, in so doing it secularizes the ultimate decision-maker. God is not dead *pace* Nietzsche. He has just changed sides from religious to secular and from divine spirit to human endeavour (Orford 2006a: 18). However, what is the point of this metaphorical apostasy? One effect is that of sophisticated ambivalence where human rights are still defensible by stating they remain the best available alternative simply as a matter of pragmatism (Hoffman 2006: 240).[8]

Yet another more ominous effect is that it strips human life of any pretence of an intrinsic value separate and apart from that granted or recognized by social consensus. Merit or utility is the new touchstone and individual life's mere existence can be construed as either a nuisance (inviting targeted assassinations or euthanasia) or an opportunity (to conduct experiments, for stem cell research, or harvest organs, etc.). This is because life as a supreme value can always be pitted against itself with individualized *lives* bearing the brunt of this high stakes contest. The law provides both the meaning and the means to drive this social process. The criminal law in particular enforces the process both at first instance and as a last resort. With criminal law extending to the international use of force in the name of humanity and for the purpose of protecting life, the process receives a global aspect and bursts its banks beyond the nation state onto the global stage. The powers of life and death are then wielded globally in the name of, on behalf of, and representative of 'humanity', in whose name life as a general principle is both protected and exposed to death.

For instance, in both Walter Benjamin's and Giorgio Agamben's work, the view expressed is that the violence of law is ultimately a power over life (Magnuson 2008: 73). Specifically, Benjamin (1978: 286) believed that law originates in its ability to decide over life and death. His argument was that, in condemning someone to death, law is not merely punishing an offence, but affirming its rule: '[I]n the exercise of violence over life and death more than in any other legal act, law reaffirms itself' (Benjamin 1978). This is because, in Agamben's (1998: 101) view, supreme power is, in the final analysis, 'nothing other than the capacity to constitute oneself and others as life that may be killed but not sacrificed'.

Carl Schmitt (2006: 12) cites Alberico Gentili as offering the first clear case of a clearly juridical as opposed to theological treatment of the nature of war when he asked theologians to be silent in what did not concern them. In so doing, justification for the use of force was shifted from the justice or otherwise of the cause to the identity of the perpetrators of force. This substituted an objective

8 See e.g. Florian Hoffman 2006: 240.

standard for a subjective stance where actors in their capacity as states could utilize force with impunity as just another political tool at their disposal.

However, through legality, objective humane ends as exceptions to the prohibition on the use of force could be the ultimate legitimation for the use of force. These would oppose the subjective standard of reason of state. In a sense, it is the geographical and political culmination of the logic of the state in monopolizing the legitimate use of physical force in a given territory extended to the globe. Given the global ramifications of modes of social control that are unbound by national boundaries, the underlying rationality can only be underpinned by replacing the reason of *state* with a reason of *humanity*, where the territory in question is the entire globe and the community under reference is humanity. In criminalizing some violence as illegal, the criminal process becomes purified of, and less entangled in, local peculiarities and parochial concerns.

The next line of inquiry below examines how the principles above relate to the distinction between spaces (war zones, the New World and colonies) and individuals (pirates, terrorists, barbarians and savages) that are open to violence (Mégret 2006: 394–5) and those places and persons not so readily amenable (Anghie 2006: 265). A space is an empty place, just as a person stripped of rights remains an individual. Space therefore matches to the individual and place to the person. Whereas the former pair is open to domination, the latter is inviolate. This describes the inclusion/exclusion mechanism of the law in concrete, historical, conceptual and empirical application as the right to life denied a whole swathe of humanity.

Persons and Spaces Abandoned to Violence

Particularly in this context, to act is to dominate and conversely to be acted upon is to be dominated (Orford 2006a: 27). Leading on, this section argues that the representative notion in law of a person as a bearer of rights and duties within a legal system is a social construct and therefore without any inherent content. The notion is only a form upon which society can act in order to endow or deny status to human lives. Giorgio Agamben (1998: 83–5) defines his notion of *homo sacer* or 'sacred man' as human life included in the juridical order solely in the form of its exclusion. *Homo sacer* is excluded from the protections of law while being included in its condemnation at the same time. This figure mirrors the sovereign who stands both within law (exercising constitutional and statutory powers) and outside the law (exercising prerogative power including suspending law itself) (Agamben 1998). To relate the two more succinctly: *homo sacer* ultimately is the figure to whom everyone is sovereign while the sovereign is the person to whom everyone is ultimately *homo sacer* (Rasch 2002: 44). When humanity is the conceptual category, foetuses in the abortion debate, human-animal hybrids in the scientific debate, refugees in the immigration debate, detainees in the terrorism debate and human–machine sentient beings in science fiction become mere staging posts in the journey to post-humanism. Luhmann foresaw this in describing social processes that were both reflexive and recursive as analogous to cell processes and therefore 'life' which utilizes communication as the unit of analysis instead of human actors as the drivers of this process.

Agamben (1998: 40) extends his study of the inner workings of power from people to places when he states that 'the state of exception is the opening of a space in which application and the norm reveal their separation', where law applies in 'ceasing to apply' leaving only the force formerly associated with the law. To sum up, the state of exception is a frame while *homo sacer* is a canvas, with the law as the paintbrush, and the politician the artist. Force and violence are indispensable to this.

Foucault (1998: 138) writes that 'the ancient right to *take* life or *let* live was replaced by a power to *foster* life or *disallow* it to the point of death'. He cites Hobbes as stating: 'Take a newborn child. Its parents (its father in a civil society, or its mother in the state of nature) could simply allow it to die, or quite simply have it put to death' (Foucault 1998: 96).This indicates to him that the law that affords protection is the same as that which allows violation. Agamben (1998: 87) notes this as well:

> The first time we encounter the expression 'right over life and death' in the history of law is in the formula *vitae necisque potestas*, which designates not sovereign power but rather the unconditional authority [*potestà*] of the *pater* over his sons. Not simple natural life, but life exposed to death (bare life or sacred life) is the originary political element.

Agamben (1998: 89) carries this forward, saying 'the first foundation of political life is a life that may be killed, which is politicized through its very capacity to be killed'. Agamben (1998: 3) relies on Foucault to hold that, because of modernity, man moved from an animal with the additional capacity for political existence to 'an animal whose politics calls his existence as a living being into question' and thus both the human species and individual have become 'what is at stake in a society's political strategies'. This development is, moreover, not limited to the domestic space and its citizens.

Classical international law mirrors this process when it divides into the 'Law of War' and the 'Law of Peace'. This distinction between war and peace provides differentiated regimes of applicable laws. In extreme cases, the use of force is allowed to affect entire populations and groups, resulting in not only military but accidental or disproportionate civilian casualties as well. Because the United Nations Charter was born in the wake of the necessity to prevent war, it represents the collective pooling of force among its members. The international system also indicates when the prohibition is inapplicable, such as in self-defence, for the lawful use of force following a breach or a threat to the peace, especially in Chapter VII and Articles 51 and 52 of the United Nations Charter. Such legalization through United Nations resolutions that authorize force in the language of 'by all necessary means' exposes whole populations to death while prescribing no penalty for their dying.

The Law of War splits in turn between the *Jus ad Bellum* (justification for the use of force) and the *Jus in Bello* (regulation of armed conflict) (Roberts and Guelff 2000: 1–3). The *Jus in Bello*, also referred to as 'Hague Law' (generally derived from the 1907 Hague Conventions), governs the conduct of hostilities and 'Geneva Law' (principally derived from the 1949 Geneva Conventions) provides for the protection of the victims of war. Hague Law renders military personnel and military targets open to the application of deadly force, while Geneva Law stipulates when military personnel may no longer be targeted, even as it protects civilians from the brunt of the *deliberate* use of force. Although both the Hague and Geneva regimes are of course not applicable prior to force being used, the two are considered discrete areas of the law with no bearing on the legality of the *resort* to force as opposed to its *use*.

The Law of Peace allows, for instance, for the general applicability of human rights law. However, even dedicated human rights instruments only protect recognized rights when it is appropriate and those not legally recognized therefore do not exist for them. Further, these instruments in any case allow derogation from the recognized rights and remain open to different regimes of the law in situations of conflict or emergency. However, there is a tendency to straddle (without erasing) the divide between war and peace for certain laws. These include non-derogable human rights and the prohibition on torture. The Hague and Geneva law regimes, while limiting the means and methods of war and assigning protections to non-combatants respectively for example, simultaneously open the use of force upon combatants and civilians. Moreover, this indicates that the law does not ignore the state of exception but attempts to capture it as well. An example is the Convention against Torture and Other Cruel, Inhuman or Degrading Treatment or Punishment (CAT) that explicitly states '[n]o exceptional circumstances whatsoever, whether a state of war or a threat of war, internal political instability or any other public emergency, may be invoked as a justification of torture' (UN General Assembly 1987: Art. 2.2).

It follows then that international law has an inside and an outside that mirror each other. That is, the international legal structure resembles a doughnut with an outer boundary and an inner core. The outer boundary allows all which international law does not forbid (represented by the *Lotus* case which found that 'restrictions upon the independence of States cannot be presumed') (S.S. Lotus *(Fr. v Turk.)* 1927: 18 (Sept. 7)). The inner core holds any and all legal obligations that are subject to the actions of the Security Council in addressing breaches of and threats to the peace (represented by the *Lockerbie* case where the International Court of Justice (1999: 15 para. 39) ruled that Security Council Resolutions under Chapter VII of the United Nations Charter prevailed over treaties and domestic laws). These actions taken by the Security Council in addressing aggression and breaches of the peace are paradoxically unbound by law but sanctioned by the law (Noll 2008: 587–9).

International law's 'inside' is the Security Council acting in exceptional circumstances to suspend the ordinary law, while the 'outside' is the not yet prohibited sphere of state action that approximates and indeed renders actual the 'state of nature'. This inside and outside mirror each other in their openness to violence, although in a state of nature there is no distinction between force and violence. This legal and constantly expanding self-referential boundary and ever contracting core of international law are crucial in resolving the ongoing tension between anomie (being completely without norm) and anarchy (being completely without rule) (Davies 2008: 78). It necessarily follows that complete freedom is only temporary and is subject to constraint in the lack of freedom from freedom itself, as it were, given unavoidable restraints in terms of the limited choices available externally. Law is then the origin and fountain of freedom and thus not subject to it. As the law expands, it reduces the chaos external to itself and the anomie internally shrinks, all in accordance with its idiosyncratic logic of assigning the code legal/illegal, just as sovereignty dialectically applies the inclusive exclusion and the exclusive inclusion (Agamben 1998: 21–2).

The process of opening or closing to violence may be mapped in terms of time. This casts the past as a violent time to be moved away from in preference for a utopian peaceful future through a present forceful struggle against violence. Individuals may be characterized as civilians, terrorists and so forth, while space may be categorized into war zones, contact zones, hospital zones, safety zones, demilitarized zones,[9] or both into 'rogue' or 'failed' states[10] either excluded or included by law from the effects of conflict. Meanwhile, normative judgements leading to applying force may include declarations of failed states, oppressive regimes, piracy and the like. The implicit assertion uniting the punitive and/or revolutionary applier of force is 'I enforce rights while you violate them'. Law enforcement is then a matter of course and the violation is a circumstance taken exception to.

Melinda Cooper (2008: 89) is a perspicuous observer of this contemporary phenomenon linking the law, life and violence/force:

> The preemptive strike has been decried as a departure from all existing principles of legitimate warfare. But it would be better understood (and countered) on its own terms, as a radically new formulation of law, one that founds the legitimate use of violence on 'our' collective apprehension of the future, however uncertain rather than the predictive calculus of risk ... Both preemption and precaution endow our suspicions, fears and panics with an active force of law.

9 See Regulation 5 annexed to Hague Convention IV, Hague Convention IX articles 1 and 2, Annex I to Geneva Conventions I and IV as well as Additional Protocol I to the Geneva Conventions in Articles, 8, 18, 26, 59, 60 and 85.

10 Devetak (2008a: 126) calls this 'strategic cartography'.

Governmental practice thus appears to be a creative wielding of productive and destructive powers underpinned by a legal regime with criminalization at the forefront. This practice of governing by production and destruction of life through wielding or withholding force and allowing or preventing violence finds itself unleashed by the forces of globalization directly onto the globe and humanity through and above state, territory and population.

Governing as Reflecting, Producing and Destroying

Thomas Hobbes used the image of the Leviathan as a striking metaphor for the state apparatus. Foucault too addressed an essentially Hobbesian description of the state as that 'artificial man who is at once an automaton, a fabricated man, but also a unitary man who contains all real individuals, whose body is made up of citizens but whose soul is sovereignty' (Foucault 1998: 34). According to Schmitt (1996b: 91–100), this fusion of man and machine in the Leviathan enabled the mechanization of man to follow the mechanization of the state. In addition, dividing human from animal shows that the state is an 'anthropological machine' that produces a gradation of humans (for example, slave, barbarian or foreigner, etc.) by the means of an exclusion (which is always already a capturing) and inclusion (which is always already an exclusion) (Agamben 2004a: 37). This is 'a ceaselessly updated decision' that, moreover, operates on 'bare life' (Agamben 2004a: 38). Human beings in civil society are cultivated and not naturally sociable as per Hobbes, Pufendorf and Foucault (Devetak 2008b: 271).

These insights articulate the claim that the political community (exemplified in but not monopolized by the state) is a machine that fosters and manipulates life and dispenses death through the mechanism of law. Giorgio Agamben has developed further Foucault's biopolitics to cover this ground. Examples include cloning, human experimentation, euthanasia and the death penalty. Additionally, with colonialism and state building, the state has also come to replicate itself as it produces humans (through the construct of legal personality). According to Agamben (1998: 26–7), law captures life not by sanction but by guilt through being indebted to the law: that is, 'the condition of being included through exclusion'. This 'guilt' refers not 'to the determination of the licit and the illicit, but to the pure force of the law, to the law's simple reference to something' (Agamben 1998).

Foucault (1998: 98) notes that although Hobbes seemed to proclaim that war was everywhere and ever present, he in fact meant quite the opposite as he believed that it was the subjects who (with or without war and defeat) constituted the sovereign that represented them. In sum, through constant divisions, the state produces life and death by creating human personality while feeding off human life with the consent of humans. Democracy is government in our name, for our benefit and by us. Sovereignty is only the organizing principle along which the process of inclusion and exclusion rules by opening and closing persons and populations to potentially deadly violence. This cascades into regulation of all forms of life. It ordinarily does not impose or recommend violence as such. It at most merely removes the consequences attached to the deliberate deprivation of life or denial of living conditions along the continuum from discomfort gradually onwards to death. The logic of this process links to a political community that may resemble but need not coincide with the state.

Foucault (2005: 252) defined 'governmentality' as 'a strategic field of power relations in their mobility, transformability, and reversibility'. He also urged the abandonment of the leviathan model, juridical sovereignty and the state in favour of analysing the 'techniques and tactics of domination (Foucault 1998: 34). Agamben's (1998: 6) own work too relies on this setting aside of traditional approaches in order to examine how power acts on actual bodies.

The conceptual apparatus of government with humanity as the sovereign and security replacing religion de-links itself from nation states (Hindess 2008: 268, Rose and Miller 1992: 176), which are in fact judged by and do not judge governmentality (Foucault and Faubion 2002: 221). For example, human rights are in a sense post-political being neither culturally nor geographically relative. Slavoj Žižek's (2008: 10–13) differentiating of subjective, objective and systemic violence may underpin the present need for moving international violence from the subjective (the terrorist/freedom fighter false dichotomy) to the objective (a distinction between legal force and illegal violence) and onward to the systemic (an international monopoly on the legitimate use of force).

Efforts to achieve this are ongoing, with attempts to include the crime of aggression within the ambit of international criminal law. After the Second World War, the victorious Allied Powers criminalized the illegal use of force as a 'crime against peace'. The Nazis and imperial Japanese were the first, and so far the only, convicted and punished 'peace' criminals. The political process leading to the Rome Statute for the International Criminal Court attempted to find or create a definition without complete success. A definition is pending with a special working group considering proposals for the same before the next meeting of the state parties to the statute (ICJ 2007).

Legalizing further the use of force by criminalizing objectively illegitimate violence as aggression will be a foundational step towards keeping legal tools for legal ends. This is because it will prevent a rule by law that mimics the rule of law by utilizing the legal system for political ends through a preponderance of military force. This ensures that a clearer distinction can be drawn between the spheres of law and politics and enables the rule of law to transcend the nation state and apply directly to the global level with an accompanying identity between the illegal and the inimical.

Thus the friend/enemy political distinction is being mapped onto the legal/illegal criminal conduct distinction. With globalization, the state is increasingly marginalized and the monopoly on the use *of* force is becoming a monopoly on the use *for* force. That is, humanitarian and security concerns increasingly underpin resort to force and claims to sovereignty in justifying resort to force are no longer legitimate. Because the state predicates itself upon distinguishing force from violence, it essentially justifies the former and penalises the latter even though they are essentially identical. In other words, the law makes a re-entry in order to distinguish between force and violence after emerging from a mythical undifferentiated regime of general and all pervasive war.

Force: The Relationship between Law and Violence

Following on from previous sections that described criminalization governing the globe and humanity with torture and thus illustrating law as linked to life and death through exclusion and inclusion (thereby producing a distinction between force and violence that enables the monopolization of entitlement to life and ability to give death), this section argues that although force and violence are physically indistinguishable they are legally distinguishable (for example, when *violent* riots by striking workers, students or whoever are *forcibly* put down by the authorities). That is to say, only the law provides a viable distinction between them. This is because both force and violence are found at the absolute limit of the law, albeit with a telling difference. Force is inside the law and violence is outside the law. Whether violence not permitted under the law is against the law would depend on the content of the *particular* law in question not the *general* amenability of violence to legalization. The mechanism of the law itself can be used conceptually, has been used historically, is being used in the domestic law setting, and can be further extended in international law by attaching penal sanctions to the unlawful use of force.

The legal narrative of the emergence from a state of nature may be summarized as violence once the rule becomes the exception, and peace as the exception becomes the rule. This inversion, though lauded in law, has had its critics. Walter Benjamin (1986: 295) for instance considered that the power of the law was its threat to mere life and therefore making law was in reality manifesting power and, in so doing, manifesting violence.

This violence of law does not simply sanction a transgressive act but instead repeats the same act without sanctioning it by treating it as an exceptional case (Agamben 1998: 26–7). The law therefore makes possible the distinction between privileged lawful force and illegitimate unlawful violence. The pre-legal state of nature is assimilated to the state of extreme violence of a Hobbesian war of all against all. The state of exception also requires, and therefore excuses, the use of violence to restore order as an emergency exigency. The emergency is what makes it exceptional. It therefore cannot be permanent because permanent conflict means (for example) no gains or spoils of war could ever be consolidated or enjoyed.

The state of exception simultaneously provides a state of no applicable law with the ordinary distinctions rendered inoperative and an opportunity for a new legal regime to instil these same distinctions anew under a different dispensation. This is then how violence always defers to law except when it does not and law never defers to violence except when it does. The key to this is the *normative* monopoly on the use of force coinciding with a *descriptive* monopoly on the use of force. The ICC as part of the constellation of international criminal justice is therefore shaping up as an apparatus for governing through trying crimes with little explicit debate as to whether this is a proper purpose for it.

The next chapter examines this issue in greater detail. It reconstructs the notion of abuse of legality as expressing the teleology of law according to the law and therefore as the principal juridical shield against political machination in discerning between law creating force and law destroying violence.

Chapter 8

Abuse of Legality: The Illegal Use of the Legal

According to Walter Benjamin 'All violence as a means is either lawmaking or law-preserving' (Benjamin 1986: 287). In this chapter the question is whether there is an a priori conceptual bar to legalizing resort to force and suppression of violence that is necessarily derived either from the nature of force or violence or the nature of law. This volume's author proposes to answer this by exploring the hypothetical scenario, as outlined in Chapter 1, to investigate whether a court of law (as the central site of legal disputation) could or must decline to hear an allegation of aggression as *ipso facto* an abuse of its (legal) process. The hypothetical answer is that it could, but only as a matter of its particular jurisdiction and not as a general principle that force/violence are not amenable to legal process. Therefore, if the jurisdiction is vested, as in the case of the Nuremberg and Tokyo tribunals, then the prosecution of aggression is not an abuse of legality.

However, when the tools of the legal system themselves are used to oppress, the task of distinguishing legality and illegality is on a terrain approximating a hall of mirrors. The Justice Trial at Nuremberg put legal practitioners on the dock for acts that only legal practitioners could do (Nuremberg Trials: The Justice Trials). The charge was for participation in a governmentally organized system of cruelty and injustice that violated the law while being perpetrated in the name of law by the Ministry of Justice, through the courts and by lawyers (Nuremberg Trials: The Justice Trials).

The Nuremberg judgment said that the 'prostitution of a judicial system for the accomplishment of criminal ends involves an element of evil to the state which is not found in frank atrocities' (The Nuremberg Trials: The Justice Trial). In such an extreme situation the legal system is itself a problem and indeed lawyers and judges the criminals by virtue of their acts and profession. This is the problem grappled with in this chapter.

Illegality Mirroring the Law

The conventional state of nature narrative regarding the advent of law is that, following generalized violence, the society chooses a leader from among them to keep the peace through and by enforcing the law. In this way the sovereign too is a creature of the law and is bound by it. However, this fable of the origins of law enforcement can be turned on its head by the return of the repressed violence, whereby the law is subordinate to power and not vice versa. In other words, force is only justifiable in protecting (during normal times) and restoring (during extraordinary times) legality. Meanwhile, in its mirror image (the abuse of legality), violence is used in the name of the law to subvert it by rendering the exception general and the general exceptional. As argued earlier, the law is the only distinguisher between violence and force. Force is therefore subordinate to law and not law subordinate to force. The latter would be a mere case of violence overwhelming the law. To counter this, it is argued that globalization functions optimally when the legal system has exclusive control of legal operation when the law is applied (as opposed to when it is made) in being independent of political intervention. With this in mind, this chapter reconstructs the notion of abuse of process as expressing the teleology of law according to the law and therefore as the principal juridical weapon against political machination in discerning between, on the one hand, law creating violence and law destroying violence and, on the other hand, law enforcement and illegal violence.

This is in order to demonstrate that because life, liberty and property may not be taken without due process of law, it means that law properly so-called can therefore never sanction deprivation of life, liberty or process outside legality by mere force. That is, there is nothing legal that is outside law: whatever is outside law is by definition unlawful.

In reference to the war on terror, the United States Supreme Court has said that the constitution and laws of the United States are designed to survive and remain in force not just ordinarily but even in extraordinary times (*Lakhdar Boumediene et al., Petitioners v George W. Bush, President of the United States et al.* Unreported No. 06–1195). Liberty and security are therefore reconciled within the legal framework (*Boumediene v Bush*). The Supreme Court cites the Magna Carta as basic and decreeing that no one shall be imprisoned contrary to the law. The constitution grants Congress and the President the power to acquire, dispose of and govern territory but not the power to decide when and where the terms of the constitution apply (*Boumediene v Bush*). Further, even when acting outside its borders, the United States does not have absolute and unlimited powers but is subject to constitutional restrictions (*Murphy v Ramsey,* 114 U. S. 15, 44 (1885)). Lastly, granting the political branches the power to switch the constitution on or off at will permits them, and not the courts, the power to say what the law is (*Marbury v Madison*, 1 Cranch 137, 177 (1803)).

Consequently, it is clear that not every mention of the code values law/non-law turns a communication into a legal operation (Luhmann 2002: 67). Even so, certain statements are difficult to classify justifiably. However, everything that cannot be brought under the scheme of law/non-law does not belong to the legal system but to its environment (Luhmann 2002: 55–6). Politics is part of the law's environment and cannot be ignored by law. This is not to say that the law should be controlled by political imperatives, however, because that would render the law indistinguishable from political expedience, which would be an abuse of legality.

This judicial decision, which parted ways with the political branches of the government, shows the built-in objectivity of the law even over its own creators and thus its ability to distinguish between the violence that endangers the law by breaking and abusing it and the violence that engenders the law in creating new legal systems from a void of undifferentiated violence. How this translates beyond the domestic legal system is addressed in the next part of this chapter.

In a recent case, the British House of Lords found a clash between the power and duty to detain exercisable on the express authority of the United Nations Security Council and fundamental human rights (*R (on the application of Al-Jedda (FC) v Secretary of State for Defence* [2007] UKHL per Lord Bingham of Cornhill: para. 39). It held, however, that the United Kingdom could lawfully, where necessary for imperative security reasons, exercise this power to intern so as to minimize human rights infringements (*R v Secretary of State for Defence* [2007] UKHL per Lord Bingham of Cornhill: para. 136). The reason for holding the proscription on internment to be qualified or displaced was that Article 25 of the United Nations Charter requires member states to accept and carry out Security Council decisions, while Article 103 provides that, in the event of a conflict between that obligation and the member state's obligations under any other international agreement, the Charter prevails (*R (on the application of Al-Jedda (FC) v Secretary of State for Defence* [2007] UKHL per Lord Brown of Eaton-Under-Heywood: para. 151).

The question is: does this mean that the Security Council absolves legal obligations as a matter of law? The International Criminal Tribunal for the former Yugoslavia answered this in the negative, saying 'neither the text nor the spirit of the Charter conceives of the Security Council as *legibus solutus* (unbound by law)'.[1] This is the only legally defensible answer because a legal system is the interlacing of legal rules and of legally regulated institutions. There is also no power in the state or in society that is *de legibus solutus* (O'Donnell 2001: 1, 45). That is, all powers are subject to the legal authority of other powers and nobody is supposed to be above or beyond the rules (O'Donnell 2001: 1, 45). Following below is an argument of how this comes to be. This is especially relevant because one of two sticking points to the definition of aggression is the role of the Security Council.

A Law-Shaped void within the State of Nature

The essence of legality is by no means anything legal.[2] The explanatory power of the concept of a state of nature as an *ex post facto* justification of the law should not be underestimated. The state of nature is a thought experiment that imagines a world without law. This means that it begins with a law-shaped void

1 See *Prosecutor v Tadić*, Case No. IT-94–1-I, Decision on the Defence Motion for Interlocutory Appeal on Jurisdiction, (2 October 1995) 35. See also Gill 1995: 48.

2 This is a paraphrase of Martin Heidegger's 'Likewise, the essence of technology is by no means anything technological' in Heidegger 2003: 279.

that consequently requires the law in order to be complete. In this way it is both reflexive and recursive: of law and from law. Thomas Hobbes' (2005: 88–90) view was that a world without law existed as *bellum omnium contra omnes*, 'the war of all against all'. In this state, any person has the natural right to do anything to preserve their own liberty or safety. People in a state of nature ceded their individual rights in a social contract to create sovereignty, retained by the state, in return for their protection and a more functional society. A human sovereign become a god to humans, *homo homini deus*, as distinct from the state of nature where humans were wolves to human, *homo homini lupus* (Schmitt 1996b: 31).

Jean Bodin (1992: 110–11) explores the notion of whether attempts at usurping sovereignty are answerable through force or through law. He cites the Greek example of Solon and the Latin example of Valerius to describe two differing approaches that are reconcilable (Bodin 1992: 110–11). While Valerius approved resort to force provided that the usurpation was proved afterwards, Solon forbad using force or killing someone trying to seize sovereignty (Bodin 1992: 110–11). Bodin reconciles these by saying that legality had to be followed except in order to restore legality. In other words, actors were enjoined to act within the law or in defence of the law. In this way everyone remained subservient to the law.

Legalizing Political Violence

The social contract therefore in a sense posits organized political violence as part of social capital (that is, a social commodity). Although Hobbes' sovereign remains in a state of nature, it is doubtful whether this notion survives into the modern version of the state, given the fate of Charles I of England and Louis XVI of France, both of whom were sovereigns that were tried and punished for treasonous acts. Even the last frontier of sovereign states, international law, has the United Nations Charter (and before it the League of Nations Charter) that circumscribes state sovereignty. 'State of nature' is therefore a boundary term in both legal and political philosophy, used in relation to social contract theories to describe the hypothetical condition of humanity before the state's foundation and its monopoly on the legitimate use of physical force. In a broader sense of the word, a state of nature is the condition that exists before the rule of positive law comes into being and is thus symbolic of anarchy. John Locke (2005: 412) argued that government should be from the people and limited so as not to violate natural rights. Further, the entire population has the right to punish an offender so that he or she will not commit the crime again and to deter others (Locke 2005: 412). Importantly, if the state turns into a tyranny, there is a right of rebellion (Locke 2005: 412). The monopoly on the legitimate use of physical force designates an essential attribute of state sovereignty formalized by Max Weber (1991: 77–8): '[A] state is a human community that (successfully) claims the monopoly of the legitimate use of physical force within a given territory'.

John Rawls (1999) describes an artificial state of nature, which he calls the 'original position'. People in the original position have no society and are under a veil of ignorance that prevents them from knowing how they may benefit from society. Because of this, they create the least self-interested and therefore most altruistic laws possible: a 'do unto others as you would have done unto you' constitution similar to that underpinning the Weberian state.

The point sought to be made is that the past cannot be undone. As a consequence, constitutionalized force is the norm while constitutive violence is not just the exception but is now illegal as well (treason under domestic law and aggression under international law). Constitutive violence would be the overthrow or renegotiation of the social contract in order to found a new beginning which, having already been done before, cannot be repeated again without penal consequences. Through the abuse of process discretion, courts are now the guardians of the social contract's terms. Therefore, as follows below, disputes that would have previously been resolved through armed conflict have been moved to legal terrain.

What is Abuse of Process?

The common law doctrine of abuse of process is best conceptually framed as the misuse of proper procedure. It is a claim usually raised by the defence in the context of a criminal trial with termination of the proceedings being the remedy sought. Even though abuse of process is most readily and almost invariably associated with human rights discourse, this, although not merely peripheral, is certainly incidental and not essential. In actuality it is less an abuse of rights than an abuse of power discourse. The essential attribute of abuse of process is a court protecting itself from an outside agency: that is, preventing its process from being interfered with usually, but by no means necessarily, by the executive. Implicit within this discourse is a dynamic of two principles: the separation of powers following on from the rule of law. This is an instance of the judicial arm exercising its jurisdiction not to exercise jurisdiction: that is, the negative exercise of power.

A court's self-image is indistinguishable from its process. The active expression of this power and duty is the hearing of a trial, while the passive exercise of this power is declining to hear a trial. A judge *qua* judge is an active entity with machinery, principles, rules and workers for whom the judge is the overall operator. Interference with any aspects of this machinery or 'legal procedure' is a central blow to the idea of the rule of law. Because the court has little else to do than hear cases, its ultimate expression of power is in declining to hear a case while fully seized of jurisdiction and thus denying other forums jurisdiction in its stead.

Under International Criminal Law (ICL), the tripartite functional dichotomy between the executive, legislative and adjudicatory competencies is far less clear-cut than in domestic law but is nevertheless ubiquitous in practice. To conclude that obscurity equals absence would be rash to say the least. This is because lawyers instinctively view power as legitimately exercised where it is not monopolized or concentrated. Diffusion and sharing of power is so much the norm as not to require explicit expression in order to be followed.

In ICL, abuse of process was first introduced by the International Criminal Tribunal for Rwanda in the Barayagwiza case discussed below (*Jean-Bosco Barayagwiza v The Prosecutor* (1999) refer to as Barayagwiza I). As international criminal judges have been wont to do, the judicial bench did not cut out this doctrine from whole cloth but borrowed it from domestic criminal law instead, specifically the *ex parte* Bennett case where Lord Griffiths said (*Reg. v Horseferry Road Magistrates' Court, Ex parte Bennett* [1994] 1 A.C. 42, 61H-62A and 62G):

> In the present case there is no suggestion that the appellant cannot have a fair trial, nor could it be suggested that it would have been unfair to try him if he had been returned to this country though extradition procedures. If the court is to have the power to interfere with the prosecution in the present circumstances it must be because the judiciary accept a responsibility for the maintenance of the rule of law that embraces a willingness to oversee executive action and to refuse to countenance behaviour that threatens either basic human rights or the rule of law.

Clearly, abuse of process within ICL is primarily a product of the common law system. Thus while examining its transplantation to the international sphere special care must be taken to focus on the essential and not incidental characteristics. The doctrine was subsequently referred to in numerous other cases at both the ICTR and ICTY. Not being based on any specific text but merely following on from the nature of the judicial function itself, abuse of process is more a term of art than a term of law. The abuse of process jurisdiction is a guarantee of a fair trial (*Ex Parte Brookes* (1984) 80 C. Appeal R. 164). In its various usages it hardly evinces a distinct common core of meaning and content, covering phenomena that are, on the face of it, unrelated. Moreover, domestic judicial opinion tends to be split as to the precise contours of the court's powers and duties in preventing abuse of process where individual liberty is at stake. One view is that the 'fruit of the poisoned tree' should not be enjoyed (*A v Secretary of State for the Home Department*, 8 December 2005, [2005] UKHL 71: para. 9) while another holds that a bad capture may just as well lead to good detention (that is, *mala captus bene detentus*) (*Ker v Illinois*, 199 U.S. 436 (1886), *Frisbie v Collins*, 342 U.S. 519 (1952), *United States v Alvarez-Machain*, 504 U.S. 655 (1992)).

Seeking a concrete meaning for the term 'abuse of process' is especially relevant now in the sphere of ICL due to the specific criticisms levelled at the International Criminal Court with reference to its potential to be manipulated for political ends in the prosecution of aggression. Given that general principles of law derived from national laws of legal systems are applicable before the International Criminal Court (Rome Statute of the International Criminal Court (1998): Art. 21), the argument is that the arguably *jus cogens* norm of secure protection of law bars deprivation of liberty without the requisite due process and therefore legal arguments should be framed with this in mind.

Whereas the first prosecutions for aggression may, legally speaking, have been based on less unequivocal ground than at present, given their success there is at present, partly because of normative provision they provided, an actual justiciable crime of aggression. The most persistent queries are with regard to the forum, jurisdictional basis, and specific content of the prosecutorial process. The technique to be employed necessarily has mostly a theoretical dimension in endeavouring to ascertain the existence, level and extent of customary principles binding among and within states.

In the formulation of a working hypothesis some considerations need to be borne in mind. Plainly, 'abuse' refers to a wrong or improper use, while 'process' is the entire course of proceedings in a legal action and 'doctrine' is a principle of law established through past decisions. However, the issue before the court where an abuse of process is alleged, unlike in ordinary proceedings, is neither for the determination of guilt nor validation of innocence of the accused. It is rather for the protection of the very integrity of the court system from being conducted in a manifestly unfair way or being misused for collateral purposes.

The abuse of process defence shifts an accuser to being the accused, examining the conduct of the prosecutor. The whole system is seemingly turned on its head; for this reason, the current research is not only highly interesting but also topical, practical, useful, realistic and feasible. Just as the abuse of process defence shifts an accuser to being the accused, accusation of criminal aggression is accompanied by unavoidable objections as to the bona fides of the accuser. Both concepts therefore conversely, even bizarrely, lead to examining the motivations and conduct of the prosecutor, not the alleged criminal.

The issue of the accused's conduct, criminal or otherwise, never comes to the fore. The issue under test is whether there are circumstances that will make the proceedings an abuse of the process of the court. Basically it is the presence of unfairness and wrongfulness to such a scale that the court should not allow a prosecutor to proceed with what may be, in all its other aspects, a regular proceeding within the rules (*Hui Chi-Ming v R* [1992] 1 AC 34: para. 57). Abuse occurs when court process is diverted from its proper purpose for some collateral ulterior motive or advantage, which the law does not recognize as legitimate. Necessarily, the circumstances in which abuse of process can arise are varied and it is nigh impossible to provide an exhaustive listing. However, there is inherent jurisdiction in every court of justice to prevent an abuse of its own process and a duty to intervene and stop the proceeding (*Mitchell & Ors v DPP & Ano.* CLR (1987) 127: per Haynes P. para. 129).

The defence of abuse of process may be used to protect the accused from infringement of their rights to liberty, freedom from arbitrary arrest and detention, a fair trial and/or due process of law. An example is the case of *Dole Chadee et al.*

v Trinidad and Tobago of 29 July 1998 CCPR-14–1/CCPR-OP-3,[3] in which the human rights committee examined the defence under the International Covenant for Civil and Political Rights. In *The Prosecutor v Siméon Nshamihigo* Case No. ICTR-2001–63-DP,[4] the International Criminal Tribunal for Rwanda examined and dismissed the defence when it was raised in the same context of procedural rights in fair trial.

Because general principles of law derived from national laws of legal systems that would normally exercise jurisdiction are applicable to the International Criminal Court, it would be well to examine these critically as a starting point. Due process is protection of individual rights through the inherent power of the court to protect its process in a manner not explicitly provided for in rules, but which may be discerned from application of relevant legal principles that the rules themselves are intended to effectuate.

Writing in the domestic context of power of the court to stay proceedings that are an abuse of the process of the court, Andrew Choo (2009: 6) has stated that a stay should be granted where 'compelling an accused to stand trial would violate those fundamental principles of justice which underlie the community's sense of fair play and decency' or where the proceedings are oppressive or vexatious. In other words, this discretion is intended 'to ensure that the repression of crime through the conviction of the guilty is done in such a way which reflects society's fundamental values' (*R v Conway* [1989] 70 CR (3d) 209: per L'Heureux-Dubé J para. 222–3). Respect and support of the community is essential in the administration of criminal justice. Therefore, 'where the affront to fair play and decency is disproportionate to the societal interest in the effective prosecution of criminal cases, then the administration of justice is best served by staying the proceedings' (*Keyowski v R* (1988) 62 CR (3d) 349: per Wilson J para. 550).

It is too simplistic to assume that the sole function of the criminal justice process is the conviction of criminals and protection of the innocent. There is a consideration that has force independent of guilt or innocence. This is the consideration of the public interest in the moral integrity of the criminal justice system.

A prosecution may be stayed if it would compromise the moral integrity of the criminal justice system, notwithstanding the public interest in the conviction of the guilty. Due process principles would require dismissal of the indictment if substantial prejudice to fair trial was used as an intentional device to gain tactical advantage over the accused (*US v Marion* 404 US 307, 324 (1971) 61). International criminal justice has been described as the absence of due process in post-war situations; the IMT and IMTFE were exemplary in criminalization but neither creation nor procedure (Köchler 2003: 9–10).

3 The authors applied for a permanent stay on the ground that their trial would be an abuse of the process of the Court, because of the extent of negative pretrial publicity.

4 Before Navanethem Pillay J. Decision of 8 May 2002 On The Defence Motion Seeking Release Of The Accused Person And/Or Any Other Remedy On The Basis Of Abuse Of Process By The Prosecutor.

In criminal law, this part of the court's jurisdiction is invoked by way of its inherent powers, constitutionalism, human rights norms and the common law. The existence and recognition of the doctrine is well settled in decided cases. It is open to a court under its inherent powers to decide that it would not be in the public interest and policy to allow a prosecution to continue.

From early times, courts have had inherent power to see that their process is not abused, so as to be vexatious and harassing, and thus can protect themselves (*Metropolitan Bank v Pooley* (1885) 10 App. Cases 210: per Lord Blackburn para. 220- 221 and per Lord Selbourne para. 214). It is open to every court to decline to hear proceedings on the ground that they are oppressive and an abuse of the process of the court (*Mills v Cooper* 1967 2 ALLER 100: per Lord Parker CJ para. 104), in relation to matters directly affecting the fairness of the trial, such as unlawful procedures or violating international law (*In R v Horseferry Road Magistrate's Court, ex p Bennett* (No3) [1995] 1 Cr App R 147: para.149).

There are similarities in approach, content and justification running through the decisions. These relate to the exercise of inherent jurisdiction of the court to protect human rights in the context of constitutionalism and the rule of law. Inherent jurisdiction is the power that a court has simply because it is a court of particular description. Inherent jurisdiction is not something derived by implication from statutory provisions conferring particular jurisdiction (*R v Forbes* ex p. Bevan (1972) 127 CLR 1: per Menzies para. 7).

The jurisdiction that is inherent in a superior court of law is that which enables it to fulfil itself as a court of law. The juridical basis of this jurisdiction is therefore the authority of the judiciary to uphold, protect and fulfil the law in a regular, orderly and effective manner (Jacob 1970: 23). The various options open to the judge when an abuse is alleged in proceedings include exclusion of evidence, orders for compensation, remission or reduction of sentence, dismissal of charges with prejudice or permanent stays on proceedings.[5]

During the trial of the Nazi War criminals, the defences of *tu quoque* and victor's justice were inadmissible, and indeed dismissed when raised, as the Nuremberg Charter itself provided the basis for jurisdiction. Justice Pal's dissentient judgment at the Tokyo Tribunal was an erudite and lengthy exposition of the abuse of judicial process in various ways including drafting of crimes, frames of reference and ambit of accused (Radhabinod 1953).

The European Court of Human Rights considered abuse of process in *Loizidou v Turkey* Application No. 15318/89 (decision of 23 March 1995)[6] and *Akdivar v Turkey* Application No: 21893/93 (decision of 1 April 1998).[7] However, in both cases the allegation of abuse was unsuccessful in terminating the proceedings, illustrating the comparative rarity of a successful defence of abuse of process.

5 See generally Choo 2009.

6 The Court rejected a Turkish allegation of abuse of process.

7 The Court dismissed preliminary objections concerning an alleged abuse of process.

In the Akayesu Appeals Chamber's Judgment of 1 June 2001 of the International Criminal Tribunal for Rwanda, the accused invoked the abuse of process doctrine in arguing for a stay of proceedings. The Appeals Chamber already had had occasion to consider the issue of abuse of process in the Barayagwiza Decision, holding that, under this doctrine, proceedings that had been lawfully initiated may be terminated if improper or illegal procedures were employed in pursuing an otherwise lawful process. The court deemed it important to stress its discretionary nature, being a process by which judges may decline to exercise their jurisdiction in the light of extreme violations of the accused's rights where full trial would be detrimental to the court's integrity.

The International Criminal Tribunal for the former Yugoslavia's jurisprudence provides the case of *Prosecutor v Slobodan Milošević* dated 8 November 2001 ICTY Case No IT-02–54 (para. 17). The *amici curiae* raised the doctrine of abuse of process already considered by the Appeals Chamber in the Barayagwiza case. The court noted that, if there were an abuse of process, it did not lead to a lack of jurisdiction but raised the question whether, assuming jurisdiction, discretion be exercised to refuse to try the accused. Consequently, the International Tribunal would have exercised its discretion to do this, had there been an egregious breach of the rights of the accused. The Special Court for Sierra Leone also embraced the doctrine but examined and dismissed it in the circumstances of the case (*Prosecutor v Brima, Kamara and Kanu*).[8]

In the case concerning legality of use of force, *Yugoslavia v 10 NATO states* (Provisional Measures), individual judges of the International Court of Justice seem to have invoked the abuse of process by a determination not to let Yugoslavia use the court for its own purposes. In their decisions to deny provisional measures, they regarded Yugoslavia's action as an abuse of the process of the court (Gray 2003: 867, 881).

In *Barayagwiza v Prosecutor*, the ICTR relied on the doctrine to order a stay on proceedings without any trial on the merits. Following is a rendition of how the judges developed their reasoning. The court approved the British House of Lord's view that, discretionally, criminal proceedings could be stayed where a fair trial was impossible and where it would be contrary to the public interest in the integrity of the criminal justice system that a trial should take place. The court found that application of this doctrine resulted in dismissal of charges with prejudice, particularly where to proceed on the charges in the light of egregious violations of the accused's rights would cause serious harm to the integrity of the judicial process.

Ex parte Bennett, where the House of Lords stayed the prosecution and ordered the release of the accused, was quoted as stating that a court has a discretion to stay any criminal proceedings on the ground that to try those proceedings will

8 Written Reasons for the Trial Chamber's Oral Decision on the Defence Motion on Abuse of Process due to infringement of Principles of Nullum Crimen Sine Lege and Non-Retroactivity as to Several Counts, SCSL-04–16-PT 31 March 2004.

amount to an abuse of its own process, either because it will be impossible to give the accused a fair trial or because it offends the court's sense of justice and propriety to be asked to try the accused in the circumstances of a particular case. Another permissive jurisdiction the court also invoked as a corollary, not examined on review of considerations of the procedural differences between review and appeal, was that of its supervisory powers. It held these as closely related to the abuse of process doctrine and useful in the interests of justice, regardless of a specific violation.

The United States Supreme Court too was quoted as stating that courts had a 'duty of establishing and maintaining civilized standards of procedure and evidence' as an inherent function of the courts' role in supervising the judicial system and process. Judge Noonan of the United States Ninth Circuit Court of Appeals indicated that a court had inherent supervisory powers to dismiss prosecutions in order to deter illegal conduct. Furthermore, such illegality need not be related to a constitutional or statutory violation. Though there was some domestic precedent (*Southeast Mortg. Co. v Sinclair*, 632 So. 2d 677(1994)),[9] by using their discretion to dismiss the indictment with prejudice to the prosecutor, they let themselves open to the observation that it was a stick to beat the prosecutor for their conduct of the case, thus contradicting the judgment itself. Judges are not in charge of prosecutions. It is trite that the prosecutor has wide discretion in prosecutions.

It is this author's view that whenever the court disapproves of a prosecution it should not dismiss it with prejudice but should stay the case. That is, it should proceed no further with it and let the file gather dust at the Registry. This power is almost analogous to that of a *nolle prosequi* exercised by Attorneys General the world over to stop a prosecution without advancing reasons. Had the judges done this the first time and on observing the fallout, which was as unexpected as it was unwarranted, they could simply have picked up the file again and started over on the strength of changed circumstances.

A stay is not *res judicata*: to undo it would not require the straining of legal credulity. Even the cases that the judges above quoted from municipal law advocated stays and not dismissals with prejudice. If, however, the infringement of the accused rights is not so great as to require such a drastic remedy, mitigation of any sentence to be imposed would be appropriate or otherwise a recommendation for suitable compensation.

Having examined what the judges have made of the doctrine in their own words, it would appear that the term abuse of process is quite malleable enough to cover a multitude of undesirable actions by different actors in the justice system. The only commonality discernible was that the actions sought to be addressed called for remedies strictly out of the ordinary jurisdiction of the judge and therefore they invoked some extraordinary judge-made jurisdiction to cope.

9 *Barayagwiza v Prosecutor*. 'The trial court interpreted the earlier order as a dismissal with prejudice and thus res judicata as to the subsequent complaint'.

This is not a criticism: far from it. If judges need to creatively use their jurisdiction to prevent wrongful use of their courts, so be it, as long as their reasoning is impeccable and based on sound legal principles. Besides, legal draftspeople cannot think of everything including the specific circumstances of cases in hand in all their infinite variety. However, contrary arguments boil down to the notion that all law enforcement is basically a triumph of consequences over risk. Not all criminals get caught, and even fewer get punished after all the resources spent on detection, investigation, apprehension and prosecution. To add another reason for setting an accused free, other than insufficient evidence, would be to stretch the system beyond its tolerances.

This, then, is the dilemma facing judges: do they set someone free on abstract principle, or enforce law and order at the expense of legalistic niceties? But this dilemma is more apparent than real. One can no more enforce the law by breaking it than have one's cake and eat it too. Because law is obeyed out of respect and not fear, it is far better to enhance that respect in a particular case where the intention is to maintain law and order generally.

The use of such supervisory powers was described by the court as serving three functions: to provide a remedy for the violation of the accused's rights, to deter future misconduct and to enhance the integrity of the judicial process. The last is the focus of this study. Serious uproar followed this action of the tribunal (ordering a stay on proceedings without any trial on the merits) and the Appellate Court was constrained to beat a hasty retreat in their extraordinary review decision of the above case under Article 25 and Rule 120 of the ICTR Statute[10] and Rules[11] respectively (*Prosecutor v Jean-Bosco Barayagwiza* Appeals Chamber Case no. ICTR-97–19-I refer to as refer to as Barayagwiza II).[12]

---

10 Article 25: Review Proceedings. Where a new fact has been discovered which was not known at the time of the proceedings before the Trial Chambers or the Appeals Chamber and which could have been a decisive factor in reaching the decision, the convicted person or the Prosecutor may submit to the International Tribunal for Rwanda an application for review of the judgment. *Statute of the International Criminal Tribunal for Rwanda*, annexed to *Resolution 955*, SC Res 955, UN SCOR, 49th sess, 3453rd mtg, UN Doc S/RES/955 (1994).

11 Rule 120: 'Request for Review. Where a new fact has been discovered which was not known to the moving party at the time of the proceedings before a Chamber, and could not have been discovered through the exercise of due diligence, the defence or, within one year after the final judgement has been pronounced, the Prosecutor, may make a motion to that Chamber, if it can be reconstituted or, failing that, to the appropriate Chamber of the Tribunal for review of the judgement'. *International Criminal Tribunal for Rwanda, Rules of Procedure and Evidence* Adopted on 29 June 1995 pursuant to Article 14 of the *Statute of the International Criminal Tribunal for Rwanda*, annexed to *Resolution 955*, SC Res 955, UN SCOR, 49th sess, 3453rd mtg, UN Doc S/RES/955 (1994).

12 Decision on Prosecutor's Request for Review or Reconsideration dated 31 March 2000 before: Navanethem Pillay, (Presiding), Asoka de Zoysa Gunawardana, Erik Møse JJ. (Barayagwiza II).

Curiously the court opened by saying 'with respect to this Motion for Review the Appeals Chamber begins by confirming its decision of 3 November 1999 on the basis of the facts it was founded on' (Barayagwiza II: para. 51 at page 84 of the judgment).[13] However, it then proceeded to reverse its earlier decision on the basis of 'new facts' that, most respectfully, were neither new (Barayagwiza II)[14] nor facts (Barayagwiza II).[15] It was beyond dispute that these 'facts' had occurred before the trial and were known, or at any rate should have been known, to the prosecutor. It was also conceded they were far more evidentiary than factual.

Further, and more unusually, the court construed the relevant provisions of the law as being merely 'directory', in contradistinction to 'mandatory' or 'peremptory' (Barayagwiza II),[16] in order to escape their literal meaning purportedly in the interests of justice. Proceeding from this, it may be inferred that, since the legal position in the decision under review was correct and the judges merely finessed their way out of it by a novel and tenuous definition, interpretation and construction of the law, there were overriding considerations that could not be ignored. The search for these considerations need not go far but rather into the court record itself, submissions of both parties and the joint and separate judicial declarations.

It is arguable that the court would not have acted in this way if it were not for the highly adverse reaction to the earlier decision by the Government of Rwanda, a 'new fact' in its own right (Barayagwiza II).[17] The relevance of this was that the government had paralysed the tribunal's operations in a strong reaction to the earlier ruling by the court. The judges did protest too much their independence from political considerations but, most importantly, in the end they found that although there was substantial interference with the accused's rights in the trial it was neither wholly occasioned nor attributable to the prosecution (Barayagwiza II).[18] Blame was shared with a third party, the Government of Cameroon, and in

---

13 Decision on Prosecutor's Request for Review or Reconsideration dated 31 March.

14 'The new facts identified in the first two periods were not known to the chamber at the time of the decision but they may have been known to the Prosecutor or at least could have been discovered'. Para 64 at p. 23.

15 'The Appeals Chamber considers that several elements submitted by the Prosecutor in support of the Motion for Review are evidence rather than facts'. Para 54 at p. 19.

16 'In the wholly exceptional circumstances of this case, and in the face of a possible miscarriage of justice, the Chamber construes the condition laid down in Rule 120, that the fact be unknown to the moving part at the time of the proceedings before a Chamber, and not discoverable through the exercise of due diligence, as directory in nature. In adopting such a position, the Chamber has regard to the circumstance that the statute itself does not speak on this issue'. para 65 at p. 23.

17 'Later, the Attorney General of Rwanda appearing as representative of the Rwandan Government, in his submissions as "amicus curiae" to the Appeals Chamber, openly threatened the non cooperation of the peoples of Rwanda with the Tribunal if faced with an unfavourable Decision by the Appeals Chamber on the Motion for Review'. Para 34 at p. 13.

18 'The Appeals Chamber considered that the human rights of the Appellant were violated by the prosecutor during his detention in Cameroon. However the new facts show

small measure by the acquiescence of Defence counsel once the accused was in the tribunal's custody and power.

However, the Appeals Chamber's earlier decision expounding on the law must be borne in mind (Barayagwiza I: para. 73):[19]

> First and foremost, this analysis focuses on the alleged violations of the Appellant's rights and is not primarily concerned with the entity responsible for the alleged violation(s). As will be discussed, it is clear that there are overlapping areas of responsibility between the three organs of the Tribunal and as a result, it is conceivable that more than one organ could be responsible for the violations of the Appellant's rights.
>
> Moreover, even if fault is shared between the three organs of the Tribunal-or is the result of the actions of a third party, such as Cameroon-it would undermine the integrity of the judicial process to proceed. Furthermore, it would be unfair for the Appellant to stand trial on these charges if his rights were egregiously violated. Thus, under the abuse of process doctrine, it is irrelevant which entity or entities were responsible for the alleged violations of the Appellant's rights. Second, we stress that the circumstances set forth in this analysis must be read as a whole. Third, none of the findings made in this subsection of the Decision, in isolation, are necessarily dispositive of this issue. That is, it is the combination of these factors-and not any single finding herein-that lead us to the conclusion we reach in this subsection. In other words, the application of the abuse of process doctrine is case-specific and limited to the egregious circumstances presented by this case. Fourth, because the Prosecutor initiates the proceedings of the Tribunal, her special responsibility in prosecuting cases will be examined in subsection 4, infra.

This should be ample illustration that whether or not the prosecutor was responsible for the infringement of the accused's rights, it is not pertinent to a finding of the abuse of process. By disregarding this it would be difficult to dispel the perception of judicial error. It is possible that Security Council resolution 955 of 1994, which saw the setting up of the tribunal under Chapter VII as a subsidiary body to itself and which provided the *raison d'*être of the tribunal as the maintenance of international peace and security through judicial means, could have been taken into legal consideration.[20] Further, by that the reaction of the Rwandese authorities

---

that, during this second period, the violations were not attributable to the Prosecutor'. Para 58 at p. 21.

19 'The Abuse of Process Doctrine'.

20 Clause 1 'The Security Council … under Chapter VII … decides … to establish an international tribunal for the sole purpose of prosecuting persons responsible for genocide … and to this end to adopt the Statute of the International Criminal Tribunal for

(Barayagwiza II)[21] may have been rendered a suitable topic of discussion on the merits of the tribunal, instead of a cause for embarrassment all round and an excuse for cynics to read realpolitik into the work of the tribunal.

By conceding that the accused's rights had indeed been violated and then reversing the earlier decision on the basis that the prosecutor was not wholly responsible (Barayagwiza I),[22] the judges floundered in a lack of objectivity.

Academic commentary has already explored the application of the abuse of process doctrine in the International Criminal Court in the context of the *Ne bis in idem* rule and time limits on prosecution (Cassese, Paola and Jones 2002: 710, 713, 874, 885). The laws applicable are the Statute, Elements of Crime, Rules of Procedure and Evidence, treaties, principles and rules of international law, including established principles of international humanitarian law and, most pertinently in this context, general principles of law derived by the court from national laws of legal systems that would normally exercise jurisdiction (Rome Statute: Art. 21).[23]

The abuse of process defence was first affirmed in the International Criminal Court on 13 June 2008 by its Trial Chamber I while hearing the matter of the Situation in The Democratic Republic of the Congo, specifically in the case against Thomas Lubanga Dyilo.[24] The court found that trial process had been ruptured to the degree that it was impossible to have a fair trial and consequently imposed a stay in the proceedings in order to protect the judicial process.[25] This application

Rwanda'. Resolution 955 (1994) Adopted by the Security Council at its 3453rd meeting, on 8 November 1994.

21 'The Prosecutor submits that her ability to continue with prosecutions and investigations depends on the government of Rwanda and that unless the Appellant is tried, the Rwandan government will no longer be involved "in any manner"'. Para 24 at p. 10.

22 'The Appeals Chamber reviews its Decision in the light of the new facts presented by the Prosecutor. It confirms that the Appellant's rights were violated, and that all violations demand a remedy. However, the violations suffered by the Appellant and the omissions of the Prosecutor are not the same as those which emerged from the facts on which the Decision is founded. Accordingly, the remedy ordered by the Chamber in the Decision, which consisted in the dismissal of the indictment and the release of the Appellant, must be altered'. Para 74 at p. 27.

23 Opened for signature 17 July 1998, 2187 UNTS 3, art 83(2) (entered into force 1 July 2002).

24 Decision on the consequences of non-disclosure of exculpatory materials covered by Article 54(3)(e) agreements and the application to stay the prosecution of the accused, together with certain other issues raised at the Status Conference on 10 June 2008. Before: Judge Adrian Fulford (Presiding Judge), Judge Elizabeth Odio Benito and Judge René BlattmannNo. ICC- 01/04–01/06 dated 13 June 2008.

25 Decision on the consequences of non-disclosure of exculpatory materials covered by Article 54(3) (e) agreements and the application to stay the prosecution of the accused, together with certain other issues raised at the Status Conference on 10 June 2008. Before: Judge Adrian Fulford (Presiding Judge), Judge Elizabeth Odio Benito and Judge René BlattmannNo. ICC- 01/04–01/06 dated 13 June 2008 at para 94.

of the abuse of process doctrine was subsequently affirmed on appeal, thereby affirming its embedding into ICL.[26] This illustrates the points discussed above that a stay of proceedings protects the (future) judicial process far more visibly than a dismissal would have done.

The tentative answer then is yes, a jurisdictionally judicial entity may as a matter of customary international law entertain an application to decline to hear a case alleging the crime of aggression as an abuse or misuse of its procedure. The application of such an allegation to the objections outlined earlier is as follows. First an argument that criminal aggression is not sufficiently defined is an argument for its definition and not against its definition. This is especially so in the context of a treaty being negotiated for that specific purpose.

Acts of what may be called criminal aggression by non-state actors are usually covered within domestic criminal law by treason laws and suchlike and even where these acts are projected far beyond state borders this is only possible with the active connivance of a state that may be held responsible.

As for the role of the Security Council being overlooked, the following chapter addresses this. Suffice to say, there is nothing to show that the framers of the Nuremberg and United Nations Charters ever made cross-reference to each other's product or intended them to be read in conjunction. My argument is that the objections to criminal aggression being legalizable are answerable under the abuse of process doctrine. In the light of this chapter framing the dispute in terms pitting legality and illegality, the next chapter looks at the contours of criminalizing aggression.

26 Judgment on the appeal of the Prosecutor against the decision of Trial Chamber I entitled 'Decision on the release of Thomas Lubanga Dyilo' The Appeals Chamber, Judge Sang-Hyun Song (Presiding Judge), Judge Philippe Kirsch, Judge Georghios M Pikis, Judge Erkki Kourula and Judge Daniel David Ntanda Nsereko. ICC-01/04–01/06 OA 12 dated 21 October 2008.

Chapter 9
Reframing Criminal Aggression from Outside to Inside Law

Having developed a novel way of looking at the debate over aggression in previous chapters, this chapter describes the debate with fresh eyes and provides new insights into processes that reach above the state to the international community and below the state to the individual in the name of humanity. It is a genealogy tracing the notion of aggression leading up to and immediately after the Second World War and as reflected by debate around the jurisdiction of the International Criminal Court (ICC). The argument presented is that the legality or illegality of the use of force presumes a legal order as a way of life to be protected by lawful force deployed, if required, against unlawful violence. This order foregrounds a right to peace (and concomitant duty to keep the peace) by backgrounding a 'right to war' which inheres in the nation state through individuals by the operation of law. In other words, the Foucauldian notion that the government's function in modernity is 'to make live' is currently achieved through legal intervention by way of correction, punishment and death deployed violently against life on behalf of life (Dillon 2007: 7, 11).

The relevance of this chapter for the hypothetical scenario, as presented in Chapter 1, is to outline the development of the relevant treaty and customary law sources of the law applicable and to determine how a court would apply legal reasoning in discerning which contested rules to apply to the disputed facts. It is also a truncated detective story that follows the development of aggression's *definability* as a crime in law, not just in terms of legal history but also as part of a broader arc of global social control. It should be noted that in the scenario the nation states are a stubborn fact of life; even as some of them wither or break up, others flourish and strengthen. However, the threats faced are transnational and the individuals responsible remain natural persons, while the concerns go beyond narrow self-interest.

A 'Right to Peace'

The first attempt to legalize war in the Western tradition was through the doctrine of 'just war'. The just war doctrine aimed to reconcile might with right though recognizing only just wars as legal and unjust wars as aggression and therefore illegal (Grotius 2005: 39). War therefore could only be a just response to aggression and in this way was the ultimate means for both restoring a 'right' of some sort that had been violated and simultaneously punishing the offender (Grotius 2005: 39). It therefore seems that, in discussing the legality or illegality of the use of force and its normative manifestation, there is a universal yet inarticulate soft law background presumption that at its simplest says 'there is a right to peace'[1] that could be violated, but such violation would attract penal consequences. This so-called right to peace and concomitant duty to keep the peace[2] inheres in the nation state but arguably also in individuals[3] through the operation of customary international law.[4] It may not be part of the positive law as such but it does provide interpretative capacity by conceiving of peace as the norm and war/armed conflict the undesirable exception.

At the foreground of this right to peace is the reality of war or armed conflict as acknowledged in the hard law. The laws that govern entry into and conduct of war and armed conflict have traditionally been divided into two: *jus ad bellum* and *jus in bello* (Kolb 1997: 553). The contemporary arguments extending *jus in bello* principles into internal armed conflict just as cogently apply to *jus ad bellum*.[5] Peace at its most basic is the absence of armed conflict. Armed conflict is resort to force by state or non-state actors which may be legal or illegal. *Jus ad bellum* law governs resort to war or force in general (the *why* questions), while *jus in bello* governs the conduct of war or armed conflict (the *how* questions).

Aggression falls on the *jus ad bellum* side of the ledger. The dearth of trials for the crime of aggression, despite the wealth of perpetrators, gives cause for comment (Paulus 2004: 21). If indeed it is irrefutable that present-day positive international law reflects the Nuremberg Judgment (Dinstein 2002: 109) and United Nations declarations,[6] is the lacuna observed in normative application

---

1 'All peoples have the right to national and international peace and security'. African [Banjul] Charter on Human and Peoples' Rights, adopted 27 June 1981, OAU Doc. CAB/LEG/67/3 rev. 5, 21 I.L.M. 58 (1982), 1520 UNTS 217 entered into force 21 October 1986 art. 23.

2 See e.g., *Resolution on Principles of International Law concerning Friendly Relations and Cooperation among States in accordance with the Charter of the United Nations*. UNGA Resolution 2625 (XXV) (24 October 1970).

3 See clause '1. Every nation and every human being, regardless of race, conscience, language or sex, has the inherent right to life in peace'. *Declaration on the Preparation of Societies for Life in Peace* UNGA/Res/33/73 (15 December 1978).

4 See e.g. Declaration of the Right of Peoples to Peace UNGA Res 39/11 (12 November 1984), which expressed 'the will and the aspirations of all peoples to eradicate war from the life of mankind' and in art. 1. 'Solemnly proclaims that the peoples of our planet have a sacred right to peace'.

5 See *Prosecutor v Dusko Tadić* a/k/a 'Dule' (Case No. IT-94-1-T) decision of 2 October 1995, 'On The Defence Motion For Interlocutory Appeal On Jurisdiction', Before: Cassese, J (Presiding), Li, Deschênes, Abi-Saab, Sidhwa JJ. paras 83 and 134.

6 *Definition of Aggression* UNGA Resolution 3314 (XXIX) of (14 December 1974), art 1: 'Aggression is the use of armed force by a State against the sovereignty, territorial integrity or political independence of another State, or in any other manner inconsistent

merely a result of realpolitik or are there largely suppressed, legally reasoned and underlying reasons subsisting?

Under contemporary international law, the prosecution of international crimes is generally the responsibility of the state as the oldest, most traditional and indeed appropriate subject of international law.[7] Although the Nuremberg Charter itself was established without prejudice to the jurisdiction of national courts,[8] it in turn was set up 'as an act of the will of the conqueror' (Glueck 1946: 25). Even with the advent of the ICC, this responsibility to prosecute is still mainly with the state as expressly provided under the Rome Statute (1998: Art. 17) on issues of admissibility. This statute provides that due regard must be given to paragraph 10 of the Preamble[9] and the first article of the statute,[10] both of which unequivocally lay stress on the principle of complementarity. It is laid down that the court shall determine that a case is inadmissible where, inter alia, the case is being or has been investigated or prosecuted by a state which has jurisdiction over it, except where the state is either unwilling or unable in good faith to carry out such investigation or prosecution (Rome Statute of the International Criminal Court 1998: Art. 17 para. 1 clause (a)). Under the Statute of the International Criminal Court, the accent and emphasis is thus clearly on the primary duty of the state to prosecute violators of international criminal law.

Further, with a few relatively minor exceptions, the statute does not create, codify or legislate new types of crime but only provides a novel collective mechanism for dealing with the most serious crimes of international concern. Even then, this is only when the state primarily responsible for investigation and/or prosecution has abdicated its responsibility and another state has not taken it upon itself to investigate and/or prosecute such a crime (Rome Statute 1998: Art. 17 para. 1 clause (a)). Moreover, the ICC has jurisdiction only over the most serious crimes of international concern (Rome Statute 1998: Art. 17 para. 1 clause (d)). The rest remain within the purview of states.

---

with the Charter of the United Nations'; art 2: 'The first use of armed force by a State in contravention of the Charter shall constitute prima facie evidence of an act of aggression although the Security Council may, in conformity with the Charter, conclude that a determination that an act of aggression has been committed would not be justified in the light of other relevant circumstances, including the fact that the acts concerned or their consequences are not of sufficient gravity'.

7 See generally Charney 2001: 120.

8 Article 6 of the *Agreement for the Prosecution and Punishment of the Major War Criminals of the European Axis, and the Charter of the International Military Tribunal.* London, 8 August 1945.

9 Emphasizing that the International Criminal Court established under this Statute shall be complementary to national criminal jurisdictions.

10 Article 1 provides that the International Criminal Court shall be complementary to national criminal jurisdictions. Article 1 of *Rome Statute of the International Criminal Court*, opened for signature 17 July 1998, 2187 UNTS 3, art 83(2) (entered into force 1 July 2002).

With particular reference to the crime of aggression, the ICC will exercise the jurisdiction already vested over the crime of aggression once a provision is adopted containing a definition and procedure of how aggression should be dealt with. However, this should be consistent with the relevant provisions of the Charter of the United Nations (Rome Statute 1998: Art. 5 para. 2).

From Geopolitics to Biopolitics

It is noteworthy that the author who popularized, and indeed coined, the term 'geopolitics' is responsible too for coming up with 'biopolitics' (Esposito 2008: 16). The two terms are linked in terms of remorselessly conceiving the world as a space populated by humans to be dominated. Geopolitical distribution signals a world divided between competing sovereign territories, while biopolitical circulation views a world in terms of biological structures and functions of species (Dillon 2007: 11). Geopolitical threat perception differs from biopolitical threat perception. The biopolitical threat is not that of an external enemy as such but within life itself. This threat to life by life is infinitely adaptable because adaptable emergence is the core vital sign of life (Dillon 2007: 12).

Geopolitical reasoning is a perfect fit with public international law because it is primarily concerned with state actors. Meanwhile, biopolitical reasoning sits easily with international criminal law that reaches below the state to the individual from above the state as a placeholder for the international community/humanity. Aggression was conceived in a geopolitical context but could only gather purchase and be applied within a biopolitical paradigm. What follows is a sketch of this movement.

The Public International Law Prohibition on the Use of Force

The Hague Peace conferences of 1899 and 1907 contained the first, albeit modest, restrictions on the use of force but did not go so far as to comprehensively outlaw its use outright.[11] Prior to this century, no prohibition of the use of force had existed and states were free to resort to war as yet another tool in the diplomatic kitbag

11 Article 1: 'The Contracting Powers recognize that hostilities between themselves must not commence without previous and explicit warning, in the form either of a reasoned declaration of war or of an ultimatum with conditional declaration of war'. International Peace Conference: Opening of Hostilities (1907 Hague III); 18 October 1907 <http://avalon.law.yale.edu/20th_century/hague03.asp> Article 7: 'The acceptance of mediation can not, unless there be an agreement to the contrary, have the effect of interrupting, delaying, or hindering mobilization or other measures of preparation for war. If mediation, occurs after the commencement of hostilities it causes no interruption to the military operations in progress, unless there be an agreement to the contrary'. *Convention (I) For the Pacific*

(Maogoto 2005: 22).[12] Public international law at the time permitted the use of force in the relations between states (Maogoto 2005). During the era of the League of Nations, its covenant went some way towards progressively regulating and restricting the use of force amounting to war between states.[13] A further welcome development was the Geneva Protocol for the Pacific Settlement of International Disputes of 1924 outlawing aggressive war and labelling it an international crime (Alexandrov 1996: 43). In the Kellogg-Briand Pact (that is, the General Treaty for the Renunciation of War 1928), the state parties to it not only condemned recourse to war for the solution of international controversies, but renounced it as an instrument of national policy and agreed that only peaceful means were to decide all disputes or conflicts among them ('Kellogg–Briand Pact 1928' *United States Statutes at Large*, 46(2), 2343 Art. 1–3) The provisions of this treaty may be taken accordingly as evidence of international customary law rules. However, the position as it stands now is markedly different.

After the First World War, through the Treaty of Versailles 1919, William II of Hohenzollern, former German emperor, was indicted for 'a supreme offence against international morality and the sanctity of treaties and essential rules of justice' (Israel 1967: 1265). However, the Netherlands, where he was exiled, declined to give him up for trial after receiving assurances that the Allied Powers would not vigorously pursue the point.

But the real watershed in terms of individual criminal responsibility came in Article 6 of the Constitution of the International Military Tribunal appended to the London Agreement for the Prosecution and Punishment of the Major War Criminals of the European Axis.

The tribunal set up had the power to try and punish persons who, as individuals, had committed crimes against peace: namely, planning, preparation, initiation or waging of a war of aggression, or a war in violation of international treaties, agreements or assurances. The judgment of the court said that crimes against international law were committed by persons, not abstract entities, and only by punishing individuals who committed such crimes could the provisions of international law be enforced (Judgment of the International Military Tribunal for the Trial of German Major War Criminals). As for the critical matter of individual criminal responsibility, the High Command case ruled that the criminality of aggressive war was attached only to individuals at the policy-making level (*United States of America v Wilhelm Von Leeb et al.* (1948) Case XII).

Settlement of International Disputes (Hague I) (29 July 1899). Repeated in *Convention for the Pacific Settlement of International Disputes (Hague I)*; 18 October 1907.

12 See also Bruno Simma et al. 2002: 127.

13 Article 10: 'The Members of the League undertake to respect and preserve as against external aggression the territorial integrity and existing political independence of all Members of the League. In case of any such aggression or in case of any threat or danger of such aggression the Council shall advise upon the means by which this obligation shall be fulfilled'. *The Covenant of the League of Nations.*

The aforementioned General Assembly resolution (UNGA Resolution 3314(XXIX) (29(1)) affirmed the rules of law developed by the Nuremberg Charter and Judgment and directed the International Law Commission to draft them into a code. Still on this point, the International Law Commission said 'the law of the Charter concerning the prohibition of the use of force in itself constitutes a conspicuous example of a rule in international law having the character of *jus cogens*' (UN International Law Commission 1966: 247).

The first time criminal aggression was defined in a legal text was for the Nuremberg trials. The Charter of the International Military Tribunal (IMT) defined the jurisdiction and set out the general principles for the criminalization and prosecution of 'the major war criminals of the European Axis countries' for inter alia aggression, as set out in the following terms:

> (a) CRIMES AGAINST PEACE: namely, planning, preparation, initiation or waging of a war of aggression, or a war in violation of international treaties, agreements or assurances, or participation in a common plan or conspiracy for the accomplishment of any of the foregoing. (Nuremberg Trail Proceedings vol. 1)

During the negotiations leading to the adoption of the text, the United States' position, as put forward by its representative Justice Jackson, was that 'sterile legalisms developed in the age of imperialism to make war respectable' justified acts which otherwise would be crimes, indistinguishable from piracy and brigandage. Jackson, however, distinguished between international law of the nineteenth century and that of the early twentieth century, which declared that war-making was not illegal as both parties to war were regarded as being in an identical legal position. This was a departure from the doctrine taught by Hugo Grotius (favoured by Jackson), distinguishing between just (defence) and unjust (aggression) war (International Conference on Military Trials 1949). According to Jackson, international law went beyond 'abstract and immutable principles' but originated in state action (International Conference on Military Trials 1949). There was therefore no need for precedent to justify the trial because when the Nazis came to power aggressive war was already illegal and criminal.

According to Jackson this followed on from the texts already cited above, together with some notable inclusions (International Conference on Military Trials 1949):

1. The Briand–Kellogg Pact of 1928 with which Germany, Italy and Japan renounced war as an instrument of national policy, which mentioned the Geneva Protocol of 1924 for the Pacific Settlement of International Disputes, that declared aggressive war criminal.
2. The unanimous resolution of the Eighth Assembly of the League of Nations in 1927, including Germany, to declare wars of aggression criminal; and (most interestingly from the perspective of this inquiry).

3. The unanimous resolution of the Sixth Pan-American Conference of 1928 stating that 'war of aggression constitutes an international crime against the human species' (International Conference on Military Trials 1949).

These justifications for prosecuting aggression readily divide into the more traditional horizontal/geopolitical plane (including Germany with its consent) and the radically inclusive vertical/biopolitical plane (including Germany regardless of its consent).

The point consistently emphasized during drafting of the IMT Charter was that only actual attack or invasion constituted aggression, and any possible arguments that such attack or invasion was in defence against political or economic measures were headed off in the drafting. This was despite the drafters' awareness that from Germany's perspective such an attack was considered a defensive action. Defining the 'aggressor' beforehand would exclude any argument in the courtroom over characterization in which the Germans would participate (International Conference on Military Trials 1949). Aggression was therefore defined to exclude 'resort to war to redress economic or political disadvantages or threats of encirclement, etc. as a defence' (International Conference on Military Trials 1949). Neither political or military nor other considerations could excuse resorting to war. That is, for the purposes of prosecution in 1945 peaceful settlement of grievances between states was considered compulsory *ex ante* due to a prohibition of aggression deemed by that point to be customary (International Conference on Military Trials 1949).

Sir David Maxwell Fyfe, representing the United Kingdom and speaking in support of Jackson, presented the available options as stark choices: firstly, exclude aggression which was the essential complaint against the Germans; secondly, allow political argument as to the meaning of aggression at trial; and thirdly, define aggression for the purposes of the tribunal. Jackson expressed his fears that, if argument was allowed over the political and economic causes of the war, controversy would arise regarding whether Germany invaded Norway just before a British invasion of Norway or whether France, in declaring war, was the real aggressor. These considerations would also apply to Russia (International Conference on Military Trials 1949). In this way, therefore, aggression was defined as a crime by reference to states but with or without their consent through the strategic use of the term 'humanity'. The usual concerns of international law – criminal law and legality – were left by the wayside in creating the new jurisdiction.

Developments Post Nuremberg

Article 2(4) of the United Nations Charter instructs states to 'refrain in their international relations from the threat or use of force against the territorial integrity or political independence of any state'. This provision is an improvement of the language of the Kellogg–Briand pact in replacing the term 'war' with 'force'. This is in anticipation of aggressors qualifying the force they use as not amounting to war.

In the Nicaragua (Merits) Case (1986) ICJ REP. 14, the International Court of Justice considered the principle of non-use of force a rule of customary international law. The court went on to say that the United Nations Charter by no means covered the whole area of the regulation of the use of force in foreign relations, and stated that relevant customary rules still applied, some of which, being in the nature of *jus cogens*, could not be varied by treaty.

According to Bruno Simma et al. (2002: 127), neither Article 2(4) nor any Charter provision provides a basis for the criminal prosecution of individuals violating the prohibition of the use of force. Therefore the international community has not yet succeeded in completely transforming the respective principles emanating from the Nuremberg and Tokyo trials regarding aggression into valid international law (UN International Law Commission 1950: 191). Another commentator has expressed the opinion that the Charter does not per se declare war illegal or criminal, but merely a breach of treaty subject to the sanctions embodied in that treaty (Green 2000). However, another view is that as pre-existing international crimes already entailed individual liability, it is therefore reasonable to extend the same principle by analogy to the international crime of aggression (Malanczuk 1997: 354). Further, under customary international law, war crimes and crimes against peace are subject to universal jurisdiction, so that all states are entitled to bring offenders to trial (Akehurst 1970 as cited in Dinstein 1996: 16).

Another matter to be taken into consideration is that the principles laid down in the Charter and Judgment of the Nuremberg Tribunal concerning individual criminal responsibility for aggression or crimes against peace had been approved by the United Nations General Assembly (Resolution 95(1)). Moreover, the initial title for the then proposed International Criminal Court statute was 'Draft Code of Crimes against the Peace and Security of Mankind' (1954) and later (1996). However, both the General Assembly and the International Law Commission remained silent on punishment as this was envisaged to be provided for in the future by the then proposed but not putative ICC (Dinstein and Tabory 1996: 16). The advent of the ICC was the occasion for slightly more than glacial progress in further codifying aggression. A question of some merit is whether the judicial enforcement of peace is compatible with the role of the Security Council. However, this is addressed by the statute itself, which gives a perpetually renewable 'veto' to the Security Council concerning deferral of investigations or prosecutions (Rome Statute of the International Criminal Court 1998: Art. 16).

The 1998 International Criminal Court Rome Conference

The ICC negotiations led to the following compromise formula regarding aggression in Article 5 of the Rome Statute, which confers aggression and withholds its exercise pending a definition:

> 1. The jurisdiction of the Court shall be limited to the most serious crimes of concern to the international community as a whole. The Court has jurisdiction in accordance with this Statute with respect to the following crimes:
>
> ...
>
> (d) The crime of aggression.
>
> 2. The Court shall exercise jurisdiction over the crime of aggression once a provision is adopted in accordance with articles 121 and 123 defining the crime and setting out the conditions under which the Court shall exercise jurisdiction with respect to this crime. Such a provision shall be consistent with the relevant provisions of the Charter of the United Nations.

However, the majority of participants at the conference to establish the ICC were in favour of including the crime of aggression. For instance, Mr Westdickenberg, who was the Germany representative, expressed strong support for inclusion of the crime of aggression (UN Diplomatic Conference 1998: 171 para. 19). He believed that a non-political, workable and precise definition of the crime of aggression could be found that conformed to the Charter of the United Nations (UN Diplomatic Conference 1998: 171 para. 19). Mr Baibourtian, the Armenian delegate, was of the view that the ICC should have jurisdiction over aggression. However, a clear definition of aggression was needed in order to avoid misinterpretation over the right to self-defence (a traditional right expressed externally by a state against other states) and self-determination (a non-traditional right expressed internally within the state between factions that otherwise owe allegiance to the state) (UN Diplomatic Conference 1998: 78 para. 83–4). The latter was problematic because it undermined the legitimacy of the state by raising a right to self-determination that seemed to trump the presumed 'right to peace'. This is one of the issues raised in the hypothetical scenario presented in Chapter 1.

Mr Bill Richardson presented a somewhat revised position for the United States from the view expressed at Nuremberg by saying that acts not clearly criminalized under international law should be excluded from the definition of aggression and that it was therefore premature to attempt to define aggression in terms of individual criminal responsibility (UN Diplomatic Conference 1998: 95 para. 61).

Leading up to Article 5 reproduced above, Mr van der Wind for the Netherlands said that it was unclear whether the crime of aggression should be included (UN Diplomatic Conference 1998: 146 paras 1–6). He suggested that although the number of states accepting inclusion had risen over the years, much would depend on the definition and the role of the Security Council. He identified two precedents for the definition of aggression: the statutes of the Nuremberg and Tokyo Tribunals and General Assembly resolution 3314 (XXLX) of 14 December 1974 (UN Diplomatic Conference 1998: 146 paras 1–6). Regarding the Security Council, the issue was whether the ICC might consider the crime of aggression only after the Council had determined that a state had committed such an act (and the ICC would then have the duty to look into the criminal responsibility of the person who had ordered that act) or whether the ICC might also consider a crime of aggression without such a prior determination by the Council (UN Diplomatic Conference 1998: 146 paras 1–6). Further, the crime of aggression had been discussed in the Preparatory Committee on the Establishment of an International Criminal Court, initially on the basis of the definition included in the Nuremberg Charter and of the definition included in General Assembly resolution 3314 (XXIX) of 14 December 1974. During those discussions, it had become clear that neither of the precedents was considered acceptable or appropriate for full inclusion (UN Diplomatic Conference 1998: 171 paras 15–19).

Mr Lloyd, representing the United Kingdom and speaking on behalf of the European Union, the Central and Eastern European countries associated with the European Union, the associated country of Cyprus and the European Free Trade Association countries of Iceland and Norway, said that the ICC should have jurisdiction over the crime of aggression, properly defined, but without detracting from the role of the Security Council in maintaining international peace and security (UN Diplomatic Conference 1998: 66 paras 31–3).

Mr Omar, representing South Africa and speaking on behalf of the Southern African Development Community (SADC), said that the ICC was a necessary element for peace and security in the world and must therefore have inherent jurisdiction over aggression (UN Diplomatic Conference 1998: 65 para. 15).

Mr Hassouna, who was the observer for the League of Arab States, expressed support for the principle of including the crime of aggression in the list of crimes within the jurisdiction of the ICC, taking into account the definition of aggression contained in General Assembly resolution 3314 (XXDQ) of 14 December 1974 and the distinction between aggression and the right of peoples to armed struggle (UN Diplomatic Conference 1998: 88 para. 67). There being no agreed definition of the crime of terrorism, Mr Hassouna stated that he would prefer not to see that crime included in the statute, but if it was included, he suggested that it might be guided by the definition of the crime of aggression and the crime of terrorism laid down in the Arab Convention for the Suppression of Terrorism adopted in Cairo in April 1998 (UN Diplomatic Conference 1998: 88 para. 67).

Mr Mirzaee Yengejeh, the delegate for the Islamic Republic of Iran and speaking on behalf of the member States of the Movement of Non-Aligned Countries, expressed disappointment over not including the crime of aggression. Mr Yengejeh's view was that the difficulties that allegedly would result from aggression's inclusion were pretexts for excluding the 'mother of crimes' as recognized by the Nuremberg Tribunal and as called for in the declaration by the Ministerial Meeting of the Coordinating Bureau of the Movement of Non-Aligned Countries, held at Cartagena de Indias, Colombia, on 19 and 20 May 1998 (UN Diplomatic Conference 1998: 321 para. 17). In saying this, the delegate was probably referring to the Nuremberg International Military Tribunal (1947: 186), which famously characterized 'a war of aggression as the supreme international crime in that it contained within itself the accumulated evil of the whole'.

In opposing the inclusion of aggression, Israel and Pakistan found themselves in close agreement. Mr Nathan, representing Israel, was not convinced that the crime of aggression should be included in the ICC's jurisdiction (United Nations Diplomatic Conference 1996: 172 paras 45–51). This was because he believed penal sanctions should be based on precise and universally accepted definitions and not politically motivated ones (United Nations Diplomatic Conference 1996: 172 paras 45–51). Although there were the precedents of the Nuremberg crimes against peace and the General Assembly resolution 3314 (XXIX), no exhaustive enumeration of acts of aggression was possible (United Nations Diplomatic Conference 1996: 172 paras 45–51). Further, according to Nathan, acts of aggression were committed by states against states. In addition, even if the crime was included, it would be subject to Security Council determination which would prejudice both the defence and the ICC's independence (United Nations Diplomatic Conference 1996: 172 paras 45–51). His suggestion therefore was that aggression be postponed for a future review conference, pending the development of an acceptable definition (United Nations Diplomatic Conference 1996: 172 paras 45–51).

Mr Mahmood, speaking for Pakistan, opposed the inclusion of aggression for its controversial nature (United Nations Diplomatic Conference 1996: 173 paras 41–3). The definition of aggression that had been adopted by the General Assembly in 1974 was considered by Pakistan as not only non-binding but more political than legal (United Nations Diplomatic Conference 1996: 173 paras 41–3). Any role for the Security Council would introduce a political element which would undermine the state sovereignty (United Nations Diplomatic Conference 1996: 173 paras 41–3). Furthermore, aggression was traditionally considered a crime committed by states, whereas Pakistan favoured the principle that the ICC's jurisdiction should be limited only to crimes committed by individuals (United Nations Diplomatic Conference 1996: 173 paras 41–3). Mr Sadi, the Jordanian delegate, stated that he would prefer to maintain the reference to aggression as a crime subject to the jurisdiction of the ICC, but was open to deferring its definition to a later stage if an acceptable formula could not be found (United Nations Diplomatic Conference 1996: 52 para. 72). This was what transpired eventually.

What the diplomats sounding a discordant note at the negotiations neglected to mention was that a clear distinction must be maintained between a finding of *factual* aggression under the United Nations Charter[14] and a charge of *criminal* aggression, such as that under the contemplations of the Rome Statute for the International Criminal Court (United Nations Charter)[15] and domestic penal legislation in Germany, Japan, Switzerland, Austria, Russia and Sweden (Gewehr

14 Art 39: 'The Security Council shall determine the existence of any … act of aggression …'.

15 Art 5(1): 'The Court has jurisdiction … with respect to … The crime of aggression'.

2003: 34–7). The former entails state responsibility, the latter, individual criminal responsibility. One is political and the other is judicial. Presumably, the latest effort under the ICC process will allay such concerns should the states have maintained their position.

The ICC Special Working Group on the Crime of Aggression was mandated by the State parties to prepare a draft definition and conditions for the exercise of jurisdiction for discussion at the next review conference that was set for Kampala in June of 2010. They developed a draft definition of the crime of aggression as (ICC 2009: 20):

> 'crime of aggression' means the planning, preparation, initiation or execution, by a person in a position effectively to exercise control over or to direct the political or military action of a State, of an act of aggression which, by its character, gravity and scale, constitutes a manifest violation of the Charter of the United Nations.

This provision is plainly a marriage between the Nuremberg definition and the United Nations General Assembly definition of aggression. This is clearly so when 'act of aggression' for the purpose of the provision means the use of armed force by a state against the sovereignty, territorial integrity or political independence of another state, or in a way otherwise inconsistent with the Charter of the United Nations (ICC 2009). This definition is explicitly derived from United Nations General Assembly resolution 3314 (XXIX) of 14 December 1974.

On 11 June 2010 the Kampala ICC Conference adopted by consensus Resolution RC/Res.6 at the 13th plenary meeting defining the Crime of Aggression just as proposed by the Special Working Group (ICC. 2010h). What the debate in the context of the ICC indicates is that the law is more or less settled but the political will to put mechanisms in place is so far lacking. However, having a law in place is one thing and interpreting it in the right spirit is quite another. Providing a legal basis for determining aggression is a necessary but insufficient first step. Interpreting the law in the right spirit by not normalizing the exceptions inherent to any law must follow. Quite plausibly having a law in place may *enable* violence done by justification or legitimation through law instead of impeding it.

The next chapter builds on this conclusion to conclusively answer the research question of whether a prosecution of criminal aggression would *necessarily* be an abuse of legality. Based on the analysis presented thus far, the chapter argues that prosecuting criminal aggression would in fact be very much within legality because although it is politicized, it is not inherently political.

Chapter 10
Legality and Resolving Ambiguity

This book began as a project investigating the transplantation of the common law notion of abuse of process into international criminal law and whether this would be adequate to protect the integrity of judicial proceedings when prosecuting the crime of aggression. Preliminary research indicated that far from being a run-of-the-mill defence, the doctrine delved right into the very purpose and utility of the law while raising the spectre of a threat to the rule of law's guaranteeing of life, liberty and property and hence represented a danger to life and the quality of life itself. This connected it directly to the problem of criminalizing violence in international law: first by querying what the utility of law was against violence, second by revealing that the distinction between force and violence is a legal distinction of what are otherwise indistinguishable, and third by laying bare the paradox of law's prevention of the violent taking of life (and degrading of living) by the means of forcible taking and degradation of life. The question raised then was that if life had been captured in the law, could it still be convincingly argued that the decision to take life was nevertheless outside the law?

This concluding chapter brings the disparate threads together and consolidates the thesis. This chapter addresses finally the basic research question posed in the opening hypothetical: must a judicial entity decline to entertain a prosecution for criminal aggression as *ipso facto*, an abuse or misuse of legal procedure? Previous chapters have traced the genealogy of aggression, through its criminalization to its relationship to law and deriving meaning, as well as illustrated how it applies in actuality.

A court as a judicial proceeding must have the necessary independence and impartiality to decline to exercise its jurisdiction in order to protect the integrity of the proceedings, and therefore of the legal system as such, by preferring not to proceed with politically motivated prosecutions. That is, if we in the final analysis understand legality and violence as a mutually exclusive but nevertheless entwined dyad, then our approach to aggression as either a non-justiciable act of state violence or as a justiciable legal fact constitutes a normative choice (that is in turn socially constituted). However, the only legally tenable position is that aggression is a justiciable legal fact regardless of its gravity.

The argument pursued throughout this thesis is that the debate on prosecuting criminal aggression at the International Criminal Court is ostensibly about criminality but in reality is a dispute about the legal global order. This order relies on the law to the extent that the independence of the law is severely compromised. The chink in the armour of the law is necessity. In customary international law, this is exemplified by the 'Caroline case' of 1842, which was contained in a series of letters between the United States and the United Kingdom. Both parties agreed that 'necessity of that self-defence is instant, overwhelming, and leaving no choice of means, and no moment for deliberation' (Miller 1934: 1836–46). This is the nucleus of necessity in international law. As necessity either knows no law or is its own law, the necessary legitimates the exceptional either by appearing to attribute to necessity the power to render the illegal legal or by releasing a particular case from the literal application of the norm (Agamben 2005a: 24). With modernity the state of necessity increasingly tends to be included within the juridical order and so it progressively becomes generalized. Necessity defining a unique situation in which the law loses its obligatory force is reversed to necessity constituting the ultimate ground and very source of the law and political action.[1]

It follows therefore that both the content of the definition of aggression and the context of the definition's application join issue as to whether the appropriate space for dealing with aggression is political or legal: that is, whether 'facts' (political reality) or 'law' (legalized justice) take precedence. Even the International Court of Justice has said it is impossible to apply the usual legal distinctions in the face of necessity (ICJ 1996: para. 105), thereby re-affirming that 'necessity knows no law', which renders definition and decision impossible in the indistinct boundary between law and politics. This *non-liquet*, or identification of a gap in the law that the law cannot answer, illustrates the 'state of exception' contemplated by the law where the law is paralysed or rendered inapplicable.

This then is the primary obstacle to overcome if the law is to provide an answer to the phenomenon of aggression. The response to this is that the law provides for both ordinary and extraordinary situations. Force and violence are extraordinary situations but nevertheless still under the law as either law enforcement or law breaking. Even necessity is no real exclusion from law because it is bound to certain terms including that it must be temporary and for the purpose of restoring legal order and not overthrowing it. Thus presumably law is the locus of the debate and principally its international criminal law subset. What are the terms of this inclusion?

The argument presented in previous chapters is that the discourse within international criminal law is a universalized penal theory, practice and set of institutions and practitioners. These work through states but natural persons are ultimately responsible as part of endogenous groups. With specific reference to international criminal law, the simultaneously universalizing and particularizing aim of the ICC has been understood as to 'consolidate an international community underpinned by the primacy of the individual' (UN 1998: Statement by Minister for Foreign Affairs of Italy). Given the confusion and perplexity in the area, how could the legal knots be untangled?

The unfolding of the paradox lies in demonstrating that society has separated law and politics by imposing rules on utilizing force and thereby suppressing violence. It follows then that while deciding between the applicability and inapplicability of

1 See generally Agamben 2005a.

legality, the will of the society has been constructed through legal texts. Peace is normality and war abnormal. The legal text is the median point from which either interpretation (utilizing subtext) or construction (following context) depart.

What then are the links between unleashing violence and abusing the law? Simply that violence, being captured in the law, can no longer be unleashed with impunity without doing serious damage to the law. Further, when it is done in the name of the law, it goes beyond breaching the law per se to abusing it by enlisting its institutions, processes and language in order to abuse human rights. Therefore when society permits law *enforcement* and abhors violence as a transgression of law, the use of legal tools for violence emerges as a real possibility. This is because the semblance of legality is used to cloak violent acts which are doubly harmful to the law and the victims of misuse of the law.

Extreme violence shows up certain inadequacies in law that go beyond mere systemic lack (of law and order resources) to conceptual befuddlement (given a monopoly on violence, when is might not right?). Nevertheless, the argument is that there is a meaningful and consequential distinction between a monopoly on the legitimate use of force and a legitimate monopoly on the use of force. That is, because the law relies on a coincidence between power and authority (Higgins 1963: 15), or principle (UN 2004), a crisis appears when these are asunder which is not caused by an excess of law but a manipulation of its instruments.

The stakes in this inquiry are quite literally life and death because the law not only regulates both the states of life and death but also defines the boundary between them. The law does this by assigning rights and duties between the living to create different forms of and entitlement to life. This 'vital' process of the law profoundly influences social relations and can be extended along a continuum beginning with life, ending with death and encompassing everything in between.

The war on terror is a case in point. It presents the opportunity to extend freedom, democracy, development, free markets and free trade globally (The White House 2002: 4), not to mention action against drug cartels, bioterror, infectious disease and mass casualty dangers, all thus linking public health to violence and to criminalization as a tool of global governance. Here crime, war and disease are simultaneously the defined enemy in a war waged on the terrain of life itself.

For the United States, the 'war against global terrorism' is ultimately about fighting for 'democratic values and way of life' (The White House 2002: 7). Furthermore, the campaign against terrorism forges new international relationships and redefines existing ones in a future-oriented manner (The White House 2002: 7). Violence is therefore being deployed to found new revolutionary legal orders.

Giorgio Agamben's notion of the state of exception describes how sovereignty now paradoxically defends the law from outside the law in the name of security, thereby blurring, distorting or erasing the lines between law and lawlessness.[2] Due to its efficacy in addressing extraordinary circumstances, this state of exception gradually becomes the rule. Governments increasingly rely on this seemingly

2 See generally Agamben 2005a.

bottomless source of power and legitimacy which, when coupling security and risk, means that even modern democratic societies are not exempt from a state domination that approaches the totalitarian.

What do we make of all this? Torture encompasses both 'disciplinary' and 'regulatory' aspects of power. Whereas discipline orders a multiplicity of individualized persons by surveillance, training and punishment, regulation is addressed to humanity globally through life from birth to death (Foucault 2003: 242–3). With regard to war that could be characterized as aggression, Melinda Cooper has identified the issue as not only the securitization of human life that incorporates 'humanitarian warfare', but '*the whole of life*, from the micro- to the ecosystemic level' (Cooper 2008: 80). Permanent war becomes simply *a fact of life*, with no other end than its perpetuation, as fears become a source and justification for ever more intrusive laws (Cooper 2008: 98).

What is the problem to be confronted by the law when the law is captured? The United States Supreme Court had the following to say in reference to the war on terror: '[T]he laws and Constitution are designed to survive, and remain in force, in extraordinary times. Liberty and security can be reconciled; and in our system they are reconciled within the framework of the law' (*Lakhdar Boumediene et al., Petitioners v George W. Bush, President of the United States et al.* Supreme Court of the United States, unreported No. 06–1195). This proposition can be juxtaposed with the Nuremberg judgement, which says that the 'prostitution of a judicial system for the accomplishment of criminal ends involves an element of evil to the State which is not found in frank atrocities' (The Nuremberg Trials: The Justice Trial *United States of America v Alstötter et al.* ('The Justice Case') 3 T.W.C. 1 (1948)). In such an extreme situation, the legal system is itself a problem and indeed lawyers and judges the criminals by virtue of their acts and profession.

This chapter addresses these ambiguities by recommending that politicians leave the law to its devices, free of direct everyday political interference, to delineate progressively the expanding boundaries of its application to life. In this instance, the solution is specifically to provide an acceptable legal definition of aggression for the purposes of the Rome Statute. This would frame the debate as law distinct from politics and move away from the decision-making procedure such as that of the United Nations Security Council to an adjudicatory forum as exemplified by the International Criminal Court. A court as a judicial proceeding would then have the necessary independence and impartiality to decline to exercise jurisdiction in order to protect the integrity of its proceedings, and therefore of the legal system as such, by preferring not to proceed with politically motivated prosecutions which would be essentially synonymous with violence.

Foucault's notion of government's function in modernity as 'making live' is by way of correction, punishment and death violently deployed against life on behalf of life (Dillon 2007: 11). Geopolitical threat perception differs from biopolitical threat perception. The biopolitical threat is not that of an external enemy as such but within life itself. This threat to life by life is infinitely adaptable because adaptable emergence is the core vital sign of life (Dillon 2007: 12). This consideration is at odds with conceptualizations that depend solely on the use of force by state actors which rely on notions of sovereignty and the like.

In the drafting of the IMT Charter, aggression was defined to exclude 'resort to war to redress economic or political disadvantages or threats of encirclement, etc. as a defence'. It described how under this definition neither political or military, nor other considerations could excuse resorting to war. That is, peaceful settlement of grievances between states was compulsory as a matter of the criminal law (Jackson 1945). Only actual attack or invasion constituted aggression, and any possible arguments that such attack or invasion was in defence against political or economic measures were headed off in the drafting of the crime (Jackson 1945). This was despite the drafters' awareness that, from Germany's perspective, such action was considered defensive (Jackson 1945). Defining the 'aggressor' beforehand was designed to exclude any argument in the courtroom over characterization in which the Germans would participate (Jackson 1945).

Based on that preliminary effort, this chapter argues that suspending the law due to violence, or in order to unleash violence in the name of the law or protecting human rights, leads to irresolvable ambiguities of entitlement to life regarding norms and exceptions, law and fact, sanctioned and unsanctioned, legality and legitimacy, and even war and peace. The chapter addresses these ambiguities by recommending that subsequent to producing the law through consensual processes, politicians should leave the law to its devices, free of direct everyday political interference, to delineate progressively (and not after the fact) the expanding boundaries of its application.

The fruit of this effort has been the discovery and exposition of an exclusionary/inclusionary biolegal project that dates back to the origin of the law and offers a glimpse into its future. This thesis's plea is for a life-affirming biolegality: an emancipating biolegality that does not rely on unleashing death and violence as its primary tool but one that looks at the fostering and nourishing of all human life as its transcendent goal. The debate on criminalizing aggression as only a single process within an overall project should be brought back to its grounding on the legitimate concerns of humanity as a whole and not on any narrow and specific interests represented in various atomized cliques, groups or special interests vying for legitimacy.

The positive aspect of legal regulation is that it seeks overall to prevent the arbitrary loss of life, liberty and property through the untrammelled exercise of raw power. By extending the logic of a monopoly on the legitimate use of force to the international community, criminal aggression can mirror the domestic crime of treason. A legitimate monopoly on the legitimate use of force would provide a self-referentially legal use of force by recourse to legal rules. This would free up the law from violence. The only exception would be a role in distinguishing between violence and force. This is because the law gives meaning and structure to ambiguous and unstructured situations. Consequently, because the law is the only viable forward-looking distinguisher between law and fact, life and death, and so forth, it is the solution to defining, containing and constraining aggression through criminalizing certain of its aspects while affirming the human in an inclusive fashion.

In this instance, the beginning is specifically to provide an acceptable legal definition of criminal aggression for the purposes of the Rome Statute that is removed from the political decision-making procedure of the United Nations Security Council. The test and proof of this proposition is the simple thought experiment outlined in Chapter 1: that is, must a judicial entity decline to entertain a prosecution for criminal aggression as (by that very fact) an abuse, or misuse of legal procedure? The answer is no. However, it may. This is in essence a question of jurisdiction, which would follow an imposed legitimate monopoly on the legitimate use of force. If the court had a definition before itself, it would try the case according to the evidence presented. If the court lacked such a definition, it could then dismiss the proceedings for lack of jurisdiction or stay the proceedings as an abuse of its process. That is, the law manifestly contains the answer to any challenges of its competence and especially so with regard to life itself. What the law needs to signify in order to attain or retain this capacity is an emphasis of the protection of life and a de-emphasis of the dispensation of death. The administrators of the law should make a point of keeping the exception exceptional in order to maintain the normal as normal. The self-recognition of law that its processes, institutions, practitioners, and language could be abused is the homage that virtue must pay to vice.

Epilogue

There is a dilemma inherent in affirming the legitimacy and potency of legality in the regulation of mass violence while recognizing the role of the law in conspiring with political authority to sectionalize crimes of aggression. One must be mindful of the danger inherent in law's capacity to become complicit in abuse of power because law mystifies domination as well as anything in the arcane toolbox of governing.

This thesis highlights the flaws both in the current normative frames for international law (humanitarian and customary) as a primary or pre-eminent regulator of mass violence, and the conjectural position of conventional legal instrumentalities and processes in presenting a detached legality capable of qualifying and controlling mass violence for the benefit of humanity rather than hegemony. Why then does law still have a place?

In the end, this author remains mindful of the strangeness involved in asserting the law together with acceptance of political reality in the political demarcation of law's application. On too many previous occasions legality has masked violence. However, this problem is not in the tool but in its wielding. This thesis has contributed a refined understanding of the relationship between law and violence. That understanding offers new directions for legality in addressing mass politically motivated violence. The thesis in the final analysis advocates for transforming the relationship between law and violence and repositioning legality within a wider regulatory space. Historically, the focus for law has by and large supported and enabled a hegemony, instead of all of humanity. However, this is not a problem inherent in the law but an abuse of legality. A genuine commitment with authority and legitimacy to act in the interest of humanity would transform the law by radical expansion of its constituency. This would be inclusive without excluding by focusing on human security instead of state security.

It is the transformation of the legality/violence relationship that is the key to unlocking the regulatory potential of legality within wider regulatory engagement. These include approaches that are other than legal (including a more prominent role for victims in the justice process, promoting investigation of 'truth' and not only finding of 'fact', as well as reconciliation in place of retribution). The law on its own can never stop, limit or prevent aggression. It is also through critical transformation of the application of law in confronting crimes of aggression on the way to abuse of power that this negative possibility can be called into account

The contribution of this thesis has been to show the amenability of violence to legality. Additionally, this amenability is linked to law's self-conscious autonomy in the face of its abuse. The study of the debate on codifying aggression for the ICC has therefore shown what the role of law should be and not much more than that. The irony in clearing up a space for law is the unintended consequence of an accompanying simultaneous demarcation of law's boundaries. While stipulating law's competencies, its scope and authority are at the same time limited to that very scope and authority. Therefore, methodologies such as joint scenario planning and mapping across various disciplines and competencies can provide the opportunity to harness skills that add a richer and more considered vision to problem-solving which, while incorporating legality as an approach, does not promote it as the sole value or raise it as an absolute principle.

References

Achebe, C. 1971. *Things Fall Apart*. The New Windmill Series, 162. London: Heinemann Educational.

African [Banjul] Charter on Human and Peoples' Rights, adopted 27 June 1981, OAU Doc. CAB/LEG/67/3 rev. 5, 21 I.L.M. 58 (1982), 1520 UNTS 217 entered into force 21 October 1986.

Agamben, G. 1991. *Language and Death: The Place of Negativity*. Theory and History of Literature, vol. 78. Minneapolis, MN: University of Minnesota Press.

Agamben, G. 1993. *The Coming Community. Theory out of Bounds*, vol. 1. Minneapolis, MN: University of Minnesota Press.

Agamben, G. 1998. *Homo Sacer: Sovereign Power and Bare Life* (Heller-Roazen, D. trans.). Stanford, CA: Stanford University Press.

Agamben, G. 2001a. *Means without End: Notes on Politics*. Minneapolis, MN: University of Minnesota Press

Agamben, G. 2001b. Security and Terror. *Theory and Event*, 5(4). [Online]. Available at: http://muse.jhu.edu/journals/theory_and_event/v005/5.4agamben.html [accessed: 13 August 2009].

Agamben, G. 2002. Security and Terror. *Theory and Event*, 5(4).

Agamben, G. 2004a. *The Open: Man and Animal* (Attel, K. trans.). Stanford, CA: Stanford University Press.

Agamben, G. 2004b. Life, a Work of Art without an Author: The State of Exception, the Administration of Disorder and Private Life. *German Law Journal*, 5.

Agamben, G. 2005a. *State of Exception* (Attell, K. trans.). Chicago, IL: University of Chicago Press.

Agamben, G. 2005b. *The Time that Remains: A Commentary on the Letter to the Romans*. Meridian, Crossing Aesthetics. Stanford, CA: Stanford University Press.

Agamben, G. 2009. *The Signature of All Things: On Method*. New York, Cambridge, MA: Zone Books; Distributed by MIT Press.

Agamben, G. 2011 *The Kingdom and the Glory: For a Theological Genealogy of Economy and Government*. Stanford, CA: Stanford University Press.

Agamben, G., Chiesa, L. and Mandarini, M. 2011. *The Kingdom and the Glory: For a Theological Genealogy of Economy and Government*. Meridian: Crossing Aesthetics. Stanford, CA: Stanford University Press.

Agreement for the Prosecution and Punishment of the Major War Criminals of the European Axis, and the Charter of the International Military Tribunal. London, 8 August 1945.

Alber, J., O'Connell, D.C. and Kowal, S. 2002. Personal Perspective in TV Interviews. *Pragmatics*, 12, 257–71.

Alexandrov, S.A. 1996. *Self-Defense against the Use of Force in International Law*. The Netherlands: Martinus Nijhoff Publishers.

Allen, K. 2007. Questions linger over Kenya killings. *BBC News* [Online], 10 November. Available at: http://news.bbc.co.uk/2/hi/africa/7088750.stm [accessed: 12 November 2007].

Alvarez, J.E. 1996. Nuremberg Revisited: The Tadić Case. *European Journal of International Law*, 7(2), 245–64.

Anderson, D. 2005. *Histories of the Hanged: Britain's Dirty War in Kenya and the End of Empire*. New York: W.W. Norton & Company.

Anghie, A. 2006. On Critique and the Other. In Orford, A. (ed.), *International Law and Its Others*. Cambridge: Cambridge University Press.

Aquinas, T. and Dominicans. 1981. *Summa Theologica*. Complete English edn. Allen, TX: Christian Classics.

Arendt, H. 1969. *On Violence*. New York: Harcourt, Brace & Wood.

Arendt, H. 2004. *The Origins of Totalitarianism*, 1st edn. New York: Schocken Books.

Augustine. 2003. *Concerning the City of God against the Pagans*. London: Penguin Classics.

Bailey, R. 2009. Up against the Wall: Bare Life and Resistance in Australian Immigration Detention. *Law and Critique*, 20(2), 113–32.

Bakhtin, M.M. 1973. *Problems of Dostoevsky's Poetics*. Minnesota, MN: University of Minnesota Press.

Baines, E.K. 2009. Complex Political Perpetrators: Reflections on Dominic Ongwen. *The Journal of Modern African Studies*, 47(2), 163–91.

Baker III, J.A. 1995. *The Politics of Diplomacy: Revolution, War and Peace (1989–1992)*. New York: G.P. Putman's Sons.

Baker, J.A. and DeFrank, T.M. 1995. *The Politics of Diplomacy: Revolution, War, and Peace, 1989–1992*. New York: Putnam.

BBC. 2012a. Kenya: Will radical Islam ruin Mombasa's charms? http://www.bbc.co.uk/news/world-africa-19650148.

BBC. 2012b. Kenya Tana Delta massacres raise election violence fear http://www.bbc.co.uk/news/world-africa-19621246.

Balkin, J.M. 1990. Nested Oppositions: Book Review of Against Deconstruction by John M. Ellis. *Yale Law Journal*, 99(7), 1669–48.

Barshack, L. 2000. The Totemic Authority of the Court. *Law and Critique*, 11, 301–28.

Beard, J. 2003. Understanding International Development Programs as a Modern Phenomenon of Early and Medieval Christian Theology. *Australian Feminist Law Journal*, 18, 27–54.

Beard, J. 2006. The Confessional Framework of Rule of Law Development: How to Offer Salvation to Willing Legal Subjects. *Nordic Journal of International* Law, 75, 409–49.

Beck, U. 2002. The Cosmopolitan Society and Its Enemies. *Theory Culture and Society*, 19(1–2), 17–44.

Bellamy, A.J. 2006. *Just Wars: From Cicero to Iraq*. Cambridge: Polity Press.

Bellamy, A.J. 2011. Libya and the Responsibility to Protect: The Exception and the Norm. *Ethics & International Affairs*, 25(3), 263–9.

Bellamy, A.J. and Reike, R. 2010. The Responsibility to Protect and International Law. *Global Responsibility to Protect*, 2, 267–86.

Benjamin, W. 1986. *Critique of Violence, Reflections: Essays, Aphorisms, Autobiographical Writings*. New York: Schocken.

Benjamin, W. 1978. *Critique of Violence in Reflections: Essays, Aphorisms, Autobiographical Writings*, 1st edn. New York: Harcourt Brace Jovanovich.

Benjamin, W. et al. 1996. *Selected Writings*. 4. Cambridge, MA: Belknap Press.

Bernard, T.J. et al. 2010. *Vold's Theoretical Criminology*. New York: Oxford University Press.

Bikundo, E. 2007. The Trial of David Hicks and the Law on the Use of Force. *Current Issues in Criminal Justice*, 18(3), 494–7.

Bikundo, E. 2008. *Law, War and Crime: War Crimes Trials and the Reinvention of International Law* by Gerry Simpson. *Melbourne Journal of International Law*, 9(1), 301–12.

Biodefense for the 21st Century (NSW). 1989. 168 CLR 23.

Bishop, J.P. 2009. Biopolitics, Terri Schiavo, and the Sovereign Subject of Death. *Journal of Medicine and Philosophy*, 33(6), 538–57.

Blake, F. 2002. Tristes Tropiques and Systems Theory and the Literary Scene. *Soziale Systeme*, 8(1), 27–37.

Bodin, J. and Franklin, J.H. (eds).1992. *On Sovereignty: Four Chapters from the Six Books of the Commonwealth*. Cambridge: Cambridge University Press.

Bohannan, L. 1966. Shakespeare in the Bush. *Natural History*. [Online]. Available at: http://www.naturalhistorymag.com/editors_pick/1966_08–09_pick.html

Boniolo, G. and Di Fiore, P.P. 2009. A Defining Analysis of the Life and Death Dyad: Paving the Way for an Ethical Debate. *Journal of Medicine and Philosophy*, 33(6), 609–34.

Borradori, G. 2004. *Philosophy in a Time of Terror: Dialogues with Jurgen Habermas and Jacques Derrida*. Chicago, IL: University of Chicago Press Books.

Bourdieu, P. 1977. The Force of Law: Toward a Sociology of the Juridical Field. *The Hastings Law Journal*, 38(5), 805–13.

Bourdieu, P. 1986. The Forms of Capital. In Richardson, J.G. (ed.), *Handbook of Theory and Research for the Sociology of Education*. New York: Greenwood Press.

Brownlie, I. 1963. *International Law and the Use of Force by States*. Oxford: Clarendon Press.

Brownlie, I. 2002. *Principles of Public International Law*, 6th edn. Oxford: Oxford University Press.

Brunnée, J. and Toope, S.J. 2010. The Responsibility to Protect and the Use of Force: Building Legality? *Global Responsibility to Protect*, 2, 191–212.

Burton, J. 1990. *The Sources of Islamic Law: Islamic Theories of Abrogation*. London: Edinburgh University Press.

Bush, G.W. 2004. *President of the United States Directive: Biodefense for the 21st Century*. Washington, DC: U.S. Department of Homeland Security.

Bussolini, J. 2010. Review Essay: Critical Encounter between Giorgio Agamben and Michel Foucault: Review of Recent Works of Agamben: *Il Regno e la Gloria: per una genealogia teologica dell'economia e del governo, Il sacramento del linguaggio: Archeologia del giuramento*, and *Signatura rerum: Sul metodo. Foucault Studies*, (10), 108–43.

Campbell, J. 1846. *Lives of the Lord Chancellors*, 2nd edn, vol. 1. U.S. [Online]: Forgotten Books.

Cappelletti, M. 1992.*Comparative Law Teaching and Scholarship: Methods and Objectives*. Paper to the International Conference on Comparative Law, Peking, 7–10 April 1992.

Carnegy, P. 1973. *Faust as Musician: A Study of Thomas Mann's Novel Doctor Faustus*. A New Directions Book. New York: New Directions.

Carr, E.H. and Cox, M. 2001. *The 20 Years' Crisis, 1919–1939: An Introduction to the Study of International Relations*. Houndmills, Hampshire; New York: Palgrave.

Carroll, R P. and Prickett, S. 2008. *The Bible: Authorized King James Version*. Oxford World's Classics. Oxford, New York: Oxford University Press.

Cassese, A., Gaeta, P. and Jones, J.R.W.D. (eds). 2002. *The Rome Statute of the International Criminal Court: A Commentary*. Oxford: Oxford University Press.

Chairman of the Joint Chiefs of Staff, Department of Defense. 2002. *The National Security Strategy of the United States of America*. Washington, DC: The White House, National Security Council.

Chairman of the Joint Chiefs of Staff, Department of Defense. 2006. *The National Security Strategy of the United States of America*, Washington, DC: The White House, National Security Council.

Charney, J.I. 2001. International Criminal Law and the Role of Domestic Courts. *The American Journal of International Law*, 95(1), 120–24.

Cheboi, S. 2008. Chaos erupts every five years in Burnt Forest. *Nation Media Group* [Online], 24 March. Available at: http://www.nationmedia.com/dailynation/nmgcontententry.asp?category_id=1&newsid=119694 [accessed: 24 March 2008].

Chesterman, S. 2009. UNaccountable? The United Nations, Emergency Powers, and the Rule of Law. *Vanderbilt Journal of Transnational Law*, 42, 1509

Chesterman, S. 2011. 'Leading from Behind', The Responsibility to Protect, the Obama Doctrine, and Humanitarian Intervention after Libya. *Ethics & International Affairs*, 25(3), 279–85.

Chin, W. 2007. Examining the Application of British Counterinsurgency Doctrine by the American Army in Iraq. *Small Wars & Insurgencies*, 18(1), 1–26.

Chomsky, N. 1993. *Year 501: The Conquest Continues*. London: Verso Books.

Choo, A. 2009. *Abuse of Process and Judicial Stays of Criminal Proceedings*. Oxford: Oxford Scholarship Online.

Close, F.E. (2009). *Nothing: A Very Short Introduction.* Oxford, New York: Oxford University Press.

Conrad, J., Matin, M.A. and Stade, G. 2003. *Heart of Darkness and Selected Short Fiction.* New York: Barnes & Noble Classics.

Convention for the Pacific Settlement of International Disputes (Hague I). 18 October 1907. [Online]. Available at: http://avalon.law.yale.edu/20th_century/pacific.asp [accessed: 17 August 2009].

Convention (I) For the Pacific Settlement of International Disputes (Hague I). 29 July 1899. [Online]. Available at: http://avalon.law.yale.edu/19th_century/hague01.asp [accessed: 17 August 2009].

Cooper, M. 2008. *Life as Surplus: Biotechnology and Capitalism in the Neoliberal Era.* United States: University of Washington Press.

Coorey, P. and Banham, C. 2007. PM tells the party: I could free Hicks – but won't. *The Sydney Morning Herald* [Online], 7 February. Available at: http://www.smh.com.au/news/national/pm-i-could-free-hicks – but-wont/2007/02/06/1170524096341.html [accessed: 7 February 2007].

Cox, N. 2001. *Republic of Fiji v Prasad*: A Military Government on Trial. *New Zealand Armed Forces Law Review*, 1–12.

Crabb, A. 2006. Law strips Hicks of UK citizenship in hours. *The Sydney Morning Herald* [Online], 20 August. Available at: http://www.smh.com.au/news/world/law-strips-hicks-of-uk-citizenship-in-hours/2006/08/19/1155408075077.html [accessed: 21 February 2007].

D'Amato, A. 1989. Can Any Legal Theory Constrain Any Judicial Decision? *University of Miami Law Review*, 43, 513–39.

D'Amato, A. 1991. Counterintuitive Consequences of 'Plain Meaning'. *Arizona Law Review*, 3(33), 1–52.

Daily Nation, In Pictures: MRC leader arrested http://www.nation.co.ke/News/-/1056/1534912/-/xsowi4z/-/index.html

Dallmayr, F. 1989–1990. Hermeneutics and the Rule of Law. *Cardozo Law Review*, 11(5–6), 1449–70.

Datta, R.P. 2009. From Political Emergencies and States of Exception to Exceptional States and Emergent Politics: A Neo-Durkheimian Alternative to Agamben. *International Social Science Journal*, 58, 169–82.

Davies, S.E. 2008. International Law and the State of Exception. In Bellamy, A.J., Bleiker, R., Davies, S.E. and Devetak, R. (eds), *Security and the War on Terror*. Abingdon: Routledge.

Dawkins, R. 2006. *The Selfish Gene* (30th anniversary edn). New York: Oxford University Press.

Dean, M. 2012. The Signature of Power. *Journal of Political Power*, 5(1), 101–17.

Declaration on the Preparation of Societies for Life in Peace UNGA/Res/33/73. 15 December 1978.

Declaration of the Right of Peoples to Peace UNGA Res 39/1. 12 November 1984. [Online]. Available at: http://daccessdds.un.org/doc/RESOLUTION/GEN/NR0/459/88/IMG/NR045988.pdf?OpenElement [accessed: 20 August 2009].

Deng, F.M. 1993. *Protecting the Dispossessed: A Challenge for the International Community*. Washington, DC: The Brookings Institution.

Deng, F.M. 2010. From 'Sovereignty as Responsibility' to the 'Responsibility to Protect'. *Global Responsibility to Protect*, 2, 353–70.

Derrida, J. 1981. *Dissemination*. Chicago: University Press.

Derrida, J. 1989–1990. Force de Loi: La 'Fondement Mystique de L'Autorite' (translated: Force of Law: The 'Mystical Origin of Authority'). *Cardozo Law Review*, 11(5–6), 920–1046.

Derrida, J. 2002. *Acts of Religion* (ed. Anidjar, G). Abingdon: Routledge.

Derrida, J and Bennington, G. 2009. *The Beast and the Sovereign: Seminars of Jacques Derrida*. Chicago: The University of Chicago Press.

Deuber-Mankowsky, A. 2008. Nothing is Political, Everything Can Be Politicized: On the Concept of the Political in Michel Foucault and Carl Schmitt. *Telos*, 142(Spring), 135–61.

Devetak, R. 2008a. Failures, Rogues and Terrorists: States of Exception and the North/South Divide. In Bellamy, A.J., Bleiker, R., Davies, S.E. and Devetak, R. (eds), *Security and the War on Terror*. Abingdon: Routledge.

Devetak, R. 2008b. Foucault, Discipline and Raison d'état in Early Modern Europe. *International Political Sociology*, 2(3), 270–72.

Dillon, M. 2007. Governing Terror: The State of Emergency of Biopolitical Emergence. *International Political Sociology*, 1(1), 7–28.

Dinstein, Y. 2002. *War, Aggression and Self-Defence*, 3rd edn. Cambridge: Cambridge University Press.

Dinstein, Y. and Tabory, M. (eds). 1996. War Crimes in International Law. *The Cambridge Law Journal*. The Hague: Martinus Nijhoff Publishers.

Douzinas, C. 2006. Speaking Law. In Orford, A. (ed.), *International Law and Its Others*. Cambridge: Cambridge University Press.

Durkheim, E. 1912. *The Elementary Forms of the Religious Life* (English translation by Joseph Swain: 1915). New translation by Karen E. Fields 1995. New York: Simon & Schuster.

Dyer, C. 2007. There is no war on terror. *The Guardian* [Online], 24 January. Available at: http://politics.guardian.co.uk/terrorism/story/0,1997247,00.html [accessed: 21 February 2007].

Eckhard, F. 2011. Whose Responsibility to Protect? *Global Responsibility to Protect*, 3, 89–101.

Edelstein, D. 2007. The Law of the 22 Prairial: Introduction. *Telos*, 141(Winter), 82–91.

Eliade, M. 1959. *The Sacred and the Profane: The Nature of Religion*. New York: Harcourt.

Eliade, M. 1996. *Patterns in Comparative Religion*. Lincoln: University of Nebraska Press.

Elkins, C. 2005. *Britain's Gulag: The Brutal End of Empire in Kenya*. London: Jonathan Cape Ltd.

Elliot, S.D. 1956. Techniques of Interpretation. In Schwartz, B. (ed.). *The Code Napoleon*. Westport: Greenwood Press.

Elon, M. 1994. *Jewish Law History, Sources, Principles*, vols 1–4. Philadelphia: The Jewish Publication Society.

Esposito, R. 2008. *Bios: Biopolitics and Philosophy* (Campbell, T. trans.). Minneapolis, MN: University of Minnesota Press.

Esposito, R. 2012, *Third Person: Politics of Life and Philosophy of the Impersonal* Cambridge: Polity Press.

Findlay, M. 2008. *Governing through Globalised Crime: Futures for International Criminal Justice*. Cullompton: Willan.

Fox, C.A. 2007. Sacrificial Pasts and Messianic Futures: Religion as a Political Prospect, in René Girard and Giorgio Agamben. *Philosophy Social Criticism*, 33(5), 563–95.

Foucault, M. 1975. *Discipline and Punish: The Birth of the Prison*. New York: Knopf Doubleday Publishing Group.

Foucault, M. 1993. About the Beginning of the Hermeneutics of the Self: Two Lectures at Dartmouth. *Political Theory*, 21(2), 198–227.

Foucault, M. 1998. *The History of Sexuality*, vol. 1 (Hurley, R. trans.). London: Penguin.

Foucault, M. 2003. *Society Must Be Defended: Lectures at the Collège de France, 1975–1976* (Macy, D. trans.). New York: Picador.

Foucault, M. 2005. *Hermeneutics of the Subject: Lectures at the Collège de France 1981–1982*. New York: Picador.

Foucault, M. 2008. *The Birth of Biopolitics: Lectures at the Collège de France, 1978–1979*. Basingstoke: Palgrave Macmillan.

Foucault, M. and Bouchard, D. (eds). 1977. *Language, Counter-Memory, Practice: Selected Essays and Interviews*. New York: Cornell University Press.

Foucault, M. and Faubion, J.D. (eds). 2002. *Power: Essential Works of Foucault, 1954–1984*, vol. 3 (Hurley, R. trans.). New York: New Press.

Frazer, E. and Hutchings, K. 2007. Argument and Rhetoric in the Justification of Political Violence. *European Journal of Political Theory*, 6(2), 180–99.

Frazer, J.G. and Fraser, R. 2009. *The Golden Bough: A Study in Magic and Religion*. Oxford World's Classics, new edn. Oxford: Oxford University Press.

Freud, S. and Jones, K. 1939. *Moses and Monotheism*. London: The Hogarth Press and the Institute of Psycho-analysis.

Freudenschuß, H. 1994. Between Unilateralism and Collective Security: Authorizations of the Use of Force by the UN Security Council. *European Journal of International Law*, 5(4), 492–531. [Online]. Available at: http://207.57.19.226/journal/Vol5/No4/art2–02.html [accessed: 19 June 2012].

Frowein, J. and Krisch, N. 2002. Chapter VII: Action with Respect to Threats to the Peace, Breaches of the Peace, and Acts of Aggression. In Bruno Simma (ed.), *The Charter of the United Nations: A Commentary*. Oxford: Oxford University Press, 701–37.

Gekara, E. 2009. Former MP pleads innocence against war crimes. *Daily Nation Newspaper* [Online], 4 December. http://www.nation.co.ke/News/politics/-/1064/817672/-/wu6ptcz/-/index.html [accessed: 11 April 2011].

Geneva Conventions of 1949.

Gewehr, J. 2003. *Defining Aggression for the International Criminal Court: A Proposal*. LLM in International Law. South Africa: University of Cape Town. Available at: http://www.publiclaw.uct.ac.za/usr/public_law/LLMPapers/gewehr.pdf [accessed: 2 April 2005].

Giddens, A. 1987. *The Nation State and Violence. A Contemporary Critique of Historical Materialism*, vol. 2. Los Angeles, CA: University of California Press.

Gignac, J. 1907. Anathema. In *The Catholic Encyclopedia*. New York: Robert Appleton Company. New Advent. [Online]. Available at: http://www.newadvent.org/cathen/01455e.htm [accessed: 11 April 2011].

Gill, T.D. 1995. Legal and Some Political Limitations on the Power of the UN Security Council to Exercise its Enforcement Powers Under Chapter VII of the Charter. *Netherlands Year Book of International Law*, 26, 33–138.

Gillespie, M.A. 2008. *The Theological Origins of Modernity*. Chicago: University of Chicago Press.

Girard, R, 1977. *Violence and the Sacred*. Baltimore, MD: Johns Hopkins University Press.

Girard, R. 1986. *The Scapegoat*. Baltimore: Johns Hopkins University Press.

Girard, R. 2011. *Sacrifice*. East Lansing: Michigan State University Press.

Girard, R., Oughourlian, J.M. and Lefort, G. 1987. *Things Hidden since the Foundation of the World*. Stanford, CA: Stanford University Press.

Glanville, L. 2010. The International Community's Responsibility to Protect. *Global Responsibility to Protect*, 2, 287–306.

Glueck, S. 1946. *The Nuremberg Trial and Aggressive War*. New York: A.A. Knopf.

Goldsmith, P. 2011. *The Mombasa Republican Council Conflict Assessment: Threats and Opportunities for Engagement: A Report based on Research Commissioned by Kenya Civil Society Strengthening Programme*. [Online]. Available at: http://www.kecosce.org/downloads/MRC_Conflict_Assessment_Threats_and_Opportunities_for_Engagement.pdf

Goldsmith, U.K. 1966. Ambiguities in Goethe's Faust: A Lecture for the General Reader. *The German Quarterly*, 39(3), 311–28.

Goldziher, I. 1981. *Introduction to Islamic Theology and Law*. Princeton, NJ: Princeton University Press.

Goodrich, P. 1990. *Languages of Law: From Logics of Memory to Nomadic Masks*. Law in context. London: Weidenfeld.

Gratton, P. 2011. What More is There to Say? Revisiting Agamben's Depiction of Homo Sacer. *The European Legacy*, 16(5), 599–613.

Gray, C. 2003.The Use and Abuse of the International Court of Justice Cases Concerning the Use of Force after Nicaragua. *European Journal of International Law*, 14(5), 867–905.

Gray, J. 2007. *Black Mass: Apocalyptic Religion and the Death of Utopia*. New York: Farrar, Straus and Giroux.

Grbich, J. 2006. Secrets of the Fetish in International Law's Messianism. In Orford, A. (ed.), *International Law and Its Others*. Cambridge: Cambridge University Press.

Green, L.C. 2000. *The Contemporary Law of Armed Conflict*. Manchester: Manchester University Press.

Greenberg, K. and Dratel, J.L. (eds), 2005. *The Torture Papers: The Road to Abu Ghraib*. New York: Cambridge University Press.

Gregory, D. 2005. Book Review: Colonial Precedents and Sovereign Powers: A Response. *Progress in Human Geography*, 29(3), 367–79.

Grotius, H. and Kolb, R. (eds). 2005. *The Rights of War and Peace Book II [1625]*. USA: Liberty Fund.

Hague Convention II 1899.

Hague IV of 1907.

Harris, G.W. 1911. Bio-Politics. *The New Age: A Weekly Review of Politics, Literature, and Art*, 10(9), 197.

Hegel, G.W.F. 1983. *Hegel and the Human Spirit: A Translation of the Jena Lectures on the Philosophy of Spirit (1805–6) with Commentary*. (Rauch, L. trans.). Detroit, MI: Wayne State University Press.

Heidegger, M. 2003. The Question Concerning Technology. In Stassen, M. (ed.), *Martin Heidegger: Philosophical and Political Writings*. London: Continuum International Publishing Group.

Heinlein, F. 2002. *British Government Policy and Decolonisation 1945–1963: Scrutinising the Official Mind*. London: Frank Cass Publishers.

Hersh, S.M. 2005. The Coming Wars: What the Pentagon can now do in secret. *The New Yorker* [Online], 24 January. Available at: http://www.newyorker.com/archive/2005/01/24/050124fa_fact [accessed: 1 December 2007].

Higgins, R. 1963. *Problems and Process: International Law and How We Use It*. Oxford: Clarendon Press.

Hindess, B. 2008. Government and Discipline. *International Political Sociology*, 2(3), 268–70.

Hobbes, T. 1996. *Leviathan*. Cambridge: Cambridge University Press.

Hobbes, T. and Tuck, R. (eds). 2005. *Leviathan*. Cambridge: Cambridge University Press.

Hoffman, F.F. 2006. Human Rights the Self and the Other. In Orford, A. (ed.), *International Law and Its Others*. Cambridge: Cambridge University Press.

Horton, S. 2009. The Bush Six to be indicted. *The Daily Beast* [Online], 13 April. Available at: http://www.thedailybeast.com/blogs-and-stories/2009–04–13/the-bush-six-to-be-indicted/ [accessed: 14 April 2009].

Hubert, H. and Mauss, M. 1964. *Sacrifice: Its Nature and Function*. Chicago: University of Chicago Press.

ICC. 1947. Proceedings of the IMT, Nuremberg, Official Documents, vol. 1. [Online]. Available at: http://avalon.law.yale.edu/imt/imtconst.asp

ICC. 1998. Press Release L/2890 Secretary-General Says Establishment of International Criminal Court Is Major Step in March towards Universal Human Rights, Rule Of Law. [Online]. Available at: http://www.icc-cpi.int/NR/rdonlyres/01668F61–04C7–405C-BE43-CA3078E9DFAD/274176/41833.pdf [accessed: 11 April 2011].

ICC. 2006a. ICC Prosecutor's Letter of 10 February 2006 re Iraqi War response. [Online]. Available at: http://www.icc-cpi.int/library/organs/otp/OTP_letter_to_senders_re_Iraq_9_February_2006.pdf [accessed: 26 February 2006].

ICC. 2006b. Session 2: NGOs and Other Experts. The Hague. [Online]. Available at: http://www.icc-cpi.int/menus/icc/structure%20of%20the%20court/office%20of%20the%20prosecutor/network%20with%20partners/public%20hearings/second%20public%20hearing/session%202/session%202?lan=en-GB [accessed: 11 April 2011].

ICC. 2009a. Annex II Report of the Special Working Group on the Crime of Aggression ICC-ASP/6/20/Add.1 [Online]. Available at: http://www.icc-cpi.int/iccdocs/asp_docs/SWGCA/ICC-ASP-6–20-Add1-AnnexII-ENG.pdf [accessed: 20 August 2009].

ICC. 2009b. Confirmation of Charges Hearing (Open Session) Page 1 International Criminal Court Pre-trial Chamber III Situation in the Central African Republic – case ICC-01/05–01/08 Confirmation of Charges Hearing – Open Session. [Online]. Available at: http://www.icc-cpi.int/iccdocs/doc/doc618933.pdf [accessed: 11 April 2011].

ICC. 2009c. Crimes of Aggression. [Online]. Available at: http://www2.icc-cpi.int/Menus/ASP/Crime+of+Aggression/ [accessed: 19 August 2009].

ICC. 2009d. ICC Prosecutor: Kenya Can Be an Example to the World Press Release: ICC-OTP-20090918-PR452. [Online]. Available at: http://www.icc-cpi.int/menus/icc/structure%20of%20the%20court/office%20of%20the%20prosecutor/comm%20and%20ref/kenya/pr452?lan=en-GB [accessed: 11 April 2011].

ICC. 2009e. ICC Prosecutor Supports Three-Pronged Approach to Justice in Kenya ICC Press Release: ICC-OTP-20090930-PR456. [Online]. Available at: http://www.icccpi.int/menus/icc/situations%20and%20cases/situations/situation%20icc%200109/press%20releases/pr456?lan=en-GB [accessed: 11 April 2011].

ICC. 2009f. International Criminal Court Trial Chamber I Situation in the Democratic Republic of Congo – Case ICC-01/04–01/06 Hearing – Open Session Tuesday, 27 January 2009 Case No. ICC-01/04–01/06 Tuesday, ICC-01/04–01/06-T-109-ENG WT 27–01–2009 1/59 NB T [Online]. Available at: http://www.icc-cpi.int/iccdocs/doc/doc623848.pdf [accessed: 11 April 2011].

ICC. 2009g. Mr Luis Moreno-Ocampo Prosecutor of the International Criminal Court Seventeenth Diplomatic Briefing Statement. [Online]. Available at: http://www.icc-cpi.int/NR/rdonlyres/B2000A0D-2159–40E6-A24F-8952FF34D3B4/281196/OTP_DiplomaticBriefing_04112009.pdf [accessed: 11 April 2011].

ICC. 2010a. Part II Resolutions adopted by the Assembly of States Parties. [Online]. Available at: http://www.icc-cpi.int/iccdocs/asp_docs/ASP8/OR/OR-ASPR8-ENG.PART.II.pdf [accessed: 11 April 2011].

ICC. 2010b. Resolution ICC-ASP/8/Res.9 Adopted at the 10th plenary meeting, on 25 March 2010, by consensus. [Online]. Available at: http://www.icc-cpi.int/iccdocs/asp_docs/Resolutions/ICC-ASP-8-Res.9-ENG.pdf [accessed: 11 April 2011].

ICC. 2010c. Statement: OTP Press Conference on Kenya, Prosecutor Moreno-Ocampo's Statement, 1 April 2010. [Online]. Available at: http://www.icccpi.int/menus/icc/structure%20of%20the%20court/office%20of%20the%20prosecutor/reports%20and%20statements/statement/20100401?lan=en-GB [accessed: 11 April 2011].

ICC. 2010d. 18th Diplomatic Briefing 26 April 2010 ICC 2010 Luis Moreno-Ocampo Prosecutor of the International Criminal Court Statement The Hague. [Online]. Available at: http://www.icc-cpi.int/NR/rdonlyres/CA355D60-EC32–467A-8CA6F7FA93D86C0B/281862/100426LMOspeechdiplomaticbriefing_final1.pdf [accessed: 11 April 2011].

ICC. 2010e. ICC 2010 Press Release: ICC Prosecutor to visit Kenya to meet victims and listen to all Kenyans ICC-OTP-20100504-PR521. [Online]. Available at: http://www.icc-cpi.int/menus/icc/press%20and%20media/press%20releases/press%20releases%20(2010)/icc%20prosecutor%20to%20visit%20kenya%20to%20meet%20victims%20and%20listen%20to%20all%20kenyans?lan=en-GB [accessed: 11 April 2011].

ICC. 2010f. Policy Paper on Preliminary Examinations DRAFT. The Hague. [Online]. Available at: http://www.icc-cpi.int/NR/rdonlyres/E278F5A2-A4F9–43D7–83D2–6A2C9CF5D7D7/282515/OTP_Draftpolicypaperonpreliminaryexaminations04101.pdf [accessed: 11 April 2011].

ICC. 2010g. 19th Diplomatic Briefing Statement Mr Luis Moreno-Ocampo Prosecutor of the International Criminal Court. [Online]. Available at: http://www.icc-cpi.int/NR/rdonlyres/F67584DE-F045–45E2–9503–8F4D16B3DEAA/282656/LMO_DiploBriefingspeech_03112011.pdf [accessed: 11 April 2011].

ICC. 2010h. Kampala ICC Conference Resolution RC/Res.6 [Online]. Available at http://www.icc-cpi.int/iccdocs/asp_docs/Resolutions/RC-Res.6-ENG.pdf [accessed 15 March 2013].

ICC. 2011a. The Appeals Chamber Situation in the Democratic Republic of the Congo Situation in the Democratic Republic of the Congo Public Redacted Version Prosecutor's Document in Support of the Appeal brought by the Prosecution against Pre- Trial Chamber I's 10 February 2006 Decision on the then prosecutor's Application for Warrants of Arrest, Article 58. [Online]. Available at: http://www.icc-cpi.int/iccdocs/doc/doc1009321.pdf [accessed: 11 April 2011].

ICC. 2011b. Widespread or systematic killings in Cote d'Ivoire may trigger OTP investigation. [Online]. Available at: http://www.icc-cpi.int/NR/exeres/85A578D5–946A-44C3–9908–1C2243062EF0.htm [accessed: 11 April 2011].

ICC. 2011c. Situations and cases. [Online]. Available at: http://www.icc-cpi.int/Menus/ICC/Situations+and+Cases/ [accessed: 11 April 2011].

ICC Document. 2007. *Informal Inter-Sessional Meeting of the Special Working Group on the Crime of Aggression, Held at the Liechtenstein Institute on Self-Determination ICC-ASP/6/SWGCA/INF.1 held at Princeton University, 11- 14 June 2007*. Woodrow Wilson School, Princeton University, United States. [Online]. Available at: http://www.icc-cpi.int/library/asp/ICC-ASP-6-SWGCA-INF.1_English.pdf [accessed: 22 January 2008].

ICC Statement. 2011. *Widespread or Systematic Killings in Cote d'Ivoire May Trigger OTP Investigation*, 6 April. [Online]. Available at: http://www.icc-cpi.int/menus/icc/structure%20of%20the%20court/office%20of%20the%20prosecutor/reports%20and%20Statements/Statement/otpStatement060411 [accessed: 19 June 2012].

ICJ. 1996. *The Legality of the Threat or Use of Nuclear Weapons (Advisory Opinion of 8 July 1996)*. [Online]. Available at: http://www.icj-cij.org/docket/index.php?p1=3&p2=4&k=e1&p3=4&case=95

ICJ. 1999. *Questions of Interpretation and Application of the 1971 Montreal Convention arising from the Aerial Incident at Lockerbie (Libyan Arab Jamahiriya v United Kingdom)- Provisional Measures Order of 14 April 1992*.

ICJ. 2007. *Special Working Group on the Crime of Aggression, ICC Assembly of States Parties, Informal Inter-Sessional Meeting of the Special Working Group on the Crime of Aggression, 6th session, ICC Doc ICC-ASP/6/SWGCA/INF.1 (25 July 2007)*.

ICJ. Questions of Interpretation and Application of the 1971 Montreal Convention arising from the Aerial Incident at Lockerbie (*Libyan Arab Jamahiriya v United Kingdom*) [1992] ICJ Reports.

ICJ. The Application of the Convention on the Prevention and Punishment of the Crime of Genocide (*Bosnia and Herzegovina v Serbia and Montenegro*) [2007] Judgment, ICJ.

ICJ. The Legality of the Threat or Use of Nuclear Weapons, International Court of Justice (Advisory Opinion of 8 July 1996) General List no. 95.

ICRC. 2007. *Report on the Treatment of Fourteen 'High Value Detainees' in CIA Custody by the International Committee of the Red Cross*. Washington, DC: Central Intelligence Agency.

International Commission on Intervention and State Sovereignty. 2001. *The Responsibility to Protect*. Ottawa: IDRC.

International Conference on Military Trials, Report of Robert H Jackson, United States Representative to the International Conference on Military Trials: London, 1945 (1949). [Online]. Available at: http://avalon.law.yale.edu/imt/jack08.asp [accessed: 15 July 2009].

International Criminal Tribunal for Rwanda, Rules of Procedure and Evidence Adopted on 29 June 1995 pursuant to Article 14 of the *Statute of the International Criminal Tribunal for Rwanda*, annexed to *Resolution 955*, SC Res 955, UN SCOR, 49th sess, 3453rd mtg, UN Doc S/RES/955 (1994).

International Law Committee. 1996. *Draft Code of Crimes against the Peace and Security of Mankind 1996*. [Online]. Available at: http://untreaty.un.org/ilc/texts/instruments/english/draft%20articles/7_4_1996.pdf [accessed: 19 June 2012].

International Peace Conference. 1907. Opening of Hostilities (1907 Hague III); 18 October 1907. [Online]. Available at: http://avalon.law.yale.edu/20th_century/hague03.asp [accessed: 17 August 2009].

Israel, F.L. 1967. *Major Peace Treaties of Modern History 1648–1967*. New York: Chelsea House Publishers.

Jackson, R. 1945. International Conference on Military Trials, Report of Robert H Jackson, United States Representative to the International Conference on Military Trials: London, 1945 (1949). [Online]. Available at: http://avalon.law.yale.edu/imt/jack08.asp [accessed: 15 July 2009].

Jacob, I.H. 1970. *The Inherent Jurisdiction of the Court*. London: Stevens & Sons.

Jantz, H. 1962. Goethe, Faust, Alchemy, and Jung. *The German Quarterly*, 35(2), 129–41.

Jenkins, F. 2004. Dialogue in the Aftermath: On Good, Evil and Responsibility after September 11. *borderlands ejournal*, 3(1). [Online]. Available at: http://www.borderlands.net.au/vol3no1_2004/jenkins_dialogue.htm [accessed: 9 October 2009].

Johns, J. 2005. Guantanamo Bay and the Annihilation of the Exception. *European Journal of International Law*, 16(4), 613–35.

Justice Report. 2011. Trials Have Not Helped Reconciliation, Survey Shows. [Online]. Available at: http://www.bim.ba/en/264/10/32161/ [accessed: 11 April 2011].

Kaka, A. 2011. Ivory Coast leader Ouattara promises legal action against Gbagbo. *Jurist* [Online]. 12 April. Available at: http://jurist.org/paperchase/2011/04/ivory-coast-leader-ouattara-promises-legal-action-against-gbagbo.php [accessed: 19 June 2012].

Kantorowicz, E.H. 1997. *The King's Two Bodies: A Study in Mediaeval Political Theology*. Princeton, NJ: Princeton University Press.

'Kellogg–Briand Pact; 1928'. *United States Statutes at Large*. [Online]. Available at: http://avalon.law.yale.edu/20th_century/kbhear.asp#treatytext [accessed: 17 August 2009].

Ki-moon, B. 2009. *Report of the Secretary General – Implementing the Responsibility to Protect, UN A/63/677*. 12 January 2009. [Online]. Available at: http://www.responsibilitytoprotect.org/index.php?module=uploads&func=download&fileId=655 [accessed: 19 June 2012].

Kiarie, Joe. 2012. Mistrust after Police fail in Tana http://www.standardmedia.co.ke/?articleID=2000066228&story_title=Mistrust-after-Police-fail-in-Tana.

King, M. and Schutz, A. 1994. The Ambitious Modesty of Niklas Luhmann. *Journal of Law and Society*, 21(3), 261–87.

Kisia, Allan. 2012. Police: We can handle Tana available at: http://www.standardmedia.co.ke/?articleID=2000065995&story_title=-Police:-We-can-handle-Tana [Accessed on 15th March 2013]

Kisner, W. 2007. Agamben, Hegel, and the State of Exception. *Cosmos and History: The Journal of Natural and Social Philosophy*, 3(2–3), 222–53.

Knight, W.A. 2011. The Development of the Responsibility to Protect – From Evolving Norm to Practice. *Global Responsibility to Protect*, 3(1), 3–36.

Köchler, H. 2003. *Global Justice or Global Revenge?: International Criminal Justice at the Crossroads: Philosophical Reflections on the Principles of the International Legal Order Published on the Occasion of the Thirtieth Anniversary of the Foundation of the International Progress Organization.* New York: Springer Science.

Kolb, R. 1997. Origin of the Twin Terms *jus ad bellum* and *jus in bello*. Paper to the International Review of the Red Cross.

Koskenniemi, M. 1989. *From Apology to Utopia: The Structure of International Legal Argument*. Helsinki: Finnish Lawyers Publishing Company.

Koskenniemi, M. 2002. Between Impunity and Show Trials. *Max Planck Yearbook of United Nations Law*, 6(1), 1–32.

Koskenniemi, M. 2004a. 'By Their Acts You Shall Know Them…' (And Not by Their Legal Theories). *European Journal of International Law*, 15(4), 839–51.

Koskenniemi, M. 2004b. International Law as Political Theology: How to Read Nomos der Erde? *Constellations*, 11(4), 492–511.

Lemke, T. 2011. *Biopolitics: An Advanced Introduction*. New York: New York University Press.

Lessig, L. 1995. The Limits of Lieber. *Cardozo Law Review*, 16(6), 2249–72.

Letsas, G. 2004. The Truth in Autonomous Concepts: How to Interpret the ECHR. *European Journal of International Law*, 15(2), 279–305.

Locke, J. and Laslett, P. (eds). 2005. *Two Treatises of Government*. Cambridge: Cambridge University Press.

Louis, W.R. 2006. *Ends of British Imperialism. The Scramble for Empire, Suez and Decolonization: Collected Essays*. New York: Palgrave Macmillan.

Löwith, K. 1949. *Meaning in History: The Theological Implications of the Philosophy of History*. Chicago: University of Chicago Press.

Luhmann, N. 1995a. Legal Argumentation: An Analysis of its Form. *Modern Law Review*, 58(3), 285–98.

Luhmann, N. 1995b. *Social Systems* (Bednarz, J.J. and Baecker, D. trans.). Stanford, CA: Stanford University Press.

Luhmann, N. 2002. *Society's Law* (Ziegert, K. trans.). Abingdon: Routledge.

Luhmann, N. 2004. *Law as a Social System* (Ziegert, K. trans.). New York: Oxford University Press.

Macleod, C. 2010. Towards a Philosophical Account of Crimes against Humanity. *European Journal of International Law*, 21(2), 281–302.

McGreal, C. 2006. Mau Mau veterans to sue Britain over torture and illegal killings in Kenya: Action alleges human rights abuses in 1950s; Case runs risk of reviving internal divisions. *The Guardian* [Online], 6 October. Available at: http://www.guardian.co.uk/world/2006/oct/06/kenya.topstories3 [accessed: 12 November 2007].

Magnuson, R. 2008. Just Barely: Agamben's Reading of Bare Life from Benjamin's Critique of Violence. *Strategies of Critique*, 1(1), 73–85.

Malanczuk, P. 1997. *Akehurst's Modern Introduction to International Law*. Abingdon: Routledge.

Mann, R. 1982. The Faustian Pattern in 'The Devils'. *Canadian Slavonic Papers/ Revue Canadienne des Slavistes*, 24(3), 239–44.

Maogoto, J.N. 2005. *Battling Terrorism: Legal Perspectives on the Use of Force and the War on Terror*. Aldershot: Ashgate.

Marchart, O. 2002. On Drawing a Line: Politics and the Significatory Logics of Inclusion/Exclusion. *Soziale Systeme*, 8(1), 69–87.

Matthews, M.W. 2008. Tracking the Emergence of a New International Norm: The Responsibility to Protect and the Crisis in Darfur. *Boston College International & Comparative Law Review*, 31, 137–52.

Medew, J. 2008. Donors not truly 'dead' when organs removed. *Brisbane Times* [Online], 20 October. Available at: http://www.brisbanetimes.com.au/news/national/donors-not-truly-dead-when-organs-removed/2008/10/19/1224351091401.html [accessed: 20 October 2008].

Mégrét, F. 2002. 'War'? Legal Semantics and the Move to Violence. *European Journal of International Law*, 13(2), 361–99

Mégret, F. 2006. From 'Savages' to 'Unlawful Combatants': A Postcolonial Look at International Humanitarian Law's 'Other'. In Orford, A. (ed.), *International Law and Its Others*. Cambridge: Cambridge University Press.

Menya, W. and Reuters. 2009. Ocampo urges Kenya unity over reforms. [Online], 1 November. http://www.nation.co.ke/News/-/1056/680212/-/item/1/-/100yn8fz/-/index.html [accessed: 11 April 2011].

Merryman, J.H. 1985. *The Civil Law Tradition*. Stanford: Stanford University Press.

Messick, B. 1986. The Mufti, the Text and the World: Legal Interpretation in Yemen. *Man: Journal of the Royal Anthropological Institute*, 21(1), 102–19.

Military Commissions Act 2006. Pub. L. No. 109–366, 120 United States Stat. 2600 (17 October 2006).

Mills, C. 2004. Agamben's Messianic Politics: Biopolitics, Abandonment and Happy Life. *Contretemps*, 5, 42–62.

Miller, H. (ed.). 1934. *The Caroline Case: Treaties and Other International Acts of the United States of America*. 4 (Documents 80–121), 1836–46. [Online]. Available at: http://avalon.law.yale.edu/19th_century/br-1842d.asp [accessed: 27 July 2009].

Minca, C. 2007. Agamben's Geographies of Modernity. *Political Geography*, 26(1), 78–97.

Minca, C. 2009. Guest Editorial: The Reign and the Glory: or, Reflections on the Theological Foundations of the Credit Crunch. *Environment and Planning D: Society and Space*, 27(2), 177–82.

Momanyi, B. 2006. Police declare all-out war on the Mungiki sect. *Religion News Blog* [Online], 20 January. Available at: http://www.religionnewsblog.

com/13330/police-declare-all-out-war-on-the-mungiki-sect [accessed: 14 June 2007].

Mondzain, M. 2005. *Image, Icon, Economy: The Byzantine Origins of the Contemporary Imaginary, Cultural Memory in the Present*. Stanford, CA: Stanford University Press.

Murray, A. and Whyte, J. 2011. *The Agamben Dictionary*. Edinburgh: Edinburgh University Press.

Mwanzia, M. 2010. Ocampo's action plans. [Online], 2 April. http://www.standardmedia.co.ke/InsidePage.php?id=2000006874&catid=4&a=1 [accessed: 11 April 2011].

Neal, A.W. 2004. Cutting off the King's Head: Foucault's Society Must be Defended and the Problem of Sovereignty. *Alternatives: Global, Local, Political*, 29(4), 373–98.

Nietzche, F. 1886. *Beyond Good and Evil*. United States: Wilder Publications.

Noll, G. 2008. The Miracle of Generative Violence: René Girard and the Use of Force in International Law. *Leiden Journal of International Law*, 21(3), 563–80.

Nouwen, S. and Werner, W.G. 2011. Doing Justice to the Political: The International Criminal Court in Uganda and Sudan. *The European Journal of International Law*, 21(4), 941–96.

NTV Kenya. 2012. Police blame Executive for failing to quell Tana violencehttp://www.youtube.com/watch?v=Dz8KWFnUels

Nuremberg Trial Proceedings, vol. 1: Charter of the International Military Tribunal. [Online]. Available at: http://avalon.law.yale.edu/imt/imtconst.asp#art6 (accessed: 23 August 2009).

Nuremberg Trials: The Justice Trial, *United States of America v Alstötter* et al. ('The Justice Case') 3 T.W.C. 1 (1948), 6 L.R.T.W.C. 1 (1948), 14 Ann. Dig. 278 (1948). [Online]. Available at: http://www.law.umkc.edu/faculty/projects/ftrials/nuremberg/Alstoetter.htm#War%20Crimes%20and%20Crimes%20Against [accessed: 6 August 2009].

Nyamboga, N. 2007. Tough choices to be made in war on Mungiki. *East Africa Standard News* [Online], 7 June. Available at: http://www.eastandard.net/archives/cl/hm_news/news.php?articleid=1143969468 [accessed: 12 June 2007].

O'Donnell, G.A. 2000. Democratic Theory and Comparative Politics. *Studies in Comparative International Development*, 36(1), 519–70.

O'Donnell, G.A. 2001. Democratic Theory and Comparative Politics. *Studies in Comparative International Development*, 1(36), 45. [Online]. Available at: http://democracy.stanford.edu/Seminar/O'Donnell.pdf [accessed: 6 March 2012].

Oketch, Willis. 2012. Arrest warrants ready for top MRC officials. Available at: http://www.standardmedia.co.ke/?articleID=2000068836&story_title=Kenya-Arrest-warrants-ready-for-top-MRC-officials [accessed: 15 March 2013].

Orford, A. 2003. *Reading Humanitarian Intervention: Human Rights and the Use of Force in International Law*. New York: Cambridge University Press.

Orford, A. 2006a. A Jurisprudence of the Limit. In Orford, A. (ed.), *International Law and Its Others*. Cambridge: Cambridge University Press.

Orford, A. 2006b. Trade, Human Rights and the Economy of Sacrifice. In Orford, A. (ed.), *International Law and Its Others*. Cambridge: Cambridge University Press.

Orford, A. 2009. Jurisdiction without Territory: From the Holy Roman Empire to the Responsibility to Protect. *Michigan Journal of International Law*, 30(3), 981–1015.

Orford, A. 2011. *International Authority and the Responsibility to Protect*. New York: Cambridge University Press.

Pakenham, T. 1992. *The Scramble for Africa*. United Kingdom: HarperCollins.

Pal, R. 1953. *Dissentient Judgment of Justice Pal: International Military Tribunal for the Far East*.

Pankhurst, R. 1999. Italian Fascist War Crimes in Ethiopia: A History of Their Discussion, from the League of Nations to the United Nations (1936–1949). *Northeast African Studies* 6(1), 83–140. Project MUSE. [Online]. Available at: http://muse.jhu.edu/ [accessed: 21 January 2011].

Patel, K. 1997. God's Little Helper. *Times Higher Education* [Online], 14 March. Available at: http://www.timeshighereducation.co.uk/story.asp?storyCode=101663&sectioncode=26 [accessed: 5 October 2008].

Paulus, A.L. 2004. Peace through Justice – The Future of the Crime of Aggression in a Time of Crisis. *Wayne Law Review*, 50(Spring), 1–36.

Pennington, K. 1993. *The Prince and the Law 1200–1600: Sovereignty and Rights in the Western Legal Tradition*. Los Angeles, CA: University of California Press.

Pert, A. 2011. Legality blurred in Libya intervention. *The Australian*, 15 April, [Online]. Available at: http://www.theaustralian.com.au/news/world/legality-blurred-in-libya-intervention/story-e6frg6ux-1226039308281 [accessed: 19 June 2012].

Peters, A. 2009. Humanity as the A and Ω of Sovereignty. *European Journal of International Law*, 20(3), 513–44.

Rabinow, P. and Rose, N. 2006. Biopower Today. *BioSocieties*, 1(2), 195–217.

Rahim, A. 1911. *The Principles of Muhammadan Jurisprudence According to the Hanafi Maliki, Shaffi and Hanbali Schools*. London: Luzac.

Rasch, W. 2000. *Niklas Luhmann's Modernity: The Paradoxes of Differentiation*. Stanford, CA: Stanford University Press.

Rasch, W. 2002. A Completely New Politics or Excluding the Political? Agamben's Critique of Sovereignty. *Soziale Systeme*, 8(1), 38–53.

Raulff, U. 2004. Interview with Giorgio Agamben – Life, a Work of Art without an Author: The State of Exception, the Administration of Disorder and Private Life. *German Law Journal*, 5(5), 609–14.

Rawls, J. 1999. *A Theory of Justice*. Oxford: Oxford University Press.

Reid, J. 2006. *The Biopolitics of the War on Terror: Life Struggles, Liberal Modernity and the Defence of Logistical Societies*. Manchester: Manchester University Press.

Reinold, T. 2011. The United States and the Responsibility to Protect: Impediment, Bystander, or Norm Leader? *Global Responsibility to Protect*, 3, 61–87.

Resolution on Principles of International Law concerning Friendly Relations and Cooperation among States in accordance with the Charter of the United Nations. UNGA Resolution 2625 (XXV) (24 October 1970).

Richey, D. 2011. ICC prosecutor certain of Gaddafi war crimes charges. *Jurist* [Online], 25 March. Available at: http://jurist.org/paperchase/2011/03/icc-prosecutor-certain-of-gaddafi-war-crimes-charges.php?utm_source=feedburner&utm_medium=feed&utm_campaign=Feed%3A+pitt%2FvLdl+%28JURIST+-+Paper+Chase+%5Bfull%5D%29 [accessed: 19 June 2012].

Roberts, A. and Guelff, R. 2000. *Documents on the Laws of War*. Oxford: Oxford University Press. *Rome Statute of the International Criminal Court*, opened for signature 17 July 1998 (entered into force 1 July 2002).

Rome Statute of the International Criminal Court (1998 entry into force July 2002).

Rose, N. and Miller, P. 1992. Political Power beyond the State: Problematics of Government. *The British Journal of Sociology*, 43(2), 173–205.

Rosenberg, S.P. 2009. Responsibility to Protect: A Framework for Prevention. *Global Responsibility to Protect*, 1, 442–77.

Ross, A. 2012. Agamben's Political Paradigm of the Camp: Its Features and Reasons.*Constellation*, 19(3), 421–34.

Sands, P. 2008. Torture Team: The Responsibility of Lawyers for Abusive Interrogation. *Melbourne Journal of International Law*, 9(2), 365–80.

Sarkin, J. 2010. The Responsibility to Protect and Humanitarian Intervention in Africa. *Global Responsibility to Protect*, 2, 371–87.

Sarkin, J. and Paterson, M. 2010. Introduction. Special Issue for GR2P: Africa's Responsibility to Protect. *Global Responsibility to Protect*, 2, 339–52.

Schabas, W. 2007. *An Introduction to the International Criminal Court*. Cambridge, UK; New York: Cambridge University Press.

Schmitt, C. 1985. *Political Theology: Four Chapters on the Concept of Sovereignty* (Schwab, G.D. trans.). London: The University of Chicago Press.

Schmitt, C. 1996a. *The Concept of the Political* (Schwab, G.D. trans.). London: The University of Chicago Press.

Schmitt, C. 1996b. *The Leviathan in the State Theory of Thomas Hobbes: Meaning and Failure of a Political Symbol* (Schwab, G. and Hilfstein, E. trans.). Westport, CT: Greenwood Publishing Group.

Schmitt, C. 2004. *The Theory of the Partisan: A Commentary/Remark on the Concept of the Political* (Goodson, A.C. trans.). New York: Telos Press Publishing.

Schmitt, C. 2005. *Political Theology: Four Chapters on the Concept of Sovereignty*. Chicago: University of Chicago Press.

Schmitt, C. 2006. *The Nomos of the Earth in the International Law of the Jus Publicum Europeaum*. USA: Telos Press Publishing.

Schmitt, C. 2008. *Political Theology II: The Myth of Closure of Any Political Theology*. Cambridge: Polity Press.

Schott, J. 2007. Chapter VII as Exception: Security Council Action and the Regulative Ideal of Emergency. *Northwestern Journal of International Human Rights*, 6(1), 24.

Seung, T.K. 2006. *Goethe, Nietzsche, and Wagner: Their Spinozan Epics of Love and Power*. Lanham, MD.: Lexington Books.

Shaw, R., Waldorf, L. and Hazan, P. 2010. *Localizing Transitional Justice: Interventions and Priorities after Mass Violence*. Stanford studies in human rights. Stanford, CA: Stanford University Press.

Simma, B., Mosler, H., Paulus, A. and Chaitidou, E. (eds). 2002. *The Charter of the United Nations: A Commentary*. Oxford: Oxford University Press.

Simons, J. 2008. Aestheticisation of politics: From Fascism to Radical Democracy. *Journal for Cultural Research* 12(3): 207–229

Simons, M. 2006. Hussein's Case Won't Bolster International Human Rights Law, Experts Fear. *New York Times* [Online], 31 December. Available at: http://www.nytimes.com/2006/12/31/world/middleeast/31history.html?_r=1&em&ex=1167714000&en=2ac46f7965649d75&ei=5087%0A&oref=slogin [accessed: 3 January 2007].

Simpson, G.J. 2004. *Great Powers and Outlaw States: Unequal Sovereigns in the International Legal Order*. Cambridge studies in international and comparative law. Cambridge, UK; New York, NY: Cambridge University Press.

Simpson, G. 2007. *Law, War & Crime*. Cambridge: Polity Press.

Skradol, N. 2011. 'There is Nothing Funny about It': Laughing Law at Stalin's Party Plenum. *Slavic Review*, 70(2), 334–52.

Skradol, N. 2012. Carnival of Exception: Gabriele D'Annunzio's 'Dialogues with the Crowd'. *Rhetorica*: *A Journal of the History of Rhetoric*, 30(1), 74–93.

Snyder, J.L. and Vinjamuri, L. 2003–2004. Trials and Errors: Principle and Pragmatism in Strategies of International Justice. *International Security*, 28(3), 5–44. Project MUSE. [Online]. Available at: http://muse.jhu.edu/ [accessed: 2 April 2011].

Sorel, G. 1915. *Reflections on Violence*. (Hulme, T.E. trans.). USA: B.W. Huebsch.

Stäheli, U. and Stichweh, R. 2002. Inclusion/Exclusion – Systems Theoretical and Poststructuralist Perspectives. *Soziale Systeme*, 8(1), 3–7.

Stahn, Carsten. 2007. Responsibility to Protect: Political Rhetoric or Emerging Legal Norm? *American Journal of International Law*, 101, 99–120.

Statute of the International Criminal Tribunal for Rwanda, annexed to *Resolution 955*, SC Res 955, UN SCOR, 49th sess, 3453rd mtg, UN Doc S/RES/955 (1994).

Stedman, S.J. 2007. UN Transformation in an Era of Soft Balancing. I*nternational Affairs*, 83(5).

Stone, J. 1958. *Aggression and World Order: A Critique of United Nations Theories of Aggression*. USA: The Lawbook Exchange, Ltd.

Strauss, L. 1953. *Natural Right and History*. Chicago: University of Chicago Press.

Strauss, L. 1967. Jerusalem and Athens, Some Introductory Reflections. *Commentary*, June. [Online]. Available at: http://www.commentarymagazine.com/article/jerusalem-and-athens-some-introductory-reflections/

Strauss, L. 1981. Progress or Return? The Contemporary Crisis in Western Civilization. *Modern Judaism*, 1(1), 17–45.

Strauss, L. 1989. Thucydides: The Meaning of Political History. In Pangle, T.L. (ed.) *The Rebirth of Classical Political Rationalism*. Chicago, IL: University of Chicago Press.

Swart, M. 2011. Tadić Revisited: Some Critical Comments on the Legacy and the Legitimacy of the ICTY. *Goettingen Journal of International Law (GoJIL)*, 3(30), 985–1009.

Tallgren, I. 2002. The Sensibility and Sense of International Criminal Law. *European Journal of International Law*, 13(3), 561–95.

Tamanaha, B. 1993. The Folly of the 'Social Scientific' Concept of Legal Pluralism. *Journal of Law and Society*, 2(20), 192–217.

Tamanaha, B. 2005. Revitalizing Legal Positivism: The Contemporary Relevance of the Separation Thesis (Legal Studies Research Paper #05–006). St John's University School of Law. [Online]. Available at: http://ssrn.com/Abstract=637184 [accessed: 12 August 2006].

Teubner, G. 2001. Alienating Justice: On the Surplus Value of the Twelfth Camel. In Nelken, D. and Pribán, J. (eds), *Law's New Boundaries: Consequences of Legal Autopoiesis*. Aldershot: Ashgate.

Thakur, R. 2006. *The United Nations, Peace and Security*. Cambridge: Cambridge University Press.

Thakur, R. 2010. Law, Legitimacy and United Nations. *Melbourne Journal of International Law*, 11(1).

The Covenant of the League of Nations. [Online]. Available at: http://avalon.law.yale.edu/20th_century/leagcov.asp [accessed: 17 August 2009].

The White House. 2002. *The National Security Strategy of the United States of America*. [Online]. Available at: http://www.state.gov/documents/organization/63562.pdf

Thomasson, E. 2009. Darfur, Kenya courts to complement ICC: prosecutor. [Online], 30 October. http://af.reuters.com/article/topNews/idAFJOE59T0NA20091030 [accessed: 11 April 2011].

Thornhill, C. 2007. Niklas Luhmann, Carl Schmitt and the Modern Form of the Political. *European Journal of Social Theory*, 10(4), 499–522.

Tomuschat, C. 2006. The Legacy of Nuremberg. *International Criminal Justice*, 4(4), 830.

UN. 1945. Charter of the United Nations, 1 UNTS XVI (entered into force 31 August 1965).

UN. 1954. Code of Crimes against the Peace and Security of Mankind (1954). [Online]. Available at: http://untreaty.un.org/ilc/texts/instruments/english/draft%20articles/7_3_1954.pdf [accessed: 20 August 2009].

UN. 1996. Code of Crimes against the Peace and Security of Mankind (1996). [Online]. Available at: http://untreaty.un.org/ilc/texts/instruments/english/draft%20articles/7_4_1996.pdf [accessed: 20 August 2009].

UN. 1998. Diplomatic Conference of the Plenipotentiaries to Negotiate the ICC Statute 14 July 1998. Statement by the Minister for Foreign Affairs of Italy. Document No. A/CONF. 183/C. 1/SR.37.

UN. 2002. *United Nations Diplomatic Conference of Plenipotentiaries on the Establishment of an International Criminal Court Rome, 15 June–17 July 1998: Official Records Volume II Summary Records of the Plenary Meetings and of the Meetings of the Committee of the Whole Document No. A/CONF.183/13 (Vol. II)*. New York: United Nations.

UN. 2004. *A More Secure World: Our Shared Responsibility (Report of the Secretary-General's High Level Panel on Threats, Challenges and Change, 2 December 2004) 4 and 77*. [Online]. Available at http://www.un.org/secureworld/ [accessed: 2 August 2012].

UN. 2011 The United Nations Security Council referred Libya by unanimous resolution. [Online]. Available at: http://www.un.org/News/Press/docs/2011/sc10187.doc.htm [accessed: 11 April 2011].

UN General Assembly. 1964. Resolution 95(1).

UN General Assembly. 1974. Resolution 3314 (XXIX) of (14 December 1974).

UN General Assembly. 1987. Convention against Torture and Other Cruel, Inhuman or Degrading Treatment or Punishment. Adopted 10 December 1984, Entry into force 26 June 1987. *United Nations, Treaty Series, 1465*.

UN General Assembly. 2005. *2005 World Summit Outcome, General Assembly Resolution 60/1 of 16 September 2005, UN Doc. A/Res/60/1 (2005)*.UN International Law Commission. 1950. Formulation of Nuremberg Principles. *Yearbook of the International Law Commission*, vol. 2, UN Doc A/CN.4/22.

UN International Law Commission. 1966. *Yearbook of the International Law Commission*, vol. 2.

UN Security Council. 1993. *Resolution 808 [1993] Tribunal (Former Yugoslavia) (22 February)*.

UN Security Council. 2004. *Resolution 1528 [2004]. The Situation in Côte d'Ivoire.*

UN Security Council. 2007. *Resolution 1739 [2007]. The Situation in Côte d'Ivoire.*

UN Security Council. 2010. *Resolution 1933 [2010]. The Situation in Côte d'Ivoire.*

UN Security Council. 2011a. *Department of Public Information News and Media Division New York Security Council 6491st Meeting* (PM) In Swift, Decisive Action, Security Council Imposes Tough Measures On Libyan Regime, Adopting Resolution 1970 In Wake Of Crackdown On Protesters*. [Online]. Available at: http://www.un.org/News/Press/docs/2011/sc10187.doc.htm [accessed: 19 June 2012].

UN Security Council. 2011b. *Department of Public Information News and Media Division New York Security Council 6498th Meeting (Night) Security Council Approves 'No-Fly Zone' Over Libya, Authorizing 'All Necessary Measures' to Protect Civilians, by Vote of 10 in Favour with 5 Abstentions*. [Online]. Available at: http://www.un.org/News/Press/docs/2011/sc10200.doc.htm [accessed: 19 June 2012].

UN Security Council. 2011c. *Resolution 1970 [2011a]. Peace and Security in Africa.*

UN Security Council. 2011d. *Resolution 1973 [2011b]. The Situation in Libya.*

UN Weapons Convention 1980.

Uniform Code of Military Justice, UCMJ, 64 Stat. 109, 10 U.S.C. Chapter 47.

United States Department of Defence. 2007. Office of Military Commissions, Memorandum for Detainee David M. Hicks 0002. [Online]. Available at: http://www.defenselink.mil/news/d2007Hicks%20-%20Notification%20of%20Sworn%20Charges.pdf [accessed: 21 February 2007].

US National Security Strategy May 2010. [Online: The White House]. Available at: http://www.whitehouse.gov/sites/default/files/rss_viewer/national_security_strategy.pdf [accessed: 19 June 2012].

Unknown. (n.d.) Debate: When to Declare Donors Dead. Times [Online]. Available at http://www.time.com/time/health/article/0,8599,1832688,00.html?iid=336x280_health2 [accessed: 18 August 2008].

Unknown. 2006. A-Gs demand immediate action on Hicks trial. *ABC News* [Online], 10 November. Available at: http://www.abc.net.au/news/2006–11–10/a-gs-demand-immediate-action-on-hicks-trial/1306572 [accessed: 13 August 2009].

Unknown. 2007. Brain, not brawn, will win war on Mungiki. *Nation Media Group* [Online], 6 June. Available at: http://www.nationmedia.com/dailynation/nmgcontententry.asp?category_id=24&newsid=99710 [accessed: 14 June 2007].

Unknown. 2007a. Police attack stronghold of blood-drinking sect in Nairobi slums. *Scotsman.com* [Online], 7 June. Available at: http://news.scotsman.com/international.cfm?id=888902007 [accessed: 12 June 2007].

Unknown. 2007b. Profile: Kenya's secretive Mungiki sect. *BBC News* [Online], 24 May. Available at: http://news.bbc.co.uk/2/hi/africa/6685393.stm [accessed: 12 June 2007]

Unknown. 2008a. Defining death: O death, when is thy sting? *The Economist* [Online], 2 October. Available at: http://www.economist.com/science/displayStory.cfm?source=hptextfeature&story_id=12332939 [accessed: 5 October 2008].

Unknown. 2008b. Kenya government accused of using murderous sect. *Religion News Blog* [Online], 10 January. Available at: http://www.religionnewsblog.com/20318/mungiki-37 [accessed: 14 June 2007].

Unknown. 2008c. UK, US scientists look to genetically modified for organs. *The Sydney Morning Herald* [Online], 8 September. Available at: http://www.smh.com.au/news/science/uk-us-scientists-look-to-genetically-modified-pigs-for-organs/2008/09/08/1220725898653.html [accessed: 5 October 2008].

Walker, A.J. 2004. When a Good Idea is Poorly Implemented: How the International Criminal Court Fails to be Insulated from International Politics and to Protect Basic Due Process Guarantees. *West Virginia Law Review*, 106(2), 245–304.

Walzer, M. 1977. *Just and Unjust Wars*. New York: Basic Books.

Weber, M. 1991. Politics as a Vocation. In Gerth, H. and Wright Mills, C. (eds), *From Max Weber By Max Weber*. Abingdon: Routledge.

Weber, M. 2004. *The Vocation Lectures*. Edited and introduced by D.S. Owen, T.B. Strong, translated by R. Livingstone. Indianapolis, IN: Hackett Publishing Company.

Werner, W.G. 2001. Securitization and Judicial Review: A Semiotic Perspective on the Relation between the Security Council and International Judicial Bodies. *International Journal for the Semiotics of Law*, 14(4), 345–66.

Windeyer, W.J.V. 1938. *Lectures on Legal History*. Sydney: Law Book Co. of Australasia Pty Ltd.

Yale Law School. 2008a. *The Avalon Project: Documents in Law, History and Diplomacy. International Conference on Military Trials: 1945 Letter of Transmittal*. [Online]. Available at: http://www.yale.edu/lawweb/avalon/imt/jackson/letter.htm [accessed: 8 May 2006].

Yale Law School. 2008b. *The Avalon Project: Documents in Law, History and Diplomacy. International Conference on Military Trials: London, 1945 Preface*. [Online]. Available at: http://www.yale.edu/lawweb/avalon/imt/jackson/preface.htm [accessed: 8 May 2006].

Yale Law School. 2008c. *The Avalon Project: Documents in Law, History and Diplomacy. Nuremberg Trial Proceedings Volume 19*. [Online]. Available at: http://avalon.law.yale.edu/imt/07–26–46.asp [accessed: 13 August 2009].

Yourow, H.C. 1996. *The Margin of Appreciation Doctrine in the Dynamics of European Human Rights Jurisprudence*. Boston, MA: Martinus Nijhoff.

Zartaloudis, T. 2010. *Giorgio Agamben: Power, Law and the Uses of Criticism (Nomikoi, Critical Legal Thinkers)*. New York: Routledge.

Žižek, S. 2001. *The Fragile Absolute: or, Why is the Christian Legacy Worth Fighting For?* London: Verso Books.

Žižek, S. 2002. Are we in a war? Do we have an enemy? *London Review of Books* [Online], 24(10). Available at: http://www.lrb.co.uk/v24/n10/zize01_.html [accessed: 13 August 2009].

Žižek, S. 2008. *Violence*. London: Profile Books.

Index

abuse of process 55–6, 91, 112, 132, 135–46
Achebe, C. 42
Afghanistan 58, 60
Africa
 cases before ICC 2, 6, 7, 17, 20–3, 145–6, 162
 sacrifice for international justice 21–2, 25, 28, 31–2
 sacrificial themes in literary works on 42
Agamben, G. 20, 22, 25, 30, 42, 55, 71, 120, 121, 122, 126, 127, 128, 160
 'bare life' xviii, 56, 120, 124, 127
 bios xviii
 critiques of 33–4
 due process 56
 homo sacer 30, 33–4, 63, 64, 75, 82, 123–4
 inclusion/exclusion 126, 127
 oikonomia 44
 power 87, 124
 sacrifice 43–4
 state of exception 41, 76, 117, 120, 124, 161–2
 on state of nature and state of exception 120
aggression
 genealogy of 147–58
 in public international law and criminal international law 6
 UNGA Resolution 3314 on 148–9n6, 152, 155, 156, 157, 158,
 see also criminal aggression
al-Qaeda 60, 113
anarchy 12, 77, 126
Annan, K. 3, 16, 19
anomie 126
Arendt, H. 42, 74
Aristotle 118
Australia
 abandonment of Hicks 59, 61, 82–3
 Mabo and Others v State of Queensland (No 2) (1992) 34–9
Autonomous Concept 103

Bakhtin, M. 45
Barayagwiza, Jean-Bosco v The Prosecutor (1999) Appeals Chamber Case no. ICTR-97-19-I 136, 140, 141, 144, 145
Barayagwiza, Prosecutor v, Appeals Chamber Case no. ICTR-97-19-I 140, 142–5
'bare life' xviii, 56, 120, 124, 127
Beck, U. 69
Bellamy, A. 6, 8, 121
Benjamin. W. 12, 56, 72, 73, 73–4, 74–5, 76, 122, 129, 131
Bible 26, 38, 121
biodefence program of US 116
biolegality xviii, 113, 118, 120, 121, 163
biopolitics xviii, 117, 121, 127, 150, 162–3
Blackburn, Justice 37–8
Blackstone, W. 38
Bodin, J. 134
Bourdieu, P. 79
Bush, G.W. 4, 115, 116

carnival 45
Carr, E.H. 21
Cassese, A. 145
Christian theology 37, 44
Cicero, M.T. 16
civil law doctrine 101
colonialism 37–8, 62, 63, 119, 127
Commentaries 38
common law doctrine 101
community

accused 23
-formation 17
images and icons of international 25–6
legal concept of international 10
state as a human 134
support for administration of criminal justice 138
complementarity, principle of 149
Conrad, J. 42, 43, 44
Constitution of International Military Tribunal 151
Convention against Torture and Other Cruel, Inhuman or Degrading Treatment or Punishment (CAT) 125
Cooper, M. 117, 126–7, 162
Côte d'Ivoire 2, 6, 16
Cox, M. 21
C.R. v C.R. (1995) 103
crimes against humanity 3–4, 6, 15, 16, 120
criminal aggression
consideration of precedents in defining ICC 155–6
defined in Nuremberg Charter 97–8, 152–3, 163
as distinct from factual aggression 157–8
ICC draft definition of 158
ICC jurisdiction over 95–6, 98, 150
ICC Special Working Group on 78, 98, 128, 158
jurisprudence on legality of prosecuting 110
need for ICC legal definition of 162, 164
Rome Conference discussion of xv, 60, 93–4, 96–7, 154–8
Rome Statute
Article 5 compromise formula 95–6, 98, 154–5
construction of clauses on 97–9
interpretation of clauses on 96–7, 98
Simpson's discussion of 85
United Nations Charter Article 39 on 94–5, 96
critical theory xvii–xviii
Critique of Violence 72, 73

Dawkins, R. 27
Democratic Republic of Congo 16, 145–6
Derrida, J. 30, 65, 73, 74, 75, 91, 119
Dillon, M. 147, 150, 162
disciplinary power 63–4, 117, 162
Dole Chadee et al v Trinidad and Tobago (1998) 137–8
Dostoevsky, F. 45
Dyilo, T.L. 145

economic theology 44
emergency powers 41–2, 63, 116, 129
'enemies of mankind' 85–6
Esposito, R. 41, 119, 121, 150
ethnic cleansing, protection from 3–4, 6
'ethnic globalization paradox' 69
European Court of Human Rights (ECHR) 102–3
considerations of abuse of process 139–40
Ex parte Quirin 317 U.S. 1 (1942) 58
exclusion/inclusion mechanism xvii, 15, 21, 23, 41, 82, 115, 119–20, 123, 127, 128, 129, 163
exegesis 94, 100, 103, 108

fact and law 67, 68, 71
Faustian pacts 33–4, 41, 43, 44, 45
Findlay, M. 70, 87, 113
force
as distinct from violence xviii, 48, 71, 129–30
distinction between monopoly on legitimate use of force and a legitimate monopoly on the use of 69, 76–87, 161, 163, 164
international law on use of 5–9, 81–2, 150–8
Justice Pal's argument against criminalizing use of 55–6, 65, 84, 139
legitimacy and legality in use of 2–3, 50
managing necessity to use 1–3

monopoly on use of force becoming a monopoly on use for 12, 78, 129, 130
regulation in conflict between law and politics 65–6, 76–87, 90, 92
setting law to one side in use of 71–2
social/anti-social binary 47, 48, 66
state sovereignty and monopoly on legitimate use of 12, 70, 78, 81, 118, 129, 134
state use of 11–13
three stages of 91–4
US force-of-law in 'war on terror' 57–61
and 'war on *Mungiki*' 61–5
Foucault, M. xviii, 63, 70, 117, 118, 121, 124, 127, 128, 162
France 107, 134, 153
Civil Code 101
Conseil d'État 103
French Revolution 49, 75
freedom 126
friend-enemy distinction 63, 64, 66, 128
Fyfe, D.M. 153

Gbagbo, L. 6
General Treaty for the Renunciation of War 1928 (Kellogg-Briand Pact) 151, 152, 153–4
Geneva Conventions 50, 57, 58, 60, 115, 125
Geneva Law 125
Geneva Protocol for the Pacific Settlement of International Disputes 1924 151, 152
genocide 6, 104, 120
ICTR definition of 104–5
protection from 3–4, 6
Genocide Convention 104
geopolitics 150
Giddens, A. 76, 77
Girard, R. 20, 25, 43
globalization 113, 122
ethnic paradox of 39
and marginalization of state 12, 78, 128–9
and monopoly on use of force 129
glory 43
governmentality 128
Guantanamo Bay 57, 59, 82, 120
guilt
absolute 20
Agamben on 127
innocence and 20, 83, 84
transfer of 26, 30, 82

Hague Conventions 67, 125
Hague Law 125
Hague Peace conferences 150
Hamdan v Rumsfeld, Secretary of Defence, et al Certiorari to the United States Court of Appeals for The District of Columbia Circuit No. 05–184. Argued 28 March 2006 and decided 29 June 2006 57, 102
Haradinaj, R. 80
Heart of Darkness 42
heaven/hell theme 41
Hegel, F. 118
hermeneutics 94, 95, 103, 108
Hicks, D. 57–61, 83, 116
Hobbes, T. 4, 41, 44, 120, 124, 127, 134
homo sacer 30, 33–4, 63, 64, 75, 82, 123–4
hostis humani generis 15–16, 75
House of Lords 10, 102, 133, 141
human rights 48–9, 125, 128
conflict between power to detain and 133
ICC and universalizing of 16
religious connotations in protection of 121, 122
of unlawful combatants 59, 83
use of force and setting aside of 72
humanitarian intervention 7–8, 13
reconciling sovereignty and 3–4
use of force in 12, 70, 78, 129
humanitarian law 7, 11, 58, 119, 145

iconography of international criminal justice 18, 25–6
immunity 115, 119
individual criminal responsibility
collective guilt and 26, 30, 82
Constitution of International Military Tribunal and watershed for 151

establishment in international law 54, 111, 154
generating scapegoats 23, 28–9
and juridification of war 84–5
logic underpinning universal justice and 23–4
for mass political violence 16–17, 23, 28–9
under Nuremberg Charter 97–8, 154
pirates and 85
trying those with greatest responsibility for worst crimes 24–5, 149
innocence and guilt 20, 83, 84
International Commission on Intervention and State Sovereignty (ICISS) 3
International Committee of the Red Cross (ICRC) 113–14, 115, 117
International Conference on Military Trials 1949 152, 153
International Court of Justice (ICJ) 6, 128, 160
genocide prevention rulings 6
on Legality of the Threat or Use of Nuclear Weapons 11
Military and Paramilitary Activities in and Against Nicaragua Decision on Jurisdiction and Admissibility (1984) ICJ REP.392. 27 June 1986 102
Military and Paramilitary Activities in and Against Nicaragua Decision on the Merits (1986) ICJ REP.14 154
International Criminal Court (ICC)
abuse of process defence 136–7, 145–6
African cases before 2, 6, 7, 17, 20–3, 145–6, 162
Cote d'Ivoire, consideration of situation in 2, 6
draft definition of crime of aggression 158
establishment 6, 16–17, 60, 154
iconographic symbolism of 18
jurisdiction 8–9, 22, 68, 95–6, 98, 149–50, 156
Kenyan post-electoral violence case 18–20, 23–5
Libya, consideration of situation in 2, 7
need for legal definition of criminal aggression 162, 164
political violence referrals 5, 8, 11, 19–20
proposed draft title for statute 154
Prosecutor 6, 7, 19, 20, 28
and responsibility to prosecute 149
Rome Conference discussion of crime of aggression xv, 60, 93–4, 96–7, 154–8
Rome Statute
Article 5 95–6, 98, 154–5
Article 10 97, 151n13
Article 13 8–9, 22
Article 15 5–6, 9
construction of criminal aggression clause 97–9
interpretation of criminal aggression clause 96–7, 98
scapegoat mechanism and 16, 20, 21, 23, 24
selective universality of 17, 20–3
Situation in the Democratic Republic of Congo 145–6
Special Working Group on crime of aggression 78, 98, 128, 158
trying of persons 'most responsible' for worst crimes 24–5, 149
International Criminal Tribunal for Rwanda (ICTR)
abuse of process doctrine 136
Akayesu Case 104–5, 140
Barayagwiza I 136, 140, 141, 144, 145
Barayagwiza II 140, 142–5
defining of genocide 104–5
discussion of factual aggression under UN Charter 97n15
Kanyabashi case 104
Siméon Nshamihigo case 138
Statute and Rules 132–3
without jurisdiction over aggression 111
International Criminal Tribunal for the former Yugoslavia (ICTY)
inherent jurisdiction of 103–4
jurisdiction of 9, 103–4, 111

- power of UNSC to create 8–9, 10
- *Prosecutor v Miroslav Deronjic* 50n4
- *Prosecutor v Slobodan Milošević* (2001) 140
- Ramush Haradinaj case 80
- *Tadić* case 5, 9, 10, 95, 103–4
- on UNSC as bounded by law 133

international law
- all states bound by rule of 10–11
- expansive interpretation of texts in 106–7
- 'Law of War' and 'Law of Peace' 124–5
- linking of political events and a general legal structure 50–2
- and national politics 69–71
- outer and inner structure of 125–6
- separation of domestic law and 48
- UNSC bound by 9–11
- use of force in 5–9, 81–2, 150–8

International Law Commission 152, 154
Islamic law 100–1

Jackson, Justice xv, 52, 54, 152–3, 163
Japan, *see* Tokyo International Military Tribunal for the Far East (IMTFE)
Jean-Bosco Barayagwiza v The Prosecutor (1999) Appeals Chamber Case no. ICTR-97-19-I 136, 140, 141, 144, 145
Jewish law 100
juridification of war 84–5, 98
jurisdiction
- basis at Nuremberg International Military Tribunal (IMT) 139, 149, 152
- of ICC 8–9, 22, 68, 95–6, 98, 149–50, 156
- of ICTR 111
- of ICTY 9, 103–4, 111
- inherent 133, 139
- over unlawful combatants 58
- sovereignty and separation from 39
- universal 154

jus ad bellum 3, 5, 125, 148
jus cogens 5, 6, 110, 136–7, 152, 154
jus in bello 5, 125, 148
'just war' 147
Justice Trial, Nuremberg Trials 83, 131, 162
Justinian code 101

Kanyabashi case 104
Kellogg-Briand Pact 151, 152, 153–4
Kenya
- colonial administration 63, 64
- Kikuyu tribe 61, 62, 63–4, 65
- Mau-Mau 56, 62, 63, 65
- Mombasa Republican Council (MRC) 40
- *National Police Service Act* (2011) 40
- political violence in 18–20, 23–5, 40–1, 61–5
- sacrificial economy 27–9
- secession threats in 39–41
- and 'war on *Mungiki*' 61–5

Ki-moon, B. 3
Kingdom and the Glory 44
Kirsch, P. 17, 93
Koskenniemi, M. 17, 18, 21

'Law of Peace' 124, 125
'Law of War' 124, 125
Law, War and Crime 78–87
lawful combatants 58, 60, 61, 67
League of Nations 54, 102, 151, 152
legal texts
- IMT and IMTFE 50–2, 53, 96, 152
- international legal instruments 106–7
- interpretation versus construction 99–112, 161
- legal training and access to meaning of 105
- literal meaning approach to 109
- living document approach to 109
- originalist approach to 109
- 'reasoned decision methodology' 109–10
- social context 52
- writer-centric and reader-centric approaches to 105–6

legal training 105
Legality of the Threat or Use of Nuclear Weapons 11
legibus solutus 10, 11, 104, 133
Leviathan 127, 128

Libya 2, 6–8
Libyan Arab Jamahiriya v United Kingdom (Lockerbie case) [1992] ICJ REP.3 11, 125–6
life and death
  and law 118–19, 161
  legality and decisions on 121–3
  persons and spaces abandoned to violence 123–7
  state and dispensing of 127–9
Lincoln, A. 71
Locke, J. 57, 134
Lockerbie case 11, 125–6
London Agreement for the Prosecution and Punishment of the Major War Criminals of the European Axis 151
Louis XVI, King 75
Luhmann, N. xviii, 91, 97, 105, 111, 119, 124

Mabo and Others v State of Queensland (No 2) (1992) 34–9
Mabo, E. 38–9
Macleod, C. 15
Magna Carta 48–9, 120, 132
Margin of Appreciation 103
Martens clause 67
Mau-Mau 56, 62, 63, 65
May, L. 15
means–end economy 11–12, 73
Metropolitan Bank v Pooley (1885) 56, 139
Milirrpum v Nabalco Pty. Ltd (Gove Land Rights Case) (1971) 17 FLR 141 37
Military and Paramilitary Activities in and Against Nicaragua Decision on Jurisdiction and Admissibility (1984) ICJ REP.392. 27 June 1986 102
Military and Paramilitary Activities in and Against Nicaragua Decision on the Merits (1986) ICJ REP.14 154
Military Commissions Act 2006 57, 60
Milton, J. 41
Mombasa Republican Council (MRC) 40
Mungiki 61–5

Napoleon's code 101
native title, establishing existence of Australian 34–9
natural law 73
Nazis 22, 51, 52, 78, 83, 128, 139
"necessity knows no law" 11, 159–60
Nicaragua v United States of America Decision on Jurisdiction and Admissibility (1984) ICJ REP.392. 27 June 1986 102
Nicaragua v United States of America Decision on the Merits (1986) ICJ REP.14 154
Nietzsche, F. 44, 67, 122
nolle prosequi 141
non-liquet 11, 105, 160
Nouwen, S. 17
nuclear weapons 11
Nuremberg Charter
  Article 1 53
  defining of criminal aggression 97–8, 152–3, 163
  individual criminal responsibility under 97–8, 154
Nuremberg International Military Tribunal (IMT) 10, 49, 65
  jurisdiction 139, 149, 152
  Justice Trial 83, 131, 162
  legal texts 50–2, 53, 96
  political subtext 50, 51, 52–3
  social context 50, 52, 54
Nuremberg Judgment 131, 148, 152, 154, 162

Obama, B. 3–4
oikonomia 44
original position 135
Othello 107
Ouattara, A. 6

Pal, Justice 55–6, 65, 84, 139
Pan-American Conference, Sixth 153
panopticism 63
paradigms 34
Paradise Lost 41
peace xvii, xxi
  capture of war by 66–7
  law of 124, 125

and links to criminal trial 19, 24, 27
right to 147–50
as the rule 2, 66, 148
sacrifice of accused for 30
Pennington, K. 10
pharmakos mechanism 23, 28–9, 30, 31
pirates 16, 85–6
political theology 44
political violence
in Cote d'Ivoire 2, 6
criminalizing of xv, xvii, 2, 61, 70, 113, 118, 123, 128, 159
individual responsibility for mass 16–17, 23, 28–9
and international law 69–71
in Kenya 18–20, 23–5, 40–1, 61–5
legalising 134–5
in Libya 2, 6–8
protection of civilians (POC) from 5
referrals to ICC 5, 8, 11, 19–20
Politics as a Vocation 12, 77
post-humanism 124
power
Agamben on 87, 124
existence and exercise of 36
supreme 122
and violence 74, 87
preemptive strikes 126–7
profanation 45
Prosecutor v Akayesu Case No. ICTR-96-4-A (Appeals Chamber) 1 June 2001 104–5, 140
Prosecutor v Barayagwiza Appeals Chamber Case no. ICTR-97-19-I 140, 142–5
Prosecutor v Miroslav Deronjic ICTY Case Number: IT-02-61-S 30-03-2004 50n4
Prosecutor v Siméon Nshamihigo Case No. ICTR-2001-63-DP 138
Prosecutor v Slobodan Milosevic 2001 ICTY Case No IT-02-54 140
Prosecutor v Tadić (1995) 9, 10, 95, 103–4
protection of civilians (POC)
law on use of force and 5–9
managing necessity of using force for 1–3
reconciling sovereignty and humanitarian intervention for 3–4
and state use of force 11–13
UN Article 39 relevant to 5

R. v Horseferry Road Magistrates' Court Ex parte Bennett [1994] 136, 141
R v Jones & Others [2006] UKHL 16 52, 102
R v Secretary of State for Defence (2007) 10, 133
R2P (responsibility to protect) 1, 3–4, 5–6, 8
Randu Nzai Ruwa & 2 Others v Internal Security Minister & Another [2012] eKLR 40
Rawls, J. 135
Regina v Dedan Kimathi [1956] eKLR 65
regulatory power 117, 162
religion
court at centre of civil 25, 30
human sacrifice 26
and origins of *terra nullis* 37–8
religious
connotations in 'authority' over life and death 121, 122
culture 43
differentiating secular and 121, 122
law 100–1
mystification of modern state 18
res judicata 141
res publica legibus solute 10
responsibility to protect (R2P) 1, 3–4, 5–6, 8
rex legibus solutus 10
Richardson, Bill xv, 56, 60n14, 155
Roman Law 10, 33–4, 101
Rome Conference discussion of crime of aggression xv, 60, 93–4, 96–7, 154–8
Rome Statute
Article 5 95–6, 98, 154–5
Article 10 97, 151n13
Article 13 8–9, 22
Article 15 5–6, 9
construction of criminal aggression clause 97–9

interpretation of criminal aggression clause 96–7, 98
Rwanda, *see* International Criminal Tribunal for Rwanda (ICTR)

sacred 27, 43, 121
'sacred man' 30, 33–4, 63, 64, 75, 82, 123–4
sacrifice 26–7, 43–4
of Africans for international justice 21–2, 25, 28, 31–2
Biblical documenting of human 26
proximity to violence and trial 25
scapegoats 16, 20, 21–2, 23, 24, 27–31
trial-as-sacrifice 27–8
sacrificial economy 16, 18, 26, 33
in Kenya 27–9
at root of international justice 21–3
society's 42–5
sanctity of human life 1–3, 23
scapegoats 16, 20, 21–2, 23, 24, 27–31
Schmitt, C. 18, 25, 44, 48, 57, 58, 63, 64, 76, 84, 100n21, 110, 119, 121, 123, 127, 134
secular
differentiation between religious and 121, 122
modern state theory derived from theology 44, 76, 100n21, 121
mystification 17, 18
secularization 25, 44, 122
Shakespeare, W. 107
show trials 83–4
Simpson, G. 23, 28, 41, 78–87
social/anti-social binary 47, 48, 66
social catharsis, international criminal justice as 27–31
social contract xix, 41, 44, 90, 134
society
exclusion/inclusion from 119–20
formation of 28, 30
global 66, 68
and its environment 66–7
law as immune system of 119
sacrificial economy of 42–5
social/anti-social binary 47, 48, 66
and state of nature 120
sociological systems theory xviii, 48, 91, 121
sovereignty 12, 71, 72, 128, 134
absolute 48
'bare' 39
concepts of 4
existence and exercise of 36–7, 39
function of 110
over the sea 48
reconciling humanitarian intervention and 3–4
social contract and creation of 41, 134
state of exception and 117, 120, 161–2
spaces and individuals open to violence 123–7
Special Court for Sierra Leone 140
S.S. Lotus (France v Turkey) (1927) 125
state
apparatus of 127
bound by rule of international law 10–11
definitions of 12–13, 74, 77–8, 127
and dispensing of life and death 127–9
globalization and marginalization of 12, 78, 128–9
secularized theological concepts of modern 44, 76, 100n21, 121
sovereignty and monopoly on legitimate use of violence 12, 70, 78, 81, 118, 129, 134
use of force 11–13
state of emergency 41–2, 63, 65, 119, 129
state of exception 22, 41, 44, 119, 124
gap in law and 11, 160
intellectual battles over 76
law's attempts to capture 125
regulation of 72
requiring use of violence 129–30
self-contradiction of 76
sovereignty in 117, 120, 161–2
and state of nature 120
State of Exception 76
state of nature
and advent of law 41, 73, 120, 129, 131–2, 133–4
artificial 135
defining 134

ex post facto justification for law 41, 133–4
lack of distinction between force and violence in 47, 126, 129
in New World and colonies 119
and society 120
and state of exception 120
symbols of international community 25

Taliban 57, 60
Tallgren, I. 17, 18, 25
terra nullius 34–9
terrorism
applying force of law to 55, 58–9
crime of 156
outside law 86
violence of 87,
see also 'war on terror'
Teubner, G. 81, 89, 90, 98
Thakur, R. 4, 5
The Idiot 45
theology
Christian 37, 44
exception analogous with miracle 76, 100n21
life and death issues 121
Things Fall Apart 42
Tokyo charter 53
Tokyo International Military Tribunal for the Far East (IMTFE)
dissenting opinion of Justice Pal 55–6, 65–6, 84, 139
legal texts 50–2, 53
political subtext 50, 51, 52–3
social context 50, 54
torture
allegations before a Spanish court 115
Convention against Torture and Other Cruel, Inhuman or Degrading Treatment or Punishment (CAT) 125
in global 'war on terror' 113–18
United Nations Convention Against Torture 114, 115
US position on 114–15, 162

Ulema 101
United Nations Charter 97–8, 124–5, 134
Article 2 41, 104, 153, 154
Article 25 10, 11, 53, 133
Article 39 5, 94–5, 96
Article 103 10, 11, 133
Chapter VII powers under 2 , 3, 6, 9, 11, 12, 22, 53, 125
United Nations Convention Against Torture 114, 115
United Nations General Assembly (UNGA) 3, 102, 103, 114, 125
Resolution 95(1) 154
Resolution 3314 148–9n6, 152, 155, 156, 157, 158
United Nations Security Council (UNSC) 41, 126, 133, 156
as bound by law 9–11, 104, 133
Chapter VII powers under UN Charter 2, 3, 6, 9, 11, 12, 22, 53, 125
Côte d'Ivoire intervention 2, 6
enforcement of peace and compatibility with role of 154
generating law and judicial institutions 8–9, 10
Libyan interventions 2, 6–8
resolutions authorizing use of force 2, 89–90
a responsibility to protect populations 3
United States of America
assaults on UN centred law 5
biodefence program 116
criminal aggression
Nuremberg Charter negotiations on 152–3
Rome Conference negotiations on 60, 155
defence discourse integrating 'whole of life' 117–18
different interpretations of R2P 4
Military Commissions Act 2006 57
National Security Strategy 3–4
2002 116, 117
2010 3–4
position on torture 114–15
recognition for Afghan state and government 60
United States of America v Alstötter (1948) 83, 162

United States Supreme Court 57, 58, 132, 141, 162
universal justice 17, 18, 19, 23
  selective nature of 17, 20–3
  substitutive logic and 23–5
unlawful combatants 57–61, 83
unwritten law 38, 106

violence
  critique of 72–6
  as distinct from force xviii, 48, 71, 129–30
  inadequacies in the law and extreme 69, 71–2, 72–6
  law and xvi, 48–50, 118–19, 161, 164–5
  military 74–5
  persons and spaces open to 123–7
  and power 74, 87
  rejection of incorporation into law 11
  state sovereignty and monopoly on legitimate use of 12, 70, 78, 81, 118, 129, 134
  victims of 66,
  see also political violence

war
  capturing by peace 66–7
  juridification of 84–5, 98
  law of 124, 125
  norm of 66–7
  Simpson on legal project of criminializing 78–87
'war on terror' 58–61, 82–3, 85–6
  characterizing 116, 161
  torture in 113–18
  US Supreme Court on 132, 162
Weber, M. 12, 74, 76, 77, 78, 134
Werner, W. 17, 18
William II of Hohenzollern 151

Yugoslavia
  UNSC intervention in 8–9,
  see also International Criminal Tribunal for the former Yugoslavia (ICTY)
Yugoslavia v 10 NATO states (Provisional Measures) 140

Žižek, S. 68, 121, 128
'zones of indistinction' 42
Zubaydah, A. 113–14

For Product Safety Concerns and Information please contact our EU representative GPSR@taylorandfrancis.com
Taylor & Francis Verlag GmbH, Kaufingerstraße 24, 80331 München, Germany

www.ingramcontent.com/pod-product-compliance
Ingram Content Group UK Ltd.
Pitfield, Milton Keynes, MK11 3LW, UK
UKHW021303190926
475701UK00009B/623
9781138246935